PRAISE FOR

FROM CUBICLE TO CLOUD

"I've known Jennifer for a few years now, and it's been a privilege to share some of the journey and see what she's achieved and continues to achieve. She is an outstanding person and exciting entrepreneur. Not in the throw-away sense—that word is too often used these days—but in the high energy, innovative way that asks questions, challenges, learns from mistakes, works hard, and is prepared to take risks. Jennifer's first chapter appropriately starts with 'take the leap.' This is an action-orientated, pragmatic book that inspires. Rather than stuffed with hyperbole, it provokes the reader to 'take the leap'—how refreshing! Happy leaping."

—DANIEL RICHARDS, Business Development Director, My Firms App

"It is simple. This book is fantastic. The world is changing, the way we do business is changing, and this impacts our small business owners. Jennifer's take on how business owners can embrace the cloud couldn't have arrived at a better time. This book provides insight that will show our business owners how to take the necessary action to continue to move business forward, in a different way. Thank you, Jennifer, for sharing this valuable information!"

—SEAN BALKMAN, VP, Solution Advisor Manager,
Small Business Client Solutions, Bank of America

"As a long-standing member of ADP's Accountant Advisory Board, Jennifer Brazer regularly shares her keen insight into the opportunities and challenges of small businesses across the U.S. that helps ADP to continuously improve our solutions and programs for the accounting community. We appreciate Jennifer's commitment to excellence and value her unique view of client accounting services in helping us build a program that supports accounting professionals' needs and helps their clients be more successful."

—ERRON STARK, DVP Channel Sales, ADP®

"I always say, look towards the experts who have figured it out, and that is Jennifer! The world is in rapid motion right now, and it is critical we find ways to focus on value-added activities in our businesses, which is why her book's timing is so critical for all of us. Jennifer takes you right to hard-hitting, insightful action steps! I will use her book as a guide to remind me of what I can do in my business, and I will share her ideas with many others."

—THERESA M. ASHBY, PhD, MBA, COO, Kaleidoscope Media Services

"Launching a company is no easy feat. *From Cubicle to Cloud* is an eye-opener for anyone considering starting a small business or improving the business they already have. It provides a playbook of practical tips, strategies, and advice gleaned from lessons learned the hard way. The timing of this book could not be better. This may be the perfect opportunity to take the leap into entrepreneurship in a virtual world."

—ALEXANDRA DEFELICE, Director of Marketing and
Business Development, Payne & Fears LLP

FROM CUBICLE TO CLOUD

How to Start and Scale a Virtual Professional Service Business

JENNIFER BRAZER

with LIZ GOLD

GREENLEAF
BOOK GROUP PRESS

Published by Greenleaf Book Group Press
Austin, Texas
www.gbgpress.com

Distributed by Greenleaf Book Group

For ordering information or special discounts for bulk purchases, please contact Greenleaf Book Group
at PO Box 91869, Austin, TX 78709, 512.891.6100.

Design and composition by Greenleaf Book Group and Kimberly Lance
Cover design by Greenleaf Book Group and Kimberly Lance
Cover illustration: belekekin / iStock / Getty Images Plus

Publisher's Cataloging-in-Publication data is available.

Print ISBN: 978-1-62634-761-8

eBook ISBN: 978-1-62634-762-5

Part of the Tree Neutral® program, which offsets the number of trees consumed in the production and printing of this book by taking proactive steps, such as planting trees in direct proportion to the number of trees used: www.treeneutral.com

TreeNeutral

Printed in the United States of America on acid-free paper

20 21 22 23 24 25   10 9 8 7 6 5 4 3 2 1

First Edition

To my husband and Chief Strategist for seeing around corners, reading my mind, and never complaining when I had to work, no matter how endless or ill-timed it was.

To the original gangsters Sheryl Phelps, Sherri McKeel, and Sharon Stewart for always making it happen through thick and thin. It was your willingness to get it done no matter what, learn, and innovate that made Complete Controller what it is today.

To Penny McCord and the Goldfish cracker story. You will have to ask Penny; it's her story to tell.

To Jacquie for listening to my dreams ad nauseam and still being willing to listen some more, and for giving me rock-solid advice, especially when it wasn't what I wanted to hear.

"Life is like a camera.
Focus on what's important.
Capture the good times.
If things don't work out,
just take another shot."
—ZIAD K. ABDELNOUR

CONTENTS

WHY YOU SHOULD READ THIS BOOK

"Opportunity is often missed because it's dressed in overalls and looks like hard work."

—THOMAS EDISON

FROM CUBICLE TO CLOUD is the story of how I developed, built, and scaled a totally cloud-based Client Accounting Services business that serves customers and tax professionals nationwide. By writing this book, I hope to challenge the accounting industry and those who provide other professional services to consider a total rearrangement of the way they think about their business model and platform for delivery.

With the virtualization of bookkeeping services and the growing acceptance of cloud technology by accounting firms, my industry is experiencing a new energy. You may already know that the Client Accounting Services industry, also known as CAS, is booming. CAS is becoming increasingly popular because it empowers customers to focus on what they do best while others handle the bookkeeping side of their business for them. Previously skeptical businesses are starting to jump on board, realizing they can save time and money by outsourcing their bookkeeping instead of hiring in-house staff or doing their bookkeeping and payroll themselves.

In my own work, I was seeing a growing need for this service, so I began to think about how I could best offer it to others. After some careful planning and consultation with colleagues and mentors, I started to build my signature offering by leveraging existing technology (e.g., QuickBooks, the internet, and cloud computing) blended with expert bookkeeping support and help for customers looking for the best auxiliary solutions to support their businesses or busy households.

If you're interested in breaking into this industry, you will be in high demand, as the need for virtual accounting services is clear. Forty-one percent of mid-sized accounting firms are already providing CAS to their customers, according to *Accounting Today's 2019 Year Ahead Survey*, with 80 percent of CAS customers stating they appreciate the value CAS offers them, as it allows them to delegate their books to the experts.

But what about other professional services? Service professionals of all types have never before had the option to remove themselves from their businesses because their professions inherently rely on them for day-to-day operations and revenue generation. And so often they are trapped in an hours-for-dollars model. Whether a doctor, lawyer, publisher, therapist, tailor, interior designer, life and wellness coach, yogi, trainer, chef, personal shopper, ghostwriter, or social media maven, you can leverage the cloud to break free from the box. Not only can you find a way to serve your customers virtually, you can remodel your pricing, use a subscription model, even pull yourself out of the delivery role by delegating your methods to a well-trained staff.

Imagine the possibilities. By leveraging cloud technology and creative strategies, you can build a professional services business that produces a steady annuity long after you are off pursuing other adventures.

So, Who Am I to Be Writing This Book?

You may be asking, "Who is Jennifer Brazer, and how is she qualified to give me business advice?" Let me share a little bit about myself. I have twenty-six years of experience in CAS, along with previous experience in construction, manufacturing, and architectural accounting. In my twenties, I was tech-savvy and ambitious. I got lucky and worked for a few small businesses that relied heavily on their financial data for success. The funny thing is, I'm not a numbers person. I picked accounting because I excelled in that area of small business management, and my job experience showed me how empowering proper financial data could be. Providing this data allowed me to start conversations about cash flow management, budgets and forecasting, labor costs, overhead costs, pricing, and positioning. I actually thought those conversations were fun because I was helping others gain better control of their finances and develop business strategies. So, while I'm not a numbers person, I guess I am a bit of a financial empowerment nerd.

For a couple of years during the dot-com investment bubble of the late 1990s, I had a boutique business plan writing service. That experience allowed me to get exposure to different business models, including customary and totally out-of-the-box examples, and I began to understand that there were a variety of ways to generate revenue and structure a business.

I learned that abandoning traditional structures could either be a very bad idea, or it could be entirely innovative. If you were around during the dot-com investment bubble, you know that it was all about companies transitioning from brick-and-mortar constructs to virtual ones. As it turns out, accounting would be one of the last holdouts to virtualization, and I just happened to be right on the cusp of that vast industry change.

It wasn't until 2017 that certified public accountant (CPA) firms began to show an active interest in cloud-hosted solutions. Many firms today are still investigating, while others are adopting these offerings at a rapid pace. One of the offerings that was previously difficult to develop, due to lack of transparency and tools, was CAS. And because of my research and a bit of trial and error, I knew exactly what to do.

THE BEGINNING

When I started Complete Controller, I was a single mom raising three teenage daughters and managing a small portfolio of customers as an outsourced controller. A major factor that helped push me toward a virtual company structure was my daughter, Sarah. She is blind and has a rare genetic condition called de Morsier's syndrome that affects her optic nerve (eyesight) and her ability to regulate hormones. Building a business where I could be at home meant everything to me as a mother.

Sarah was never one to complain, and she eagerly did everything her sisters did—ballet, swim, choir, and some things they didn't, like orientation and mobility training, guide dog acquisition, braille challenges, and culinary school, to name a few. Three kids are a handful. Three kids with a very active social life and disability services, even more so.

While I enjoyed the freedom of being my own boss, taking time off meant money out of my pocket. A sick kiddo might cost me $30 for a doctor visit, $5 in gas running around town, $15 for a prescription, and $20 for whatever over-the-counter stuff was needed to make them comfortable. But the big hit was the $300-plus in lost billable hours. My time was unpaid, whether it was for a sick kid or a vacation. I had to give up income to be present, which was becoming a problem.

When you are a single mom with three kids, every decision to spend time with them is a costly one; however, the decision to spend time with a customer instead didn't always feel good either. I was stuck in the guilt juggernaut. When I focused on my career, inevitably, I was guilty of missing something with the kids, and when I focused on the kids, I was guilty of not giving my all to my customers.

I had a close friend at the time who was an attorney and a really smart guy. We had a pivotal conversation one day where he told me, "Your hours are your inventory. You only have so many hours in the day, and so much the market will bear for your hourly rate. Hourly rates will limit you. The key is to find a way to make money that is not associated to hourly performance. Sell professional services based on value and performance rather than hourly rate."

This was my introduction to value-based pricing. In the professional services industries, the concept of value-based pricing was still quite rare in 2007. Sure, there were attorneys charging a flat rate for legal entity formation or trademark filings and CPAs charging a flat rate for income tax returns, but my specialty was periodic accounting. I had no way to apply that advice to my current gig, but a seed had been planted.

THE CATALYST CUSTOMER

One of my customers at the time was a self-storage property management company that helped the owners of self-storage facilities maximize their gross potential and their occupancy. They had contracts with nearly twenty facilities across the nation. I met with them a couple of times a month to help with their bookkeeping.

One day my customer called to tell me that he wished I could do bookkeeping for all of the facilities he managed, which unfortunately I couldn't do since they were so spread out. He certainly didn't have it in the budget to fly me out to each facility. His issue was that, while he was including bookkeeping services in his contract to his customers to be competitive in the market, his process was inefficient. He was dropping off boxes of records to a local accounting firm, only to pick up financial reports weeks later. He never knew how much the cost would be until after the work was done because the firm billed by the hour. His reports were always at least one period behind because he had to wait until they completed the work. And since bookkeeping wasn't the highest revenue service the firm had to offer, it generally took a backseat to more lucrative projects. My customer was under contract to perform at a fixed rate and he needed timely data to make accurate decisions, so these late reports were making him look bad.

This was a defining moment for Complete Controller. I walked away from that conversation knowing there was an opportunity to be had. After much consideration and a long talk with a technology expert, I went back to my customer and said, "If I can find a way for me to be able to do all of the accounting for your facilities, regardless of location, and do it at a price point that meets your budget, will you bring me those customers to serve?" His nod fueled my decision to start one of the first totally virtualized accounting services and make sure that it was built for a national reach.

I call myself the Queen of CAS because I created the perfect marriage between service and technology, allowing me to build a leading virtual accounting service that employs efficient processes while maintaining the personal touch. Today, Complete Controller is one of the most reputable outsourced CAS departments in the nation. We get referrals every day from tax professionals who need a reliable solution for their small business customers and aren't yet interested or able to launch that solution themselves.

This book will discuss my journey to the cloud as I went from solopreneur to CEO of one of the first totally cloud-based accounting services in the country. Complete Controller started serving customers in 2007 and now has virtual offices in Costa Mesa and San Jose, California; Seattle; Denver; Austin; Raleigh; Atlanta; and New York City. We serve small businesses and households of any size and budget and provide a turnkey CAS department to CPA firms that want access to trained staff and a cloud platform with a national reach.

My mantra for my team has always been, "If you are going to do something, make it perfect." I always used to say, "You are already in there tackling the job. It's silly not to take that extra thirty seconds or two minutes to figure out how to do it right, how to do it clean, how to make it lay flat, and how to make it better for next time. Don't do it just to check it off your list. Always learn. Always evolve. Always innovate."

What's in It for You?

Some of you may be wondering what you're going to get out of this book and our time together. I believe you should read this book if you are ready to step away from the old way of doing business and embrace the virtual experience that is the cloud. In this book, you will also get a firsthand account of the steps I took—my own "secret recipe," if you will—to make Complete Controller what it is today.

This book will fan the entrepreneurial flame in your belly, whether you're an accountant or other service professional ready to step away from the confines of your office or cubicle and do your own thing. You'll find that I prefer to say "customers" rather than "clients" because it keeps me thinking of each sale as a quantifiable action that can happen without my involvement, rather than a relationship that is unquantifiable and relies on me for trust and reinforcement. I believe this strategy is especially poignant for service providers because we often find ourselves locked in by expectations of personal relationships with the people we serve. The book *Built to Sell*, by John Warrillow, explains this concept well, and I recommend it to anyone managing a business, whether or not you ever plan to sell.

THE FOUR LOGOS

PRO TIP

PEN TO PAPER

SPOTLIGHT

TOOLS

You will also notice some icons that are being used throughout. In each chapter, I share Pro Tips with you to give you additional information to help you along the way. At the end of each chapter, you will find a Pen to Paper activity to help you stretch your business muscles as you learn how to build a virtual professional services offering. My experience in developing and running a cloud-based bookkeeping service will create the backbone for the advice I give and provide some entertainment as we explore my bumps and bruises. As you read, it is my hope that you will always think of how that experience might affect your business plans, whether you are creating a book-keeping service, a division of your own firm, or a professional service that is totally outside of the accounting industry. Some chapters will feature Spot-light sections that shed additional light on the content. And throughout, I will mention various tools, which are compiled for you in the Appendix.

By the time you finish this book, you will be ready to make your own cloud-based professional service business model. This book is here to help you. Use it as a guide. Take my ideas and add to them. Learn from my mistakes and make your own recipe. In the chapters ahead, you will learn how I leveraged the cloud to disrupt client accounting services and how you can do the same to deliver your professional services more profitably and cohesively than ever before.

PART ONE

SCREW GUILT

"You cannot live to please everyone else."

—OCTAVIA SPENCER

TAKE THE LEAP

EVERY TIME YOU HAVE a new idea, ten other people are also having the same idea, so they say. This may be true, and the only thing that separates entrepreneurs from the rest of the pack is that they will actually do something about an idea. It astounds me when someone shares a new business idea with me, and five minutes into our conversation it becomes apparent that they haven't even performed a simple Google search to see if someone else is already doing it.

When you come across this person, although they have the best of intentions, know that they are not an entrepreneur. The very first thing a true entrepreneur will do with a juicy new idea is dive deep, proving it, testing it, creating a prototype, spending late nights and long weekends doing nothing but research and development, improving it, test marketing it, and many times, discarding it as a good idea, but not worth the investment.

True entrepreneurs thrive on this process; it fuels their very core.

Anyone can have a good idea, but it is a select few who will execute those ideas and an even slimmer few who can generate enough profit doing it.

And I'm here to show those of you who have a million-dollar idea how to leverage the cloud so you can streamline your processes and maximize your profits. It's challenging to start and scale a new business. Choosing the cloud as your platform for delivery and business headquarters presents a whole new set of challenges. In this book, we will explore:

How to recruit, train, monitor, incentivize, motivate, and mentor your staff without meeting them in person. How to price, package, and present your service so its value is recognized and desired without sitting across the table from your customer. How to attract and build trust and reputation with customers, colleagues, and vendors without in-person interaction. How to develop roles and processes to support your model and measure business performance without ever walking the floor of a physical office. How to overcome doubt, naysayers, and traditional model rigidity for your industry. How to keep the faith, even when capital and courage runs thin.

How I Made the Switch

As a single mom working in a hours-for-dollars consulting capacity, my goal was to develop a business that was working for me instead of just a glorified job where I was working for others. I wanted to collect the checks while other people did the work. And I believe that is the true model of a business versus a sole proprietorship—an entity must be autonomous, not reliant upon one person for its survivability.

As soon as I sniffed out an opportunity for building a business around providing accounting services with the capacity to reach beyond geographic constraints, I started my quest to see if it was possible. Technology was key, so I went about determining if a hosted environment was possible and whether others had done it before me. This was before the time when the words "cloud technology" had become widely understood by consumers.

In 2007 there were surprisingly few players in the market. My research uncovered plenty of companies that provided bookkeeping services as their core offering and plenty of midsize to large CPA firms that offered business management services to their customers. Meanwhile, the companies that touted "virtual accounting" were few and far between. In looking through some old notes on market competitors, I was reminded that it was a Chinese company that had the service offering that came closest to the model that was taking shape in my mind. They were not only offering to host QuickBooks but were also offering to do the bookkeeping work and had provided a process for the customer to get information to them.

So, I used their company as a springboard when creating my own business model. And you can do the very same with the concepts I share with you in the pages ahead. The brilliant thing about competitive analysis is that you can add what you like to your model and leave the rest. Often you find that the competition is not doing something that you would do. They are missing a critical segment of the market, their messaging is weak, they are using the wrong platform for delivery, or pricing or positioning themselves differently. By doing a little competitive analysis, you are in a sweet position. Someone else has already performed the research and development and executed on the first proof of concept. Now all you need to do to answer opportunity's knock is to differentiate yourself.

Embrace Change

Most people are leery of change and like to know what's hiding around the corner. Regardless of your profession, there are challenges that arise when making that leap from working for a firm or as a solopreneur into developing a full-blown business or building a virtual department within a firm. In many ways, the latter of those scenarios is the more challenging proposition.

I am not going to kid you; it is not easy to get people to change the way they are doing things. Change is difficult. Customers don't like change. Staff members don't like change. Firm partners don't like change. The billing department doesn't like change. You catch my drift. So, if you are creating or restructuring a department within your current firm to "go virtual," you are going to run into a lot of resistance. Right off the bat, getting your firm's leadership to adopt any kind of new process and new way of dealing with customers will be rough. Then to implement it in a profitable way will be a challenge, and we all know, without executive buy-in, you aren't going very far.

That said, I am sure as heck going to give you a convincing argument to present to them. If anything, I'm hoping this book will spark some ideas about how you would want to model your business for the cloud while bringing further innovation to your industry. Really cool things happen within the cloud sandbox. There are lots of tools and techniques to play with, and if you can get it all to play off of each other, it can be very fun. The key is to create a virtual business model that is fruitful for your customers, staff, and vendors.

Trial and Error

We all know that something that works for one person or company may not work for another. And that's okay. It's just how things go. However, there are some general practices that we've honed through simple trial and error that I'm going to share with you.

When Complete Controller was starting out, we were constantly testing strategies and new ideas. It was like throwing spaghetti against the wall. You may have to do a little bit of that, and we definitely had a few years when we would throw a noodle against the wall only to watch it fall to the floor. So, we'd throw a different one. Eventually, one stuck, and then our job was to find out what the consistency of that noodle was and continue to throw it against the wall, every day, all day long.

You should expect to do the same when building a virtual model for your business. But you will have an advantage over us since you'll be able to use what we've learned about our noodles to save yourself some time, energy, and noodles.

I'm a firm believer that if I tell you the why and the how, then you can make your own good choices. I even raised my kids that way. Rather than just saying, "Don't run across the street without me." I showed them why. I took them out to the curb and said, "Do you see this car right here? Do you see how you are shorter than the windshield? When it's moving, it can't see you. It's supposed to be on the street, and you are supposed to be on the curb. It's not expecting you to be in its way. Because of that, until you get taller than that windshield, I want you to make sure that you have someone who is taller holding your hand when you cross the street."

Now my kids have a logic trail. Now they understand the why, so they know how to solve the problem for themselves. Find someone taller and convince them to hold my hand so I can cross the street. Bingo!

This book is packed with not just what I did, but why I did it. So you can create your own logic trail and apply my lessons practically to your unique experience.

Old Ideas

Truth is, we can't move forward unless we know what is holding us back.

Every industry has its pillars (a.k.a. the mindset and approach) that may need to be dismantled for your business to successfully virtualize and differentiate itself from the competition. In my case, I was creating a new business formation in an industry that is resistant to change on its best day and carried many preconceived notions about how things "should be" done. I knew these old ways of thinking had to go. Here are some of the dusty ideas I was fighting to overcome:

☑ **The primary purpose of the work is for taxes, not business management.** I often say that firms are doing bookkeeping incorrectly. Why? Because they do it with taxes in mind, on a cash basis. While that's great for the CPA at the end of the year when they are filing taxes, unfortunately, that's not necessarily the best basis in which to run the financials for customers who need to make business decisions based on their numbers. The problem is that a lot of accountants don't know how to properly use the software to get an easy cash basis to accrual basis flip. They default to doing it on a cash basis so the customer isn't complaining that they are having to pay for redo work at the end of the year for the tax return. When the CPA makes adjustments and updates at year-end, the customer is like, "Wait a minute, I paid you to do my books all year long! Why am I paying you again to fix your own work to do my tax return?" Customers don't get it. As a result, the bookkeeping is done improperly, ineffectively, and inefficiently. We can do better.

☑ **The work is done because of customer demand, not because it can be leveraged for greater and more sustainable profitability.** Up until a year or two ago, most CPA firms only had a CAS department because they had to. Ask most CPAs and they will tell you that they did not go to school for all those years and take difficult tests so they could be overpaid for a service they don't want to be doing—in this case, bookkeeping. They are doing it because their customers demand it. So, they housed CAS under a name like business management services. Or, typically if it's a solopreneur, they just call it bookkeeping services. However, more recently, the industry has experienced a shift. Rather than CAS continuing to get shoved aside, accountants are realizing that this service can be profitable and can lead to other services that are also very profitable. Sexy, right? That's something people want to build. With the seed having been planted and virtualization becoming so prolific, it's time to fully leverage this model. Some have expanded on CAS by adding tax advice or business strategies, but not me. I'm going to show you how I did it, so you can do it, too, in any business.

☑ **You should use the 9-to-5 model.** Simply put, this hinders efficiency, productivity, and profitability. I'm not the first one to say this and I won't be the last: The 9-to-5 model is irrelevant to the way we work in today's 24/7 world. Requiring staff members to work on-site, in cubicles, dress a certain way, and engage in office culture is not necessary anymore. Think about it: Aside from the overhead of maintaining a physical location, your firm has to keep these people trained, happy, and busy for eight hours a day. When you are driven by the idea of having to keep someone busy, you are less focused on developing efficient practices, and you lose the incentive to have them minimize the number of hours that they are spending on a particular task. You have the customer wanting to spend less and get more, and you have staff members wanting to fill up their eight-hour days so they don't lose their job. Then you have firm managers trying to make sure those eight hours are filled while trying to keep their customers happy when they are billing them at the end of the month. Squeezing a profit out of this conflicting model is almost impossible. It's an old model that is no longer sustainable. So, let's change it.

☑ **Invoicing should be done upon delivery of the work.** Accountants, for as far back as I can remember, have always invoiced their customers after they have completed the work. But why? By the time the customer has the work in hand, they are no longer motivated to pay. Let's switch it up on them instead. In the last five or so years, with the proliferation of software-as-a-subscription, the value-based pricing model has emerged. Gone are the days of billing after the fact. Accountants are definitely late to the party on this one. For years doctors have insisted on receiving payment at the time of service, and smart attorneys won't start work without a retainer in place. Our profession is beginning to gather retainers and value-priced services that can be proposed at a fixed fee, but we can take it one step further. At Complete Controller, we have used a true financial-services-as-a-subscription model right from the start. In this book, I'll share how we did it and how we determined what should be included, what shouldn't, and why.

PRO TIP

Think about the traditional norms in your industry and the impact they have on profitability, efficiency, transparency, and scalability. How would you redesign the model?

At Complete Controller, we turned our back on these old models and mindsets, because we believed our services could be delivered differently and better. I set out to create a company that could liberate me from the hours-for-dollar model and operate on its own. The ultimate goal: Get paid for bookkeeping services while other people were doing the work. It was that simple. It didn't come overnight, but I am proud to say, we have created a well-oiled machine that has transformed how CAS is performed and delivered. Now I am here to help others in any field do the same.

Pen to Paper

There comes a time in every entrepreneur's life when the burning desire to change overpowers the need to stay the same. The story is different for each of us, but the result is the same. We take the leap. As you prepare yourself for action, my advice is to embrace only ideas that serve you and reject traditional constraints. Using the cloud as a delivery system and headquarters frees you from some of the more obvious limitations. This is your opportunity to create a business just the way you would want it to be. Start by putting on paper the industry norms you do not want to follow. Be as specific as you can and be sure to include what you will do differently from your colleagues so that you have your own niche in the marketplace.

2

DEVELOPING YOUR BUSINESS MODEL

AS I STARTED TO develop the model for my cloud-based business, I faced expectations both within myself and from other people that I had to shatter. My industry had a lot of stuffy, old ways of doing things, and it wasn't quick to change. It had been operating in an hours-for-dollars model, a.k.a. "your deliverable was your time, and anything you produced was valued based on how long it took to create it," for so long that people were really used to that. And on the staff side, the exchange transaction was also hours for dollars, plus benefits and paid time off. They were also used to that and it was expected. I talked about the old approaches in the introduction and previous chapter and how the model is just, well, old-fashioned. Irrelevant and dusty.

Bottom line, the traditional formula wasn't going to work for me. It practically ensured that my profit margins would be too skinny to sustain any substantial business value. Besides that, scalability would be impossible, so the chance of growing beyond a boutique size was slim. I had to let myself say, "You know what? I have to not care what other people think right now." This seemed counterintuitive because you want to start a business that makes meaning in people's lives. People's opinions do matter. But not at the expense of your vision. In my case, I was going to make bookkeeping profitable, sustainable, and scalable. And if that meant I had to disrupt the status quo for some folks, so be it.

Stop Trying to Make Everyone Happy

*While your business startup is fueled
by the flame in your entrepreneurial belly,
its longevity will be fueled by
a burning passion for success.*

To keep the fire burning, protect it from being smothered under obligations that drain you or the business of its light.

 PRO-TIP

Pick your must-haves and your absolute have-nots and create your model so it upholds your values.

One thing I've learned—if you want to make sure there is always an unhappy party to every transaction, make people-pleasing a part of your business model. When you subscribe to this practice, one person will be happy at the expense of everyone else, until they aren't happy anymore. It's not only a killer for business efficiency and reputation, it will also drain the passion right out of you.

So, I stopped—

- ☑ Trying to look to traditional methods as an example of what I should do

- ☑ Worrying about meeting the expectations of colleagues

- ☑ Catering to the customer that demanded special attention

I had to say, "Screw guilt!" If I could completely move beyond the traditional model and expectations, what would this company look like? As I got out my whiteboard and started to lay out ideas, I chose a few strategies that were totally outside the box at the time. My competitors may have offered similar services, and at least one offered a similar platform, but I wanted to take this opportunity to create a business model that incorporated learning from all of the small businesses I had worked with in the past. I wanted to create something different that provided greater flexibility to my customers and my employees.

The Service Plan Menu

I started by looking at the things I wanted to avoid. I had seen many small businesses struggle with collecting their money after the fact. They usually settled for leaving some on the table as uncollectable after weeks or months of nonpayment by customers who simply ignored the bills, had unrealistic expectations and complaints, or were suffering from cash flow problems. It seemed illogical that the person who could least afford to lose earned income—the person working hours for dollars—was the one shouldering all of the risk for their customers' business decisions and behavior.

Even if customers were paying on time, with after-the-fact billing, there was always the moment when the invoice had to be delivered and the payment received. This was yet another business process that had to be maintained and was often awkward for the service provider, whose specialty is providing a service, not billing and collections. Ask any solopreneur and you will find that the most awkward moments of their professional life have been around billing their customers. In order to avoid collections, I knew that I could avoid that discomfort by creating a subscription model, but to do so, I had to know the price for services in advance.

PRO TIP

Remember that value-based pricing is just that. It has nothing to do with the hours it takes you to complete the task you are pricing. It has everything to do with what people will pay for that task to be completed. Start by looking at what they are paying to your competitors, even if your competitors are using other methods. If you can price a service or combination of services at value and then deliver it more efficiently, the spread is your profit. Now you are rewarded for improving the efficiency and quality of your model rather than the amount of time it takes you to do the work. Wouldn't it be great to get eight hours of work done in two hours? Only if you are value priced.

This was my chance to price my accounting services based on value rather than hours. To do this, I created a Service Plan Menu of value-priced packages ✖ that met customer needs based on the frequency with which they wanted their bookkeeping updated. Anything that couldn't be anticipated in a service plan became an add-on that the customer could select to customize their experience. With value pricing, the move to a subscription model was only natural. Customers who were used to value pricing for their gym membership, for example, had no problem paying in advance for the period of service or access. I think the fact that we were a technology solution as well as a service provider allowed us to have better adoption of the subscription concept, but it was a tough sell at first. When I created our Service Plan Menu, software-as-a-subscription was not yet a broadly used business model and wouldn't be for at least another three to six years.

Take Yourself Out of the Equation

Once I had my pricing model down, I needed to look at staffing and how I planned to run my business. It's all the buzz to talk about how, if you're working *in* your business, you aren't working *on* your business. But for accounting service providers, we *are* our business until we grow to the point when we can delegate. Or we might grow by adding other people who are working in the business—adding partners and associates as many accounting firms do.

During conception is the time to build your business model so that it does not rely on you to perform the work. If you do not get your head around what that looks like now, you will struggle to extricate yourself later. At first, of course, the business is only you. But as you hire staff to fill roles, you will need a plan for peeling back the layers, one by one.

Right from the start, others did the bookkeeping work while I worked on administration, marketing, customer experience, and quality control. Then I peeled back by having the quality control managed by others while I worked on administration, marketing, and customer experience. Then I peeled back another layer by having the customer experience handled by others while I worked on administration and marketing. See where this is going?

Having done this, I was ultimately left with my role as CEO, allowing me to manage administration while being free to flex my visionary muscles and develop the relationships that keep us at the cusp of innovation in the industry. And you can do the same.

> *I urge you to model your financial projections assuming that other people will be doing the work.*

It will make your margins thinner, but you will be expecting that and account for it in each decision you make. By layering yourself out of the business, you empower it to become self-supporting and remove constraints on its potential customer capacity, allowing you to generate more profit in the long-run as you grow and even when you scale back, if needed.

Pen to Paper

Now that you know in what ways you differ from the traditional model, it's time to create your model to support what you want to be. To do this, you need to consider the characteristics that mean the most to you. For me, it was efficiency, profitability, scalability, transparency, and autonomy. What are the characteristics you desire? To help you get started, answer the following questions:

- ☑ If you didn't care what other people thought, how would your model look?

- ☑ Will you employ value pricing?

- ☑ What will your menu options be?

- ☑ Will your service be a subscription?

- ☑ When and how does the customer pay?

Once you have modeled the offering, start on the delivery, knowing that you will write each role and then peel back through delegation and start to tailor the roles.

HANDLING COMPLAINTS

THERE IS NOTHING MORE mortifying to any small business owner than to receive a customer complaint. If you are going to challenge the norm, disrupt your industry, and develop a model that isn't expected or even accepted, complaints will come. It's a good idea to have a strategy for fielding them right from the start; otherwise, they can tempt you to stray from your vision. I speak from experience when I say that I wish to avoid complaints at all costs, but that isn't really true. I wish to avoid complaints from unreasonable customers who do not appreciate our work.

Complaints from reasonable and respectful customers are fodder for customer experience improvements.

Meanwhile, every complaint has the ability to take the wind out of my sails, so I built a critical piece into the business model to help separate the reasonable feedback from the unreasonable demands: shared responsibility.

The Customer's Role

I put my customers' success into their own hands by creating sound and clear processes for them to follow. It's okay to put relationship expectations on your customers as long as you communicate clearly about how they can be achieved and provide any tools customers need to be successful. I define their role with clear guidelines to make it apparent that if they fail to hold up their end of the deal, our relationship will fail. To do this, I need to be concise and specific with my processes, give them a friendly nudge when those aren't followed, and make sure they take ownership of their required tasks.

 PRO TIP

If your customers fail to meet the relationship expectations, even with your tools and coaching, make it a hard stop. Don't ever do their work for them or work around them to deliver an incomplete product or service. The minute you do, they will come to expect it and stop contributing to (read: valuing) the relationship. It's human nature to value something more when you have invested in it through some contribution.

The processes I created for Complete Controller customers to follow addressed four crucial relationship expectations:

- ☑ Timely access to information

- ☑ Transaction recognition

- ☑ On-time document submission

- ☑ Honest and transparent business practices

Timely access to information. Because my business depends on receiving timely and accurate information from multiple financial sources, access to all of those sources is paramount to our success. It is the customer's role to make sure we have that access. Today, my company will not service customers who decline direct access to all points of information that affect the financials. PERIOD.

Transaction recognition. We are only as good as our ability to apply past experience and a thorough understanding of the business model to decipher transactions and determine how best to record them. Sometimes we get stuck, and it is the customer's role to "unstick" us by showing up for a meeting or a call or answering an email, so we can get what we need to keep things moving forward.

On-time document submission. We require source documents for each transaction, and our customers, some of whom are audited regularly, are particularly sensitive to the need for precise receipt-level document storage and retrieval. It is the customer's role to feed us those source documents by any of the multiple means we provide. Many of our customers have us manage and pay their vendor bills or payroll, and it is their role to submit bills and timesheets to us by our deadlines.

Honest and transparent business practices. Our involvement forces financial controls on customers that aren't used to having that level of accountability in place. We alert them to bad business practices when we see them, like commingled funds, improper payroll tax management, improper documentation, or poor cash procedures. If the customer squirms and tries to get us to cosign their questionable practices, we decline. We have a zero-tolerance policy for funny business. Either they change their ways, or we respectfully decline to serve them.

We lay out these expectations during the customer onboarding in a *Getting Started Guide*. Written in a simple format, we talk about each task that we need them to perform, any related deadlines, and all of the tools they can use to execute those tasks efficiently.

As part of the customer experience,
we are always looking for ways to improve
the tools for automation and delivery of
information from the customer.

The more automated the process, the more efficient, timely, and accurate the data will be. In a perfect world, we could completely bypass the customer and not require any interface with them to get the data we need. But this is not a perfect world.

Know Your Strengths (and Those of Your Staff)

Early on, I realized I had to shift taking complaints to other people. The founder of a business is the best person and the worst person to field complaints. What I found as the company grew is that I would take the complaints personally, be discouraged, become angry, step on the toes of my staff, take sides (staff versus customer), and feel inclined to over-repair the problem, which only increased the customer's expectations and reinforced that we weren't doing enough when they complained.

Let's face it, some of these business owners have been kicking their bookkeeper around for years. Unfortunately, we seem to be the scapegoat of choice! I also found that a small, pesky percentage of customers would yield the sword of "Jennifer told me that you would (fill in the blank)," against my staff to get services that they imagined or pretended I had promised them.

The whole process was creating a divide between my staff and me, my staff and the customers, and the customers and me, and it was draining morale all the way around. So, I shifted the complaint-taking role to the relationship builder in the company—the salesperson. That went over like a lead balloon. The salesperson lost some of his innocent belief that our company was impeccable, beyond reproach. And now the salesperson was getting upset with the accounting staff for screwing up on "his customer." Suffice it to say, this was a bad move.

I finally landed on the perfect solution. All the customer needed was someone disconnected from their team—someone they believed had the authority and power to change things—to listen to their problem and moderate a solution. It couldn't be me or the salesperson, but it had to be someone who understood the role of the accounting team and the role of the customer, knew the processes, and could point to them. It needed to be a neutral party whose goal was to find a solution rather than assign blame.

I have the perfect person in my company who now serves that role. She also does many other valuable things, but she is our designated customer service contact, and that is because of her unique ability to make people feel heard, gather the facts, speak frankly and openly with all involved problem solvers, and define each person's role in the solution.

But in finding this person, I first needed to figure out which characteristics indicated who could best handle this challenging, sometimes confrontational role without it making so much as a ding in their morale. By watching my team members as problems arose, I saw that this person was eager to learn more and jump into conversions about solutions. She wanted to know and be involved. When allowed to do so, she accomplished fair and equitable resolutions.

I could have recognized this person's strengths faster had I known about strengths testing. I highly recommend it. It's a fun and revealing exercise that can help you identify people who stand out with unique strengths and see which ones your successful team members have in common. All of my upper management have taken the CliftonStrengths assessment—I know their strengths, and they know each other's.

 PRO TIP

Check out the Gallup CliftonStrengths assessment. It's a game changer. https://www.gallupstrengthscenter.com

Stand Your Ground

Plenty of colleagues and potential customers pushed back against my unconventional business model. They were uncomfortable with a value-based subscription, paying in advance, and not having the work quantified by hours. As for the customers' responsibility to give us access, when we were first starting out, bankers would flat out tell our customers not to provide us with direct access to their accounts. We also experienced resistance from customers who were not ready for the shift of the bookkeeper role from "servant of their needs" to a "highly trained expert" who was bringing new solutions and processes to the table.

They did not like the requirement to conform to financial controls and abandon some of their loosey-goosey small business practices. In a business environment that was so boutique, they were used to being treated as unique and special. I get it, and we make customers feel special in different ways, but the foundational constructs of our new business model couldn't be based on singling out any one customer's unique needs.

I have to admit that I gave in to all sorts of special requests in the beginning, usually out of fear of losing the customer. However, I quickly found out that those customers who had self-dictated special needs were almost always unappreciative and unforgiving on the other side. While it was painful to lose income during our leaner years, perhaps losing the customer was exactly what the company needed.

STRADDLING TWO HORSES

The challenge is not lost on me. A lot of solopreneurs are really going to get this piece because maybe they have ten customers, and if they remodel their business practices, they might lose, let's say, five customers as a result. That is half of the customer base! This is why, if you have the opportunity for a fresh start, it's always best to model your new business the way you want it and promote and present it that way right from the start. If you don't have that opportunity, pitch your revised business model to your current customer base. Convert those who are on board with it while building a base of new customers who are not aware of your old ways. Eventually, you will feel the pressure to leave the remaining nonconformists behind.

I finally had my "a-ha" moment around clients I was still driving to for hours-for-dollars service and decided, "If I have to drive there, I'm not going." I had right around fourteen customers at the time. Some had been onboarded to the Complete Controller platform where they were being handled by Bookkeepers, but the rest I was still driving to serve on-site. A seemingly small incident provided the pressure I needed to make that critical decision.

I was driving to a customer that I knew in my heart I shouldn't be serving anymore, trying to not lose my bread and butter. On the drive, my phone blew up with a fire drill on the Complete Controller side—a problem that, if I were in front of my computer, would be a quick fix. Instead, I was in my car, heading to a customer's house where I needed to give them my undivided attention. After all, they were paying me by the hour to serve them at an appointed time, our arrangement under the old model. It's not like I could ask them to wait while I fixed the problem. It was at that moment I realized, "This isn't working anymore."

At the conclusion of that appointment, I said, "I need to let you know that this is going to be my last time coming in." I had previously told her about Complete Controller and now it was time for the "come-to-Jesus" moment: "Either you're able to see yourself as a fit with Complete Controller on one of our service plans and we'll pair you up with a Bookkeeper and get you started, or we're going to have to part ways." She had looked at the pricing for Complete Controller, and it was more than she was used to paying, so she decided that it did not make sense to sign up. She was not happy that I had put my foot down, but it was a defining moment for me. I had cut the last tether.

SPECIAL NEEDS

Not surprisingly, that wasn't the last time I would need to put my foot down or say no. Customers pushed the envelope and made demands for things that were outside our service plans to be included in their fixed monthly cost. I even had merely potential customers tell me during a sales pitch that I should be doing it differently. I eventually recognized that as long as I was the one selling the service, they would continue to behave that way. They had the decision-maker's ear, and that gave them license to float their ideas for changing my business model. Sure enough, after hiring a salesperson, the demands quieted. But not before I learned some painful lessons.

We have a very successful customer who manages multiple fine dining restaurants in Orange County, California. He is demanding and sometimes quick to temper. We have to be careful not to give in to too many late-night calls and fire drills, or he comes to expect it, and like most savvy business owners, he is extremely budget-sensitive and balks when he gets the bill for extras. I liken his behavior to my coming by one of his restaurants at breakfast time, telling him I'm a top customer and I want breakfast, so he makes me breakfast out of the kindness of his heart, even though they don't serve breakfast—then when the bill comes, I complain about it.

Here's the thing: My processes are efficient. If you want me to do it differently according to what makes you comfortable, but your way takes more time, are you willing to pay more to dictate my process? Am I willing to let you? Is it a good idea for a chef, an interior designer, or a mechanic to tell me how to do bookkeeping?

> ## Changing the process to meet
> ## a single customer's needs has a serious impact
> ## on the business.

You lose efficiency and you lose respect from the customer. Why? Because now they're the ones deciding how the work should be done. You also wind up losing money. And I will tell you that every single time I received a serious complaint that involved wanting a refund or being unwilling to pay for services, it involved a customer for which we had made some kind of special accommodation.

Bookkeepers have historically been lower in status when it comes to accounting and business management teams. Some business owners are accustomed to calling the shots and pushing us around. So, how do we dispel that expectation? For starters, we begin the relationship on our terms. It is by accepting our terms that we agree to meet their needs and bring great value to them. It's the smart move to set the rules of the game up front and not waiver from those by doing something totally customized or outside of your normal process, just to appease one customer. You see, that deviation from the norm is almost always a failure point. That's the very nature of a deviation. Because it's a deviation from your process, you have no supporting processes or quality control in place for it. The very fact that you are deviating from your process exponentially increases the chance that something will go wrong at some point around that deviation, and that's bad business.

Meanwhile, be open to feedback. Constructive criticism is the most valuable thing that a customer can give any business. And sometimes they are yelling when they give it, so you have to have a tool for avoiding the immediate answer. If there is a problem needing immediate attention, handle it. Then pause before committing to any changes, ask them to give you a moment to look into it and promise to circle back. Now weigh the feedback carefully. If they have brought your attention to a universal need, a gap in your offering or quality, then you have to address it, because if you don't, then you're missing an opportunity. Find an efficient and profitable way to address it and nimbly incorporate it into your process.

PROTECT YOUR REPUTATION

As Complete Controller grew to have a few hundred customers, squashing special demands became more of a reputational issue. You get to a certain size and your reputation is everything. Your brand is what you have to protect. Those of you who are taking an existing business or department virtual will relate to this because you experience greater reputational risk when you change the rules on established customers.

We invest time and money to get customer leads and develop our relationships. One bad statement or opinion from a customer can be detrimental to our brand and reputation. We had a customer with multiple locations who had us bent over backward with special needs. He was a little tough to serve anyway because he had a direct and brash way about him. But we were used to working with varied personalities, and as long as we accommodated their needs and they weren't abusive, we found that we could have a symbiotic relationship.

One night, however, this guy had "one too many" and called me up to rake me over the coals. And he said, "You should know that I have a huge social media presence and I'm going to use that influence to ruin your company." I was so upset. I was upset with myself for having accommodated him. I was upset with him for stooping so low as to take a swing at the business that I had put my blood, sweat, and tears into. And I was really upset because the point of conflict was something to which he had contributed. That was when I realized that I would just have to respectfully say to some people, "I don't think this is the right solution for you."

PRO TIP

You can fire your customers. I know you have heard this before and you might be thinking, "I cannot afford to fire my hard-earned customers." I encourage you to do the math. How much time and effort does it take to build a strong five-star reputation in your market? Is your difficult or unstable customer paying you enough to risk that investment? How many hours are you spending to maintain the tough customer relationship? Could you be serving two ideal customers with those hours? Are they robbing you of scalability? I'm not telling you to back down from the challenge to do better. I'm telling you to listen to that gut that knows this customer poses a risk to your reputation or profitability that you are not willing to take.

Today, our sales team follows this approach. If a prospect is giving them too much pushback and trying to challenge or redesign the solutions we are offering before even becoming a customer, our salesperson will say, "Well, it sounds like we might not be the best fit for you. Maybe there's another solution out there that is going to work better." That typically works well. Once a prospect or customer realizes that you're not going to bend to their custom demands in order to get them or keep them, they fall in line quickly, if they truly do want your services. And the ones that don't get in line? They have permission to leave and leave happy. Treat them as well going out the door as they were treated coming in the door. In the end, we're all just people trying to get by, and you never know when they are going to turn around and come right back.

Let your customers miss you. Let them feel the loss of your services and decide if they want to return.

You won't keep everyone happy. At some point, you have to be true to your business, your baby, and not feel guilty about the small percentage of people who can't wrap their heads around your pricing model or don't want to be responsible for updating their technology or internal processes. There will always be someone out there who will cater to their needs for a price, but I propose that you not be one of them.

Just saying "Screw guilt" when you have failed to meet someone's needs isn't easy, and service professionals find it particularly challenging because our value has been based on people's acceptance of us as a provider and recognition of our skill. Our value has also long been associated with an hours-for-dollars construct. I encourage you to challenge that dusty value perception. As a profession, it is fully within our power to dictate how our services are delivered and not take any crap from people who think they know better about how our business should be structured.

Do not miss out on helping hundreds
of customers because you changed for one.

Pen to Paper

You've reached a place where you know what traditional constraints you will be rejecting, what items will be on your menu, and what roles you need to support it. When you are breaking the mold, one thing you can be sure of is pushback. Defining your customer's role in the relationship will reduce friction and increase perceived value. It also helps you to separate constructive feedback from destructive complaints. To help you define their role, consider the following:

- ☑ How will your customers be required to participate?

- ☑ How will you tell them about their role and what tools will support them?

- ☑ What will be your method for fielding and settling complaints without compromising your vision?

4

KNOW
YOUR VISION

THE BEST WAY TO nip guilt in the bud is to be true to your vision for the business. I found having a clear vision to be immensely helpful during the early stages of building my business, and you will, too. In order to be true to your vision, you need to know your vision. Your business model will differ from mine since it will reflect your own personal values and profession. But having that clear vision will be pivotal when working to keep guilt at bay.

Once you've developed your vision and laid out your business model and how it works, you're going to be unstoppable. Yet, I'm not going to sugarcoat it: You'll also be tested along the way.

You'll still have those challenging moments with customers, and you'll run into obstacles and criticism. When that happens, go back to your vision. By doing this, you will become increasingly able to set aside those nagging feelings that maybe you should do that something special or different just to please one person. Instead, you can ask yourself if the action will help to move the ball toward the goals you have set. If not, it will be easy to accept that you don't have to do it. It's really that simple.

Once you have a good idea of what you want your virtual business offering to look like, perform the competitive analysis to see what others are doing and decide on the nonnegotiable parts of your service model, then you'll be ready to start laying out your business processes, which we will explore later in this book. For now, remember to

know what you want

and to stay true to your vision.

Research, Research, Research

Before developing my own processes, I set out to find who was already doing what I wanted to do. I learned as much as possible about the business models of my competitors and colleagues in the market. Leaving behind the ideas that didn't impress me, I used the pieces that did, as sparks for my own model innovations. That's when I found the Chinese company that was doing something similar. They had created a hosted environment and were providing bookkeeping services, similar to what I was offering. I liked that part of what they were doing, but I didn't like the rest. I didn't like how they were charging for it or how they were marketing it.

So, I took some bits from that company and then found another company that was offering virtual chief financial officer (CFO) services. They had put together monthly packages, which I really liked. But I didn't want to get into the CFO side of things, because I had never been a CFO and felt that role was outside of my wheelhouse. I also didn't want to stretch myself too far, at least to start. But I did like the idea of pricing packages in a way that you could see what kinds of services you were entitled to.

That inspiration helped me advance my ideas about the pricing model for my business. I implemented the Chinese menu idea where customers would get, say, a complete dinner with appetizers and main entrée and dessert for a set price, with à la carte add-ons to customize the experience. Though I really didn't find anyone who was doing it exactly that way, I knew that my vision was possible.

Most of my competitive analysis took place by Googling. I mean, I was creating a virtual business, and a web presence would be crucial as that's how most people would find or learn more about my company. It made sense to look for competition on the web since those that didn't have a strong presence weren't going to be fighting for my business. I also made phone calls to companies I was curious about—and inquired as a potential customer. Once I got someone on the phone (you might be surprised to learn that a great deal of people did not call me back and clearly did not have a sales process in place), I'd ask things like, "What is it that you're offering? What does it look like? How do you do it?" And just like a potential customer, I would introduce some of our barriers and see how they addressed them.

Really, any good sales team knows that anyone they are pitching could potentially be somebody who is shopping them in competitive analysis. That's just how it works. Once I dug in and found out what competitors were doing and how they pitched their service and how they proposed to do it procedurally, then my attention turned to understanding standards for best practice. I started asking myself, "What is going to meet that ethical threshold? That security threshold?" Part of my research was determining which regulatory bodies monitor and control the quality of the services I planned to offer, along with what they expected.

It is no small feat to learn regulatory nuances, especially for a company serving all fifty states. For instance, in California, you can call yourself an accounting service if you are providing bookkeeping services. In Texas, however, you have to call yourself a bookkeeping service and cannot use the term "accounting service" unless you have a CPA who is a 51 percent or greater shareholder running the day-to-day operations of the company. This is just an example of the types of details related to our industry that come up when looking to serve the national market. The cloud opens the door for you to offer your services nationally or even internationally, but you will need to do your homework to make sure you are addressing these regulatory nuances for each state and country you plan to serve.

In addition, in my profession, I also knew that security would be a big deal. My technical engineer and I needed to fully understand and implement the security standards that were expected for securing people's books and tax returns, their vendor receipts, their sensitive financial documents, their billing documents, and their credit card and check information. The system had to be at least as secure as online banking. When we were laying the foundation for this, we researched how security was handled around medical offices and law firms, because we knew we would be serving those industry types. And the truth is, you can't serve that caliber of customer unless you can demonstrate that you have the same or better security than they have.

Map Out Your Processes

Early on, before I even took on my first customer, I modeled the flow of information to us and then delivery back to the customer. Ironing out that process was critical to going virtual. Back then, if customers wanted to get information to their bookkeeper, they typically dropped it off in a shoebox or had their bills sent directly to their accounting service or business manager. It wasn't as easy and efficient as our process now, thanks to technology. So, I needed to lay the groundwork for how the process was going to work in the most efficient way possible. This early process-building also allowed me to see if we needed to create or introduce tools for support.

PRO TIP

Solve the most obvious problems first. For me it was how to get documents and information from our customers. What are your barriers? What have competitors done to solve them? Define a process that overcomes the barrier the way you want to do it. Then tackle the next barrier. Once you have worked through the obvious ones, you will have a framework in which to develop an order of operations. This is where the rubber hits the road.

I will admit that at first, my process was rudimentary and full of gaps. You have to start somewhere. Don't be hesitant to put pen to paper and start laying it out. Eventually, I ironed out the wrinkles and was satisfied that we had a smooth initial process that fit the model I was building. As you mesh information delivery processes with internal processes, you are essentially building a machine. You have your intake, fuel injector, carburetor, and exhaust. Your oil and fuel go in, and everything's running together in perfect harmony. Once you have the machine, you can teach someone to operate it. Give them a manual and some instruction, so they know how to turn it on, how to make it go, how to stop it. I needed to create a machine that could be run by anybody that I trained to run it because that would ensure that the business could operate without me.

Find the Right Mentors

The most valuable assets you can have as you are developing your business model are mentors who are willing to give you honest feedback *for free*. Pick people who have nothing to gain from your success. I strongly suggest that you do not pay for advice unless you are engaging in a professional, guided training or mentoring program. The truth is that every person who is being paid for their services is motivated to continue being paid—whether by referring you to a friend who will provide a commission for the referral or establishing the relationship in hopes that you will invest with them at a later date or coaching you in hopes that the coaching relationship will never end. In other words, they are positioning themselves for continued profit. It is not in their best interest for you to no longer need them.

Just look at your own experience. You want to be paid for your advice. Often, accountants will help by giving someone hourly QuickBooks training in hopes that, at some point, the trainee will get busy and engage them to do the work for them. There is nothing wrong with that. It is a viable business strategy, and there are times when you may need to call upon these folks for support in their specific areas of expertise. When you do so, just don't fool yourself that they have your best interests entirely at heart. For honest feed-back that is free of ulterior motives, choose mentors that are doing it because they are at a point in their success at which they need to give back. These are the best mentors because they have reached an understanding that giving back is the key to purposeful living.

Tell your mentors your ideas for overcoming barriers to market. Run your proposed processes by them. Sometimes just verbalizing a process will help you to see its flaws or merits more clearly. Sometimes people need to tell you that they aren't buying what you're selling. That's why you want to find people who are willing to tell you the truth, not just what you want to hear. You need to know if your ideas are so far outside the box that they create fear, or if you aren't communicating the value proposition correctly. Mentors are perfect for sifting through all of these unknowns as you develop your vision and model for delivering it.

Flying without a Net

For those of you who are taking the great leap from solopreneur or chancing a large investment, the idea of letting go of what you know for something entirely unknown can be terrifying. My outsourced controller customers that I had to drive to serve in-house were my bread and butter. But if I hadn't let them go, I would have allowed them to eat up chunks of time that I would otherwise have spent on my new venture.

There is a moment in every entrepreneur's experience when you realize that you need to surrender the safety net to jump and see if you can fly.

For the new entrepreneur, the first time they jump, it feels like reckless abandon. Seasoned entrepreneurs seem to be able to spot opportunities and jump with what appears to be unparalleled confidence. It looks that way only because they have honed the skill of sniffing out risk versus return, and they typically have a high risk tolerance (usually covered by other successes) that allows them to chase opportunities others might leave on the table.

If you have reached the point at which it is more important to provide the new business with your full attention rather than split your time trying to hold on to the safety net, you must act. Sometimes people see the success of entrepreneurs and don't see the process—the blood, sweat, and tears—that got them there. A new business is like a baby. For it to grow into a healthy child, it will need nurturing, planning, nourishment, and guidance, and it has the best chance to succeed if it has your full attention and dedication.

When you are just starting out, this might mean taking on roommates or sleeping on your friends' couches and sustaining yourself on ramen noodles for a while—it is the true entrepreneur who knows it is worth it. I don't say this lightly because for me, creating Complete Controller was a huge sacrifice. My initial influx of capital came from my dad, who died from mesothelioma, an aggressive lung cancer. The amount was less than $50,000, but I was able to pay for the technology I needed and float the company until we could break even.

As a family, we struggled in those early years. I remember early on we had a four-bedroom house in Southern California, and I had four roommates—one of whom was sleeping on the couch. I was working in the dining room because every bedroom was rented. Eventually, I moved out to the garage and worked from there.

Small business owners sometimes frustrate me. They'll have the private school and the big mortgage and the fancy car, yet their business is struggling. If there's anything I can change in the world of financial empowerment, it's this:

Your business is the lifeblood of your lifestyle. You need to feed and reinvest in your business for it to be survivable, and sometimes that means downgrading how you live.

No one will care if you are eating ramen noodles for a year or sharing a car with your spouse as you are building your empire. Business owners can get too caught up with what other people think. This is not to say that you should dive foolhardily into any great idea you have. The trick is to do your homework, test the market, create a proof of concept, and then know the right time to jump. And of course, hold true to your vision and screw guilt all along the way.

Pen to Paper

Your vision is starting to come together now, and it is time to find the obvious barriers and develop processes for overcoming them. Competitive research is a powerful tool that allows you to be inspired by the ingenuity of your colleagues and provides the spark you need to birth ideas about how to differentiate yourself. To help you get started, do the following:

- ☑ List your top five competitors.

- ☑ Share what they are doing well that you would like to emulate and what they are doing poorly that you will not.

- ☑ How have your competitors overcome industry barriers, cloud barriers, and perception barriers?

- ☑ What are your barriers?

- ☑ What are the processes you will put in place to overcome them?

Once you've written your answers, bounce your ideas off of someone you respect to get some constructive feedback.

PART TWO

MAKE MEANING

*"There really is only one question you
should ask yourself before starting any new venture:
Do I want to make meaning?"*

—GUY KAWASAKI

5

MAKE MEANING FOR
YOUR STAFF

IN THE LAST CHAPTER, I talked about how important it was for me to have a vision when I was building my company. Like me, you'll find that having a clear vision is necessary to keep you from being swayed by every special request or circumstance you encounter so you can stay true to yourself and avoid diluting your efforts and value. I've learned that if I test each business practice against one central idea—How does it make meaning in people's lives?—I stay true to my vision. This does not mean making everybody happy, which comes from a place of fear. Instead, I look at how I make meaning from a place of passion.

One of my greatest passions is financial empowerment for small businesses. I love the entrepreneurial personality. I love the ingenuity. I love the risk. I think creating and building a small business takes guts, passion, and faith. Small businesses are the lifeblood of our nation, even our world, and yet, I believe that these dynamic and valuable people are undersupported in their endeavors. Businesses are an expression of our passion and creativity. They are our art and "brainchild." To serve and empower this dynamic segment, as I've had the opportunity to, is both an honor and a responsibility.

When I started Complete Controller, I hired two women, each with young kids at home, to be my first Bookkeepers. They were both very smart; one had previously worked for a Big Four accounting firm. These women were extremely skillful, strong multitaskers, and great strategists. Since our company was in the cloud, they were able to work from home, which appealed to them and *allowed me to tap into a skilled labor resource that was otherwise basically "off the market."*

One of the benefits of watching the virtualization of the bookkeeping industry unfold is seeing so many people who previously had not been able to contribute to the accounting profession—because of traditional model rigidity—do very good work. This made meaning for them, just as it has for countless other professionals who have discovered the benefits and flexibility of working from the cloud. Over the past decade, as the work-from-home model has become more widely accepted, skilled professionals that don't have opportunities in their town or can't make the office commute have been able to flex their expert muscles, and we have had the benefit of leveraging their skills in the marketplace. It has really warmed my heart to see this.

We were trendsetters because in 2007, working from home was not the norm for our industry. But I understood the need for flexibility in scheduling because of my own experience of being a single mom. That heightened my desire to be able to give people who were in similar situations the opportunity to not just have flexible employment, but to make a really good living without ever leaving home. I also liked the idea of averting the need to promise a set number of hours each week to my staff, a strategy that was necessary to my profit equation.

The cloud affords you the opportunity to tap into skilled labor without regard for geographic constraints. Think about it: Although you are head-quartered in New York or Los Angeles, you no longer have to pull only from those talent pools, you can hire from Kansas City or Raleigh and pay a fraction of the cost for comparative skills. You also have the ability to headhunt the talent you truly want without negotiating a relocation plan into the employment agreement. Another sweet feature of a cloud-based workplace is the ability to break through traditional time constraints. Later in this chapter, I will present more about how I structured the roles within my company to be deliverable-driven rather than time-driven.

To employ these strategies, you don't just create a cloud workspace and tell staff to log in and do their work as usual. Instead, you will need to model the business processes to support new ways of doing things. If you are moving to the cloud from an already established business or moving a department to the cloud, consider starting from scratch and tossing away the processes you currently use instead of trying to make them fit your cloud-based business model.

To find, keep, and foster the growth of a skilled labor force in the cloud, you first need to recognize that the incentive system and motivators for your staff may be far different from what you are used to.

For instance, if a staff member is working at the office and the technology goes down, they can go to the break room and chat or go to the file room and file. In the cloud, they have nowhere to go. So keeping the technology in good working order is paramount. Second is creating processes and the accompanying training, so staff members know what to do and how to do it. After all, they won't have you in the office next door to bother with questions about what to do next. Finally, there has to be a method for tracking and accountability that incentivizes staff members to achieve the desired goals (e.g., efficiency, accuracy, timeliness).

How We Do It

Now that you have a general sense of the importance of making meaning for your staff, I want to show you how we do this at Complete Controller. I'll use our Bookkeepers as an example. This role is customer-facing and integral to our company, and because we promote from within, every Complete Controller Accountant has been a Bookkeeper at some point on their path.

Our Bookkeepers are highly skilled and competent people. We prequalify them as QuickBooks ProAdvisors, having a four-year degree in accounting or commensurate experience working directly under a CPA or CFO, and a solid history of performing small business accounting. We hold them to high standards and require they champion the Complete Controller trusted brand. And they come from all walks of life, which I love.

Maybe they are a CPA who doesn't want to work in that big accounting firm anymore. Or they are an entrepreneur who is tired of running their own bookkeeping company. Perhaps they are looking for more flexibility in their work life. Or maybe they just wanted to put their accounting skills to good use in a unique virtual work environment that allows them room to grow and advance, if they so choose, right from the comfort of their own home. Regardless of their reasons, we make meaning for our Bookkeepers by making it easier for them to do their jobs and giving them control over their own destinies.

WE PROVIDE A SOLID TECHNOLOGY PLATFORM

We provide a platform on which our staff can do their work easily. From anywhere. The technology infrastructure where our customer work is performed is our responsibility. It's our role to keep it supported and always up and running, and to be quick to troubleshoot and address any problems that occur.

Our technology platform needs to be reliable, consistent, and accessible. As a cloud-based company wanting to attract intelligent and hardworking talent, we're telling them they can work whenever their customers need them and on their own terms—as long as they are meeting deadlines and are impeccable about their work. If this strategy is going to be successful, we need to have a system that doesn't work against that goal.

We give our Bookkeepers the tools they need to perform their work. Each Bookkeeper has their own cloud desktop full of tools, including time records, scopes of work, email templates, instruction sets, and all of the programs they need to manage their workflow, like calendars and emails. ⚒

Their desktop is also a single point of access to all of the customers they serve. All they have to do is find a customer's shortcut and drill down to their desktop to begin working.

To increase efficiency and reduce frustration, we standardize our customer desktops, so everything is in the same place for each customer. This keeps our processes consistent and streamlined for staff. For example, our Bookkeepers know that each customer desktop will have a shortcut to the QuickBooks file and a paperless filing cabinet with all of the necessary records. Any technologies that need to be accessed by Accounting or integrated with the general ledger software are on the desktop as well. These may include bill-pay software, payroll processing company logins, payment processing software, e-commerce sites, point of sale system access, and more. Finally, there is a holding place for customer paperwork and one for the Accounting team's work in process. Our Bookkeepers efficiently manage their customers' needs without having to go to one application, close it out, and then go to another, use multiple windows, or perform work outside of our secure environment. Instead, the entire back office is in one place.

Behind the scenes (where the customer can't go), there are checklists for each customer's periodic work and a unique briefing of customer tasks broken down by frequency. These tools create a seamless workflow, allowing a Controller (the Bookkeeper's counterpart in the two-person customer-facing Accounting team) to fill in for their Bookkeeper when the latter is on vacation or a new Bookkeeper to take over an account without loss of knowledge and continuity.

Each desktop is set up the exact same way because it makes our staff more efficient. It's easier for them to function because they always know where to go to find exactly what they need. We are sticklers about standardization, how paperwork is filed, how it is named, how each shortcut is named, and what tools appear on the desktop and why. While your business may be in a different field, you can do the same when you build your own virtual environment. Think about the staff time you will save simply by standardizing the work environment.

Not only does this standardization increase efficiency, it allows our Operations team to better monitor quality control. Think about it: You can easily see if something is different from the norm if you have created a norm. In our case, because the environment is standardized, it takes almost no time to identify the staff members who aren't compliant.

The beauty of working from the cloud is you only need an internet connection and a computer with your software and tools to perform your work.

> *Our cloud platform allows our Bookkeepers to efficiently manage all of their customers from anywhere in the world where there is an internet connection.*

That means they can work whenever and wherever they need to work. Our staff is free to do that. And it means the world to them.

One of our early Bookkeepers, who had a young daughter, suffered an unfortunate separation with her husband. Her parents lived in England, and she told me, "You know, Jennifer, I want to go stay with my parents. They will help me with my daughter. I promise you that my work product will not fail, that I will still be there for you just like I am today." I said, "Well, it's an experiment. Let's give it a shot." And sure enough, she was there for a whole year and then she came back, and we never suffered from her being there. I didn't even really notice that she was overseas to tell you the truth. It just didn't matter. It was a nonfactor. She arranged her work time so she could communicate with her customers and other staff members. She made it seamless, showing up for what she needed to do. She was accurate and timely about her work product so there wasn't a problem.

Make Meaning Spotlight: Made in the USA

Although the Bookkeeper just mentioned was allowed to work overseas, it's important to note that I don't hire outside of the United States. I know many of my colleagues are tempted to do so, and I know people who have made a great business out of outsourcing accounting talent from Singapore, India, and elsewhere. Some firms utilize these services or have their own overseas staff. We choose not to do it.

Here's why.

I want to make sure that anything we do, we do under the laws of this land. Good luck prosecuting someone from Taiwan for stealing your client's bank account information, right? This is more than just what we are doing for our customers. This extends to what my staff is doing to complete their contracts for Complete Controller. I want any work performed on my behalf to be held to US standards of business practice. I want to be able to call them on the carpet if anything goes awry.

Granted, so far we have successfully avoided any major conspiracies, embezzlement, or fraud. Nothing more than falsification of hours has occurred. Regardless, I'm glad we have the ability to report any wrongdoing and have the offender fired, arrested, or otherwise brought to justice. That is only going to happen if they're here in the United States.

Bottom line: I feel more comfortable that way, my insurance company feels more comfortable that way, and my customers feel more comfortable that way. Yes, my margins are slimmer, but I sleep better at night.

And look, we are proud to give Americans jobs. I started this company in 2007. The economy went gangbusters until 2008 when everything crashed. America was in a state of desperation and the ability to work was incredibly valuable. For people to work without paying for nursery school or auto fuel was even better. I was able to find talent in places all across the nation. Their talent empowered Complete Controller to provide services, and Complete Controller empowered them to make a good living, and that made meaning for them and for me.

WE PROVIDE EXTENSIVE TRAINING

We are big on training. We want our staff to know the technology they are using, understand the tools available to them, and be well versed in the Complete Controller way of managing their work.

I believe the best way to ensure any staff member's success is to train them thoroughly and create feedback loops. We begin by clearly stating their role as well as their purpose within the company and to the customer. We tell them what we are relying on them to do and what their customers will be expecting of them, based on their service plans. Then we pay our staff to learn the Complete Controller way.

There are often many ways to accomplish the same goal. We pick the way that we believe will have the best outcome in the most circumstances and write our protocol accordingly. Our processes ensure success for the Bookkeeper and delivery of an excellent product to the customer. And by standardizing the way we deliver each task and making everything deadline driven, we make it easy to see if something is falling out of line.

In addition to giving our staff scopes of work and other training materials to teach them our techniques, we provide checklists and templates to guide their work. We also perform periodic internal peer review and facilitate collaboration between team members. The intent is to give them all the support they need to feel like they are not alone in the world, even though they have no physical contact with their co-workers.

Meanwhile, we don't spend much time having meetings about topics that don't directly affect work life. Our Accountants generally prefer to be task-oriented and stay focused on their customer relationships, and that is right where we want them. We don't want them to be distracted by office politics. If they are superstars, work best on their own, and have great relationships with their customers and supervising Controller, they won't need much interference from us. While we love supporting our staff by sharing knowledge and providing continuing education and access to a large body of expertise, we equally value their autonomy. They are trying to be efficient, earn a good living, and make their customers happy. Therefore, anything we do must empower that objective. Our support and training make meaning for them.

WE HANDLE CUSTOMER ACQUISITION AND
WE COLLECT PAYMENT

This alone is a strong argument for abandoning self-employment to work for a company. Many solopreneurs loathe the sales and collections part of the business, so we make sure our Bookkeepers aren't bothered with these pesky tasks, and your staff will appreciate it, too.

Generally speaking, accountants are not big fans of closing sales and collecting fees from their customers. Chasing past-due payments is as painful in their minds as lying on a red ant hill. Sound familiar? My experience with small businesses has shown that a large percentage of service professionals feel the same way. These providers are skilled at their profession or craft, but somehow when it comes to getting the customer to sign on the dotted line or hand over a check, the business side of business goes sideways.

Ever notice how the sales process for most outpatient surgeries and dentistry is handled in two steps? First, the skilled expert does their job and makes a recommendation for improvements. Then someone entirely separate from the medical procedure discusses the charges for those improvements and payment arrangements. They have it figured out. The psychology behind this process allows the patient to separate the business from the professional service being provided, and the doctor or dentist isn't pulled into conversations about money.

Of course, this isn't a practical approach for the solopreneur or even a firm partner who is responsible for generating their own customer relationships and producing billable services. As soon as you are able to have someone separate perform that role, I think you should. Our Bookkeepers dislike sales and collections as much as the average service provider, so we make meaning for them by shielding them from that side of the business and having a separate staff person handle those functions.

Our Bookkeepers do need to follow our processes to ensure they secure approvals for custom request work and keep the customer closely informed about progress and time spent when performing scopes of work that are outside the service plan. And they need to use their expert skills and training to deliver on each customer's service plan in a timely and accurate manner.

We handle the rest. Which brings us to our support roles: technical support and customer service.

WE HANDLE TECH SUPPORT AND CUSTOMER SERVICE ISSUES

As with sales and payments, we don't want the Bookkeepers focusing on the nitty-gritty billing and technical issues that come up. Instead, we want to keep them focused on customer relationships.

To allow for this, we have several layers of technical support. The customer Help Desk troubleshoots landmines around getting connected to our platform, printing locally, sharing clipboards, adjusting screen resolution, and user authentication. Tiered support handles conversions, integrated applications, plug-ins, email, mobile applications ✖, customer relationship management (CRM) ✖, and the customer database.

If a customer has a technology problem, you might think it would be more efficient and cost-effective to have the Bookkeeper troubleshoot it first. It's not. Our Bookkeepers are there to fulfill a specific role, and we protect them from efficiency-draining, unexpected, and unmanageable tasks such as technical support. If it is not a QuickBooks setting, the customer gets their help from technical support, not the Bookkeeping team.

Customer service is another support role that is best handled outside of the Bookkeeping team. Common customer service issues include billing questions, upgrading or downgrading services, terminating service for an entity, suspending service or creating a payment plan for a customer struggling with cash flow, or handling a customer venting frustrations. While customers should bring bookkeeping concerns up with the supervising Controller, sometimes those concerns land elsewhere, so we want to provide support for those times.

Like technical support, customer service can drain a Bookkeeper's efficiency, but most important, it can drain morale. Separating the roles allows the Bookkeeper to maintain their momentum with the customer. Many tech and customer service issues are outside of the Bookkeeper's ability to fix, authorize, or manage anyway, so making the customer go to them for everything would only cause the Bookkeeper to have to say "wait," and it would create a longer path to resolution. Instead, they make an introduction directly to the person who can solve the problem.

The separate roles also provide the customer with a new set of ears to hear their concerns. Have you ever noticed how an understanding customer service representative can make you feel heard, and that's all you need to get back on the proverbial horse and ride? We provide that support so our Bookkeepers can focus on what they do best, and a bump in the road doesn't damage that valuable customer relationship.

WE MAKE IT WORTHWHILE FOR STAFF

We reward good work. When our Bookkeepers are efficient, accurate, and timely, with good customer satisfaction, they are compensated accordingly. We tie their compensation to the accomplishment of these goals by measuring their performance using key performance indicators (KPIs).

A system of enrichment based on performance provides staff members with control over their own financial destiny.

I highly recommend this for your own company. Rewards go a long way in boosting morale and can come in many forms: praise, money, time off, prizes, etc.

Here's part of our secret sauce: We only pay for hours that are actually worked, and those hours are related to specific tasks, according to the customers' service plans within a given Bookkeeper's portfolio and any required internal work such as continuing education. To accomplish this, we use a work tracker 🛠; I highly recommend this tool for monitoring staff activity in the cloud. In the early days, we were seeing that the amount of time staff members spent studying the training materials varied greatly. Time is money. And since we were paying them to learn, we had to come up with an expectation of how many hours it should take to fully review the materials and a way to track how much time each employee was taking. That was when we first put our work tracker in place to measure actual learning time. We set parameters that measured idle versus active time and even honed it so we could see every mouse click and task being completed. Now we give new trainees a maximum number of hours for training that we will pay for.

All work, just like training, is performed within our secure cloud environment where our work tracker allows us to see every click and keystroke. We are transparent and tell staff members that we have the work tracker. Each week, a staff member's work tracker hours are compared to their recorded time, and we ask for clarity on any deviation between the two. Those deviations are recorded on that staff member's time record for all to see and we have an acceptable deviation rate that, if exceeded, is grounds for immediate termination.

Right from the start, we set the expectation that we watch carefully what work is performed and how long it takes. Every bookkeeper starts with our company at the same hourly rate and is given the same criteria for increasing that rate over time. We lay out the path for them based on performance indicators that they can easily track, so they know the right time to ask for a raise.

We do not dictate when our staff clocks in or out, and we do not control schedules.

We only require that staff members meet the bookkeeping and communication needs of their customers and supervising Controller, and that an accurate product is delivered without fail according to the set deadlines.

Because of the flexibility of our cloud workplace, instead of saying, "Promise me eight hours a day between 8:00 a.m. and 5:00 p.m. PST," I can say, "Promise me you will complete this phase of the deliverable by this deadline." With a model of only paying for actual hours worked and being deadline and work product driven, how do we make meaning to our Bookkeepers' pocket-books? Bonuses, of course.

WE SET AND MONITOR KEY PERFORMANCE INDICATORS

We set KPIs for each Bookkeeper, so they know exactly how they are performing. Each KPI measures their quality of work and their ability to produce that work efficiently. Note: There are many benefits to having strong oversight and internal controls, but not everyone wants to be held to that standard. Some squirm under scrutiny. We find those aren't our people. Our bonus structure is designed with efficiency as the baseline. Efficiency earns the bonus. Short-falls in the other measured areas cause discounts to that bonus. Here is how it works:

Efficiency

To qualify for any bonus at all, a Bookkeeper must be efficient. Efficiency is so important to our model that a Bookkeeper who cannot make the grade during any given period is in jeopardy of being immediately terminated. That includes Bookkeepers who have just completed their training. Our processes are so concise and our support so complete that there is no reason for inefficiency. We don't set the bar at an uncomfortable level, but we do incentivize those who limbo low—the lower, the better.

To measure efficiency, we look at a Bookkeeper's total portfolio value (base subscription fees for all of the customers a particular Bookkeeper serves) divided into the cost of hours it takes to perform those services. At Complete Controller, if a Bookkeeper's cost is under 40 percent of their total portfolio value, that individual is considered efficient and the bonus is earned. If a Bookkeeper's cost is over 40 percent, they are considered inefficient and may be terminated. If they are deemed efficient, then we move onto the next KPI.

Timeliness

Not surprisingly, we have a lot of deadlines. Timeliness means that the work you are performing is completed by a certain deadline. We have a deadline for bank accounts to be reconciled, a deadline for the "Ask My Client" report to go out, and a deadline for the books to be reviewed with the supervising Controller during a period closing appointment. We also have deadlines for payables, payroll, annual tasks . . . you get the drift.

Everything in our business is deadline driven, and if you miss one, and we determine that it was not an isolated mistake, the consequences are dire. As I write this, we just terminated a staff member for failing to meet the deadline of distributing report packages with disclaimers on or before the fifteenth of the month. Today is the sixteenth. I know it sounds cutthroat, but the type of person who finds it acceptable to miss a deadline even though they know 1) it is a promise to a paying customer, 2) their supervising Controller will have to step in and complete the task, and 3) it is grounds for termination, does not value timeliness. If they can sleep at night when they have missed a deadline, they aren't our type, and we release them to go find work with a company that doesn't mind their work being late.

With all this talk about efficiency and deadlines, it's clear to see that we are running a well-oiled machine here, but we want it to be a precision, high-performance machine, and that's where the next KPI comes into play.

Accuracy

The line of work I am in is great because it's really easy to measure accuracy. Numbers don't lie, and you can see very quickly if something is wonky. For example, we provide a report package for customers who do not regularly access their books on the platform. It is the only work product they get for the money they pay. As a result, it is extremely important that our packages be a reflection of our brand, delivered on time, and accurate to the best of our ability.

As our Bookkeepers prepare these periodic report packages for their customers, they first have to set a closing appointment with their supervising Controller. The Controller and Bookkeeper review the period work together, watching for anomalies and errors. The Bookkeeper is given corrections and released to send the reports out once those corrections are made.

Then we review each report package delivered. If we see that the corrections were not made, reports weren't in the right order, the disclaimers weren't properly stated, the reports were sent to the wrong person within the company, or the reports were not compiled or named properly, then the Bookkeeper loses a portion of their bonus.

Customer Satisfaction

This is an easy one. If we do not receive a customer complaint during the period, we assume customer satisfaction. If we get a complaint, a portion of the bonus is forfeited. We have other ways to check this KPI that we will talk about later in the book.

What we do is pretty straightforward: We provide our Bookkeepers a way to work within a virtual environment, get paid for the actual work they do, and bypass the rigidity and limitations of the 9-to-5 world. They get to work in their comfy clothes with their dogs at their feet, while skipping the commute and the office politics. Their goal is to produce a timely and accurate work product efficiently, with good customer satisfaction so they can earn bonuses.

PRO TIP

Reward good work and terminate those who can't meet expectations.

While we want to enrich our staff members who meet and exceed their KPIs, we can't be afraid to terminate the ones who don't. We have created the model and showed them how it works. We provide tools and support and see what they do with it. Their destiny is in their hands. The reality is we have a lot of people who can and do succeed. They earn a bonus each period that shares a percentage of the profits from their portfolio with them. Less time spent to service the portfolio means better efficiency and greater profit. The more profit in their portfolio, the bigger the bonus. The most efficient Bookkeepers are offered new customers first because they have great profit margins. Imagine what all of that free money does to a Bookkeeper's effective hourly rate.

What they quickly discover is the more efficient they are, the more customers they can handle. And as long as they handle them in a timely manner and perform accurate work, we will continue to give them customers and their portfolio value will continue to grow. The longer they retain a customer, the more efficient they will become at doing that customer's work. By incentivizing retention and profitability, the company wins, the Bookkeeper wins, and this makes for a whole lot of meaning. And the best part is they can do it all without ever having to leave the house!

Pen to Paper

Your staff will be your most valuable asset, and the cloud model has opened you up to a vast talent pool of skill and expertise. It's up to you to create an environment that keeps them engaged, motivated, and in control of their own destiny. To do this, you will need to reduce frustrations by providing reliable technology, being concise with expectations, and setting KPIs that come with incentives (like bonuses). To get started, answer the following:

- ☑ How will you develop an environment that makes meaning for your staff without simply adding on fluff to a traditional model?

- ☑ How will pay be structured?

- ☑ What KPIs will be important to monitoring success or failure?

MAKE MEANING
FOR YOUR VENDORS

IN THIS CHAPTER, YOU will learn how to cultivate valuable vendor relationships. What does that actually mean? It means partnering with vendors that provide a reach that matches yours, offering good branding and co-marketing opportunities, sharing your values of virtualization and access, and regularly demonstrating they are nimble innovators.

If your business model includes advising customers about helpful technology and service solutions, your vendor relationships will be very important. Your vendors will train and support you and even pay you to learn about their solutions. These experiences will, in turn, empower you with solutions for your customers. When something goes wrong, you will want to know that you can rely on those vendors to support you. And, there are some really cool ways that you can develop a bond by supporting them as well. It's that spark that builds mighty relationships.

When customers arrive on our doorstep, for example, we have no control over what components are in their tech (or service) stacks. As a result, we get to work with a broad spectrum of software that solves business problems across multiple areas of need—e-commerce, payment processing, inventory management, invoicing, project management, service management, you name it—for a multitude of industries. If a solution is working particularly well for one or two customers and it functions elegantly and includes valuable features, then we want to learn more about it because of the potential for other customers to benefit from it.

Before making any referrals, we go directly to the vendor and ask a variety of questions: What training is available? What marketing materials are available? Do they have a partnership opportunity with or without a revenue stream?

A vendor revenue stream is a great thing, because it can pay for your costs to have conversations and field questions about that service or product, take time to understand its features, go through the training and then turn around and train your staff and finally onboard your customers to the new solution. We call that revenue stream "alternative revenue," or alt. rev. for short, and when you have enough customers on a service or technology that is generating alt. rev., it can become a profit area.

We always want to look at a vendor with objective eyes. Knowing that a tech or service stack is only as strong as its weakest link, we want to know about the vendor's security protocols. We want to know other people's experiences using the solution. If we discover a solution that looks promising at a vendor fair or from a vendor approaching us at a conference, and we don't have a customer using it, we wait for the vendor to refer a customer that is using it so that we can test it out. Vendors see us as a potential honeypot, and sometimes they are eager to have us refer their solution to our customers before we have had a chance to test it on a customer we have in common. When this happens, we say no way. A vendor must refer at least one customer to us so we can see the solution working in a real-world scenario before we will consider referring it.

Having a customer in common allows us to get into the nitty-gritty and find the weaknesses within the technology. Because let's be real, when technology vendors are marketing to you, they are going to pitch all of the pros to the system. They are not going to point out the vulnerabilities, so we have to do a good job at poking around.

Sometimes beta testing software is necessary, especially if you are considering adding it to your service model or internal tools. During beta, if we find something we want a software to do that it can't, this is where the developers have their opportunity to show us they are nimble innovators. If they knock our socks off by being responsive, making the changes that need to be made, and doing so in a timely manner, we know we will enjoy working with them, and we feel confident referring them to customers. That's a valuable partner.

PRO TIP

You want to work with nimble innovators, because they are going to be best able to recognize and address your needs swiftly.

Two vendors that we rely on heavily within Complete Controller are ADP and Intuit. To me, the reason they have been so successful is that they listen to the experiences of their users. They are investing time and energy into constant innovation. They have advisory boards. They have feedback opportunities. They have in-person events where they feed you all day, train you, and ask for opinions on their product functionality. They are consistently doing great things to support continued innovation in their products. So, look for those key partnerships you can cultivate with your vendors. There will always be those few who stand out and go the extra mile and provide the level of service your customers have come to expect from you.

Choosing Vendors

We try to partner with multiple vendors within any given genre to best serve our customers' needs, vetting and testing as many as possible. For instance, for payroll processing, we have vetted and tested and will highly recommend ADP, Paychex, Intuit, and Gusto. Those are our four. We have quality assurance from them. We understand how they operate, what they do, and who they are—and we have partnership agreements for alt. rev. with all of them. Having multiple relationships allows us to make three recommendations when a customer asks for a vendor referral. This gives our customers a choice and relieves the risk associated with making that choice for them, in case the customer has a bad experience. A great value-add service is to offer to shop the vendors for your customers, making the selection process as painless as possible by gathering information about features and pricing and presenting it to them.

Here's what we look for in a vendor partnership:

- ☑ **National reach.** As a virtual company, this is the very nature of our business. We need our vendors to have market share all across the country. Be sure your vendors' reach matches or exceeds your own and talk with them about the strategy for making referrals from anywhere within their reach area without having to use multiple sales representatives.

- ☑ **A single point of contact for our customers.** There is nothing more frustrating to a customer than being shifted from person to person and never knowing who will be handling their account. We insist that our vendors provide Complete Controller customers with a single point of contact for their account. We call that person or team our dedicated corporate representative. For example, our payroll referrals all go to the same person within each payroll vendor company, and that is the person who reaches out to the customer to establish a quote, sign the customer up, and address customer service issues as they arise.

- ☑ **Training.** Not only do vendors need to provide training, they also must be nimble innovators and be open to feedback. We want to feel heard and see our feedback going to good use.

- ☑ **A high level of support.**

Everyone wants to feel special. As a company, we want to make sure our customers feel that way because they are aligned with us and we have their backs.

☑ It would be a vendor's worst nightmare for a customer to start complaining about their service to us because we can turn off the referrals. This motivates the vendor to pay attention when a customer has feedback or needs support. We know that some customers are hard to please, and we aren't unfair with our vendors. But if a particular service or program just isn't making the grade, we will reexamine our referral relationship.

☑ **The best pricing possible.** Due to our large number of customers, we can push our weight around to get the promise of better-than-retail pricing. And vendors are motivated because the probability of getting a customer from us is high. Again, using payroll as an example, all of our vendors have agreed to compete at lower-than-retail pricing or give us wholesale pricing that we can pass along to our customers. They also know that we refer to three providers, so behind every referral email from us is an urgency to be the first to pick up the phone or answer the email to win that business. Our customers are getting choices and great pricing, we are the hero for making the referral, and the vendors are getting customers.

☑ **The partnership generates alternative revenue.** This goes without saying. We want to build partnerships with vendors that can provide a revenue stream. Remember, we talked about how that revenue stream helps to pay for the time, training, and effort that go into vetting, establishing, and referring a vendor. After you recoup your costs, these streams, although they seem like more of a trickle at first, can become large, meandering rivers. It's important to have controls in place to protect these revenue streams. Internally, we require all referrals to copy our Account Services department so they can be tracked, and we don't allow our staff members to refer to any solution that is not approved by Complete Controller or any contact of their own who is not a designated Complete Controller rep. It is against the rules for a staff member to circumvent our relationship and make referrals to earn alt. rev. on the side. Our company refers vendors for technology and services—payroll, benefits, wealth management, insurance, loans and other debt products, banking, payment processing, collections, business valuations, entity formation, credit building, and more. Every time we make a referral, we earn alt. rev. either by way of commission or the wholesale product pricing that we can pass along to our customers with a below retail markup. Many of the revenue streams are ongoing based on the customer's continued relationship with that technology or service provider, and they can survive the customer life within our service portfolio.

Long after we are no longer serving a customer, we continue to earn on many referrals we made during our relationship. This survivability of the revenue stream causes our earnings per customer to be much greater than others within our industry.

☑ And, because it is recurring revenue, it serves to increase the value of our business in the financial-services-as-a-subscription sector. Our goal is to have alt. rev. cover the entirety of our technology costs. As I write this, we are one-third of the way toward reaching that goal. I encourage you to leverage alt. rev. to increase profitability, survivability, and value within your professional services business. It adds to the top line with little to no labor costs after the initial referral is made.

Educate and Automate

Once you have established a relationship with a vendor and decided you want to refer them, the next step is to make it easy for your staff to identify a need and make that referral. We start by allowing the vendor to give their demo and have a Q&A session with our staff so they can understand the problem that vendor is solving. Then we create referral email templates that are designed and worded carefully to be in line with our brand and messaging and make those templates available in our staff members' toolboxes so they can make a referral with a quick double-click. These templates copy our Account Services department for easy referral tracking. No reason to drain efficiency having staff members penning their own referral templates and trying to remember who the dedicated corporate rep is at that particular vendor company. What a pain that would be! No one would ever want to make referrals because it would just create more work.

Be an Active Partner

Aside from sending referrals, we make meaning for our vendors by giving them honest feedback, marketing their products and specials to our customers, and sharing our partnership publicly. For example, one of our payroll partners asked us to test a new product innovation and provide honest feedback about our experience. In exchange, they framed the product testing as a case study and created media about our company, its demographics, and our findings during the test. It was a perfect give-and-take as we had enough customers in common to provide substantial feedback about the performance of their new product, and they had the brand clout to get our case study seen on a national level. They even used it for marketing purposes during their product rollout, which gave us even more exposure and gave their product even more credibility. These are the types of vendor relationships that make meaning.

PRO TIP

Align yourself with vendors that can give you exposure to a greater audience. Then leverage that relationship. For example, if you have a referral relationship with a leading hair products company, make sure the vendor reps who fostered that relationship with you are all connections on LinkedIn. As a leading company, they have more influence than you. So, when you create a post talking about a rave review you just saw on their product, they will like and share it to their larger, more integrated, and influential audience.

I love helping journalists out with information for their articles and research. I was a member of HARO (Help A Reporter Out) for a couple of years and still dabble. It is a service that allows journalists to query participating topic experts and choose content from the multiple responses they receive. It gives me an opportunity to be the expert source and to give my vendors some exposure as well. Any vendor that meets muster with us has a solid resume, and by sharing that vendor with the media and on social media, we boost their reputation and make them stronger. Because I have a reputation for entertaining potential vendors and being willing to test their solutions, I get exposure on webcasts and in articles discussing innovation and opportunities in the market. This positions me as a thought leader, which helps my company to maintain its brand in the market.

Recently, I joined one of our vendors at an annual accounting conference and trade show to do an onstage spotlight about our experience with them. I discussed our decision to integrate their product into our solution, how we utilize it, the strategy for marketing it to our customers, and our adoption rate and price point. Our story gave legitimacy to their product and allowed the audience to visualize how they might integrate it into their model. The vendor was so grateful for my participation that they had anyone on their team who had been involved with training my staff and onboarding their product give us five-star reviews and express what a pleasure we are to work with. Wow, now that makes meaning.

The more we talk about our vendors, meet them at events, recognize their strengths, and address weaknesses with a willingness to find solutions, the stronger our relationship becomes. My hope is that they will think of us when they run across someone who needs bookkeeping. That outcome aside, when we make them stronger, we empower them to serve our customers better.

Every touch is an opportunity to exercise our vision to create long-lasting, fruitful relationships. Strategically, by looking for ways to reduce friction, empower innovation, and increase profit, you can make meaning for your staff, customers, and vendors alike.

Pen to Paper

Partnering with reputable and innovative vendors can springboard your business exposure and help you to stir up positive reputation through brand association. Each person who is thinking positively about your company, wanting you to make referrals, and investing time in the relationship with you creates positive energy. Be discerning and only select vendors that meet the criteria that will bolster your business image and top-line revenue. Leverage those relationships for exposure and give back.

Try the following exercise:

Create a cluster drawing.

Put your core services in the center of a piece of paper. Now, think of as many complementary or auxiliary services and products as you can. Add these to lines that extend from the center. Hint: You may decide to simplify your core services as you surround them with opportunities to generate revenue without doing the work. Now list a few vendors in circles at the tips of each of the services and products you identified. Choose only vendors that meet your requirements, e.g., trusted brands, national reach, dedicated rep.

Once you have these vendors listed, reach out to them to learn about their revenue sharing programs, training, and support. The more you know, the better you will be at making your selections. In some areas, it may be smart to identify more than one vendor so you can provide customers with a choice. As an example, I've included my own cluster drawing in the appendix.

7

MAKE MEANING FOR YOUR CUSTOMERS

THE CORPORATION THAT OWNS Complete Controller is Make Meaning Corp., named after the concept in Guy Kawasaki's book, *The Art of the Start*. Kawasaki teaches entrepreneurs that as long as we're making meaning in people's lives, then we are creating value. All successful businesses add value, and customers are willing to pay for value. In fact, the exchange of dollars for value is the very definition of business.

To be frank, the goal of any for-profit business is to make money. So, if your primary goal is to make money, you have to get people to value what you're selling, and to do that, you have to make meaning. You have to do something that impacts people. Maybe it excites them or solves a problem for them or saves them some time or money. The virtual styling companies Stitch Fix and Bungalow Clothing offer a great example of businesses that have broken through traditional model rigidity to bring their services to the cloud.

As a business owner, you might start by asking, "How do I make my company or my offering attractive?" While this may have some success, it may not completely address your target customer. To make meaning for your customer, you will need to go deeper and ask, "How am I making meaning for this person?"

By asking this specific question, you take a closer look at the values of your target demographic. Going back to the virtual styling service example, let's say you have decided you want to offer an online fair-trade styling service that uses clothing and accessories made by workers who are paid a sustainable living wage and stylists who work one-on-one with the customer to create a more personalized experience. By catering to a specific niche market and offering them that extra feature of direct access to their stylists, you have just made meaning for your customers that differentiates you from the competition, who uses a computer algorithm to surprise its customers each month with clothing and accessories that may not fit their taste or budget. You have also made your service marketable to a segment that is impassioned about choosing to work with empowerment companies.

Early on, my vision was to bring our customers a solution that provided them with all of the services they were used to in the traditional bookkeeping model but for less money, less time investment, and greater accessibility. Once we were up and running, busy making meaning for our staff with a dynamic, flexible, virtual culture, and making a positive impact on the small business market, we stumbled upon a way to bring value to a whole new market segment—our customers' CPAs and other experts. Because we were hosting customer data on our cloud platform and had made it so our Bookkeepers could have a single point of access to all their Complete Controller customers on their own desktops, we realized how easy it would be to do the same for CPAs or wealth managers who had multiple customers in common with us.

At the time, it was hard to get information out of customers and everything wasn't yet online and accessible. So, we started providing access to that information on our platform just to be helpful. As things evolved, we were able to improve on our single sign-on and user experience to provide the CPA/Experts with a higher level of control and access to programs that facilitated the tasks they were commonly performing. By providing bookkeeping, source documents, and information about their customers' businesses in a standardized way and making it accessible through a single login to a desktop that contained tools for exporting data, interfacing with practice software, and storing working papers, we were able to reduce the amount of time that it took for them to get their jobs done, saving them hours of time-consuming work like audits and tax returns.

Pretty soon, CPAs were coming to us saying, "Where has this been and why didn't I know about it?!" That's when we realized how deeply we were making meaning for them. By working with us, they were able to get work done faster and easier, with overall better quality. The solo tax practitioner, for example, could serve their customers without the cost of cloud technology and skilled staff, because we were supplying those rudiments free of charge. The light bulb went on. We could serve as the turnkey CAS department for CPAs large and small. This ultimately changed our go-to market strategy. I used to put small business owners first. Now, we intentionally target two segments of the market, small business owners and CPA/Experts, who have become our lifeblood.

Our Customers

In the following sections, I will break down how Complete Controller makes meaning for our two major customer segments. As you read about my experience with these two customer types, ask yourself how your business makes meaning for each segment you touch, both referrers and end users. Sometimes the attributes that are most valued by one are very different from those valued by the other.

CPA/EXPERTS

We love our CPAs and hold them in very high esteem. They are like gold around here. And notice that I have added Experts to this category. That is because CPAs are not our only referral source. We have CFO service firms and business managers that use us exclusively as their bookkeeping offering. We also get referrals from business coaches, bankers, capital investors, wealth managers, and other experts because when their customers use our service, we give them timely and accurate financial data and full transparency into how the small business owner is performing.

In turn, it is our goal to make their lives easier so they will love us and send us more of their customers. As I mentioned earlier, we began to make meaning to this group quite by accident. We didn't intend to directly market to CPA/Experts, but we did want to give them access to their customers for whom we were providing services. Once we saw how much they valued that access, we began to look for ways to add more value in the relationship. We now serve as the turnkey CAS department for hundreds of CPA firms across the nation. If you are wondering how this strategy could work for your small business, try thinking about potential referrers. If you are launching a virtual service department within a larger firm, will existing firm members make referrals? How can you make meaning to them? Can you turn your referrers into customers by providing unique access, shared data, or white labeling?

Access

Using our technology platform, CPA/Experts have a single login point of access, or single sign-on, to each of their Complete Controller customer's desktops. Remember, the desktop holds the QuickBooks file shortcut and paperless filing cabinet as well as links to all of that customer's other (hopefully integrated) business solutions.

When we first started out, accessibility was a *big* value point. The standard was that, either, the books and records were not accessible to the Bookkeeper because the customer had them on their computer, or they were not accessible to the customer because the CPA had them on their computer. There were options for logging into a customer's computer remotely or exchanging portable files so work could be done and later merged into the parent file. In my experience, both of these methods proved clunky, time-consuming, and unreliable, which led me to require that all customers be hosted by us so there was never a barrier to fulfilling our three core promises: accessibility, accuracy, and timeliness. Although this limitation created a barrier to entry for some customers, it provided us with control over access, thereby increasing efficiency, decreasing costs, and creating standardization and quality control.

Standardization

Access is great, but wouldn't it be sweet if across multiple customers everything was in the same place, named the same, and run the same way? I bet you're starting to see a pattern. We don't just standardize things for our staff. We also do this for our customers and their CPA/Experts to make meaning for them so we can present a consistent product while using our resources efficiently. And while your standardization process will differ from ours, the concept will be the same for your business, regardless of size or industry.

We manage our customers' books according to the service plan they choose, and we manage their document storage with the same level of precision. We file vendor bills, insurance policies, entity formation documents, tax records, 1099 filings, vendor W-9s, payroll journals, financial reports, customer invoicing or contracts, and more in the filing cabinet on each customer's desktop. Our filing cabinets are impeccably maintained, our quality control team makes sure of it. Why? So tax preparers and auditors can reference the source documents they need with ease.

By the way, it is a pain to gather all of these documents, and any CPA will tell you that their customers are spotty at best when providing everything requested. We saw this as an opportunity. We now make meaning for our CPA/Experts by doing the document-gathering for them. They can rely on us to hound the customer and rest assured that we will get the job done.

Each customer's desktop contains a status report that lets visitors know when our engagement with the customer began, what service plan they subscribe to, if there is a cleanup or catch-up scope in progress, what periods are closed, any special circumstances or concerning conditions that we have around that customer's bookkeeping, and whether the books are ready for tax prep.

This simple tool allows us to communicate what is going on with the customer and prevents CPA/Experts from going into an account and saying, "Geez, Complete Controller doesn't know what they are doing! These books are not right at all." Our goal here is transparency and communication. We want the CPA/Experts to know what is going on at all times, and we especially want them to know when something isn't our fault.

We only mark the books as ready for tax prep when we have completed the fiscal year-end checklist of tasks to ensure the greatest accuracy, the best accrual to cash basis flip, a clean tie-out to last year's trial balance, and all payroll reports are on file for the year. We perform an internal tax readiness review before releasing the books so we can know that we are putting our best foot forward and fully supporting the tax preparer.

Expert Team

Each customer's desktop also contains a Contact Card with names, roles, emails, and phone numbers for the team that serves them. This makes it easy for the CPA/Expert to get in touch with the right person to get questions answered or work performed. How much better is it to discuss accounting with an accountant rather than a mechanic, an attorney, a dermatologist, or a shop-keeper? As a point of contact for the CPA/Expert, we understand their needs and strategies, have knowledgeable answers to their questions, and have the bandwidth to diligently pursue further information from the customer when needed. We make meaning by doing the grunt work for our CPA/Experts.

Noncompete Promise

To be clear, we are not trying to fill the shoes of the tax professional or any other expert. We are not taking on that role. We do not want that liability. And we don't want to bite the hand that feeds us. I have colleagues that run successful bookkeeping services and include tax preparation for their customers. That is not me.

I talk later in the book about how even a department within a firm should have separation from the rest of the firm through branding. I think it is also important to make sure our staff does not step on the toes of tax advisors, auditors, wealth managers, or other members that serve that same customer. This can be avoided through strong role definition. If a customer asks us a tax strategy question, for example, we see it as an ideal opportunity to steer that customer to their CPA/Expert for an answer. That shows the customer that we value the CPA/Expert in the relationship and shows the CPA/Expert that we can make meaning by delivering opportunities for them to shine.

Reciprocation and Loyalty Bond

We love to send referrals to those with which we already have a customer in common and the relationship is strong. It's part of our "Give It Away to Keep It" philosophy. We get a steady stream of customers from Google, events, and refer-a-friend, and of course, we immediately seek to establish a relationship with that customer's CPA. In some cases, the customer wants to make a change or does not have a CPA, and they ask for a referral. We give them three options so they can find the one that fits their budget and personality. Any customer that was referred to us by a CPA/Expert has our promise that we will never refer away from that CPA/Expert. That's our loyalty bond. A single customer can't equal the value of a CPA/Expert relationship that will bear fruit for years to come. If a customer expresses concerns, we let the CPA/Expert know, providing them with the golden opportunity to repair the relationship. How many times are you unaware that a customer is thinking of leaving until they are already out the door? We make meaning by giving them the inside advantage. And you can do the same for your referring customers.

SMALL BUSINESS OWNERS

We also make meaning for our small business owners. I like to break these customers into three types:

1. **Small business owners who want/need to get their books done because they know their CPA is going to ask for it at the end of the year.** We save them money and we save them time because, well, they don't want to deal with it. These customers are like, "Hey, I'm a gold medalist. I'm off doing these advertisements and sponsorships, traveling the world, and then during my season, I'm working out. I don't have time for this. You need to just manage it all and make sure that my CPA gets what they need at the end of the year." All they care about is that their bookkeeping is accurate and completed on time. (As an aside, we've managed bookkeeping for Olympians, supermodels, musicians, and television and movie stars. Imagine the nondisclosure

agreements we sign!) We make meaning to these customers by giving them peace of mind.

2. **Small business owners who are interested in using their numbers to manage their decision-making.** These customers want us for day-to-day managerial purposes. While they are typically interested in saving money, they also want access to valuable information that allows them to make smart decisions about their business, now. They don't want another thing to manage. They don't want a person to come in and need attention, time, and a workspace. They want someone who can gather, distill, and report information quickly and accurately. Industry experience is paramount. They want someone who knows how to do a budget, a pro forma, a cash flow statement, and specialized industry reporting. They also like the Controller layer of expertise. They expect us to know the best practices and industry norms for reporting, invoicing, collections, pricing, inventory management, and more. While it is important to them that we are affordable and not intrusive, we make meaning for these customers by giving them timely and accurate information. Great examples of this customer include the fine dining restaurateur, venture capital firms, or multi-partner law firms. (By the way, these customers are our sweet spot—they need us, our model makes sense for them, and they stay forever).

3. **Small business owners who need an accounting service because they are too busy doing other things—usually things that create complexity.** This is a customer with more sophisticated needs. They are typically involved with a board of directors, bank, or regulatory agency and they may be required to produce audits. Perhaps they deal with work in process calculations, certified payroll, or other intricacies that are beyond the typical office manager or bookkeeper skill set. They might have payroll in multiple states or sales in multiple countries, or run a national e-commerce website. Nonprofit organizations with grant funding, franchises, and multiple entity structures belong in this category. The business owner is busy running and growing their business,

and while they want access to expertise, they don't necessarily want to hire a full-time person to fulfill that need. They may or may not have any accounting background, but they are usually able to look at the numbers and see how their business is performing by using the typical financial reports. While they may have a bit more business savvy than the managerial operator, they don't have time to be involved in producing those reports, and they need to know for sure that the reports are accurate when they get them. They can tell if the reports are wrong, but they are not going to be involved in correcting mistakes. They also won't be involved in any troubleshooting or dealing with the regulatory agencies or ancillary business services. They want all of that to be managed for them. We make meaning for these customers by providing expertise.

Valuable Products and Services

A large part of the expertise we provide for our customers is our broad knowledge of the technologies that drive business solutions. We can really bring value when we pull together all of the components and design them to be as integrated as possible.

At Complete Controller, we make a point of bringing up the customer's tech stack during onboarding and again when we see things changing in their financial performance. Framed as part of the streamlining processes conversation, we review the components and make recommendations if we see gaps or overlap. We remind customers that we have a broad knowledge of what's out there and how each solution integrates, unlike a consultant who is more likely to have concentrated knowledge in one solution.

Our experience, access to data, and knowledge about industry best practices put us in a position to make meaning. Remember your cluster diagram? I believe any professional service can find a way to have conversations with their customers that steer them toward other valuable products and services. At the very least, that exchange of ideas and sharing of experience will increase the relationship trust bond. At the very best, it will lead to customer decisions that improve their lives and increase your top line.

Pen to Paper

You might think you know who your customer is. But take some time to think outside of the box. The people who refer customers to you can also become potential customers through sharing data, access, white labeling, and more. If you can become a part of their menu of services, the results can be electric. To know your customer better, answer the following:

- ☑ How does your business make meaning for these people or organizations?

- ☑ How do you make meaning for your end users?

Break your customer targets down by segments and list the ways your business makes meaning for each. Sometimes the features that matter so much to one customer segment don't matter at all to another.

PART THREE

BOOTSTRAP BOOGIE

"Having the least usually forces us to make the most of what we have."

—MOKOKOMA MOKHONOANA

BOOTSTRAP BOOGIE

YOU DON'T NEED SEED money to start a business. Despite the popularity of investing in your own wealth and ventures using other people's money (OPM), I see more businesses fail that accept pre-revenue startup funding than those who bootstrap their business right from the start. Even on *Shark Tank*, it's rare to see a business that hasn't already proven their concept get an investment. Why? Because the act of bootstrapping forces ingenuity and the wise use of funds. A business that can only grow by the reinvestment of its own profits quickly learns where that reinvestment will make the most impact to the bottom line and creates early practices that position it for success in the leanest of times. It is through bootstrapping that a business can achieve true scalability.

I signed my first subscription-paying customers in May 2007. By August, I had hired my first Bookkeeper and by November, my second. In July 2008, I lost a group of three self-storage customers that had come in through my colleague at the property management company, the catalyst customer mentioned in the Introduction. They left because of a failure in our process. The mistake was costly to their business and could have really hurt us if they had made us pay the losses or given a bad review. Thankfully, the only repercussion was the sting of losing three full-service customers in one fell swoop at a time when three customers made up one-fifth of my entire portfolio.

After that, business was steady until March 2010. That was to be the last growth month of any consequence for more than a year. The recession had caught up to my small business target market and they were shifting their strategy from, "Let's have someone else do this work so we can focus on growth," to "We can do this work ourselves so we shouldn't pay someone else for it." The purse strings were cinched, and by the fourth quarter of 2010, I hit an all-time low. During that entire quarter, the company made less than its second quarter in business. The business desperately needed my undivided attention in order to thrive.

In every startup, there is something I like to call a jumping-off point. That moment when you have to decide whether to stick it out or call it quits. The first quarter of 2011 was my jumping-off point. I had to decide if I was going to become wholly and solely dedicated to Complete Controller or let it dwindle and die. It was a grueling decision, but in February 2011, I said goodbye to my last drive-to-serve customer and focused entirely on the new virtual company. The company steadied with me at the helm full-time, although customer acquisition was matching attrition, and the monthly subscriptions were stagnant.

I had to solve the customer acquisition problem—and fast. I also needed to improve quality to reduce customer attrition. Finances were tight. I was making decisions about what bills to pay. I even let my Franchise Tax Board corporation fee lapse, which is something you have to pay every year to be a corporation in California. It was $800 a year and I needed that money to pay for the things that didn't generate revenue like technology and keeping the lights on. When you're bootstrapping, sometimes you have to make tough decisions, and this was one I had to make early on.

On the personal side, I had four roommates and I was working at my dining room table. My thoughts were always on how to make ends meet and how to grow the business so the next month would be different. Single mom, with no other wage earner in the household—at this point I had jumped wholly into the business without a safety net. There were no more bread-and-butter, drive-to-serve customers to cushion the fall.

If you have started your own company without funding, this probably sounds familiar to you. And if you haven't taken the leap yet, I'm here to tell you that you will be tested each step of the way. However, if you believe in your vision and are passionate about what you do, you can be successful.

Desperation breeds ingenuity. For it is in your darkest moments that you will learn some of the foundational principles for your company's scalability and survivability.

Early on, I decided that Complete Controller was going to be a million-dollar company. The financial model worked. It worked on paper and it worked in reality. But there were lessons I had to learn and steps I had to take to get the company where it is today. In this chapter, I'll take you through my journey from struggling startup to multimillion-dollar firm. I will be sharing the lessons that I learned from my own bootstrapping experience and how you can apply them to your own self-funded virtual business or use them to build a survivable and scalable business even if it is funded by OPM.

Barriers to Growth

Once I had my company up and running, I began to notice some areas that really needed attention. I call these areas barriers to growth. Every startup has them and will experience them at different points along the journey. The key is to identify them early on and take the proper steps to remedy them. If you are not able to make an honest assessment of your barriers to growth and address them, your likelihood of success is low. Here were mine:

☑ **Perseverance.** We can't talk about barriers to growth without bringing up perseverance. Hey, I get it. It can be scary when you're starting out, particularly when you're bootstrapping. You'll need a hefty dose of it throughout your startup journey, which is why I'm bringing it up first. Throughout this chapter, you'll see how unfailing drive and determination to see my vision through to completion kept me going every step of the way.

- ☑ **Cash flow.** Bootstrappers like me have to use their existing funds to get things started. My entire initial investment was dumped into developing the technology side of my business, because it would be a main driver of my virtual services, and I wanted to offer the best that I could to my customers. I'm not going to kid you. There were some lean times, but I'm glad I stuck it through. The sacrifices and challenges were well worth it in the end.

- ☑ **Marketability.** Your business, regardless of type, will need to be marketable. I knew I had my work cut out for me because virtual accounting services were not yet widely promoted concepts in 2007. Even in 2011, as the concept was beginning its emergence, we were a truly virtual company in a not-so-virtual world. But I knew that would change, and I'll show you how I handled this barrier in the pages ahead.

- ☑ **Customer acquisition.** You can't have a business without customers. So, how do you get them and, more importantly, keep them? I learned early on that I needed a good sales team to help me out in this area. I like the accounting side of my business, but that does not make me naturally adept at sales. If anything, the two types of people are not generally alike at all. I was inept, to say the least, and needed to bring people on board who could help me grow the business, and that's exactly what I did. If you find yourself in a similar position, let go of the need to do everything and hire an expert. While you will feel an initial financial pinch, the long-term benefits of this investment will pay you back handsomely.

- ☑ **Quality control.** Now that you have customers, you want to impress and keep them, not only for the steady flow of income, but also for referrals. Creating a streamlined and efficient service takes effort and continuous review. This is where quality control comes in. It's not something you do once. This lesson reared its ugly head time and time again as I was starting out, and we still work on improving our services and fine-tuning our quality control processes. Mistakes are expensive and repeating them, even more so. This is why we work hard to streamline and standardize our services, and I recommend that you do the same.

When you first start a business, these barriers aren't always evident. They show up, though, as the business struggles to grow. Think like a bootstrapper and know that the solution to overcoming a barrier isn't always to throw money at it. Sometimes the solution involves some time or restructuring. As with any bootstrapped startup, our early years were the toughest financially. Having made it through, I became comfortable with bootstrapping. I liked the feeling of being debt-free and nimble. And as we grew, I continued to implement techniques to keep us sleek and scalable. Bootstrapping isn't the easier, softer way, but I am a firm believer that it is the *best way*.

 PRO TIP

When your business is up and running, you will begin to notice barriers to growth. We can call them shortcomings. It's your job to find and apply solutions that fit the business model and do not sacrifice your vision. Do not ignore these shortcomings. Denial will not make them go away; instead it will ensure that they cause inefficiencies as you try to work around them instead of solving them. You can't fix what you don't recognize. Start by taking an inventory of your business's barriers to growth. Notice which areas are not performing the way you wish they would and create a plan to address them.

Lesson 1. Pay for the Work with Revenue from That Work.

This lesson has cash flow written all over it. Fortunately, I chose a subscription model for my business. The subscription model was not only a brilliant strategy but a necessary one. I didn't have excess capital to pay my staff up front and hope I would get paid on the back end. Plus, I didn't want to take that risk. I would rather have the potential downside of a fixed fee for recurring services than the certain downside of uncollectable fees for services already performed.

Limited capital also affected the decision for my employees to be hourly and part-time. By making no promise of salary, I lost any potential benefit derived from their ability or desire to work more than forty billable hours, but that more than paid for itself with the peace of mind that I was only paying for the hours they actually worked. It was imperative to have a structure that carried the greatest promise of profit. If I made the process efficient and the work environment stable and predictable, it would take my staff less time to perform their work, they would be happier, and my margins would increase.

I put a process in place to pay my staff once a month, on the fifteenth, for the time worked in the prior month. That pay strategy, coupled with a subscription that charged the customer at the beginning of the month, made sure the capital that I used to pay the staff was the very revenue I had earned for their services. And if a customer was late to pay, their service was suspended, causing the staff to cease all work on their behalf. In this way, I never fronted work to anyone.

Then I ran into a situation where a customer asked for a substantial scope of cleanup/catch-up work to be performed hourly. I invoiced my customers on the twenty-sixth of each month for the amount of their subscription plus any add-ons for the period. That invoice is due by automatic payment on the first. Cleanup/catch-up scopes were add-ons along with any hourly custom requests—anything that was not predictable and so could not be folded into a subscription.

When the aforementioned cleanup/catch-up scope showed up on my staff member's time record, I had already sent the bill for the period to my customer.

By gathering my staff's time records at the end of the month, after the subsequent month's billing had been prepared and sent, I was left holding the ball for the hourly work in excess of an entire billing cycle. So, I staggered it.

I instructed my staff to give me their hours from the twenty-sixth of the month through the twenty-fifth of the following month. That would cover the closing of the period and reporting, as well as the day-to-day servicing on the account up to the twenty-fifth. The subscription payment that I had received on the first of that month would be paying for those services. Then, any hourly custom work would make it onto the billing because I already had it in hand when the bills were being produced on the twenty-sixth. Cleanup/catch-up and hourly custom work was now paid on the first as well, allowing me to collect those funds before paying my staff on the fifteenth for those very same services.

PRO TIP

Only pay for approved work.

By staggering the reporting of staff hours from the customer billing, we were able to invoice and be paid for all work before paying our staff, but things did not always go as planned. Every so often, we would have a customer complain about the hourly service add-ons that showed up on their invoice. They might give us some pushback saying they never approved that scope of work and weren't going to pay.

Here's the thing,

it's always best never to have a dispute,
but if you are going to have one, you want to have
all of the evidence that you did things right.

So, in these instances, we went about making sure those hours were always collectable by following a simple process that I refer to as cover your a** (CYA). Whether a request for add-on or hourly custom services comes during a conversation, in a text, or by email, a follow-up CYA email must be sent detailing the request. We deep dive into CYA in Chapter 15.

When this process is followed precisely, it alleviates about 98 percent of disputes. The other 2 percent generally fall silent when we send them a copy of their written approval. And only on the rarest occasion do we have a customer resolutely deny their approval, even though it's in writing, usually with some off-the-wall justification.

Those clients who refuse to pay are not ideal customers for Complete Controller, and now that we are bigger, we can let them know that we believe there is a service out there that will serve them better. In fact, we say we are so sure of it that we are giving them their books and records back (as soon as they pay us) while wishing them all the best.

When the CYA process is not followed precisely, our staff member risks immediate termination or forfeits those hours if they are disputed by the customer. Basically, by not following that simple process, they render us impotent to collect the revenue for those services. It becomes a he said/she said argument, and in those cases, the customer is always right. Providing services without proper approval is a big loser. No one likes nasty surprises on an invoice and that's exactly what the staff person is setting their customer up for when they ignore protocol. Not only is it inconsiderate, it's also bad for business.

PRO TIP

Hire ahead of need and only pay for hours worked.

I mentioned that we only hire part-time staff. That is not to say that everyone working for us is part-time. On the contrary, they are able to grow their portfolios as large as they need or desire, and we have many staff members working full-time. But they do so of their own volition and there is no agreement compelling us to provide full-time work. That relieves a tremendous amount of pressure from the company to create work and satisfy a need for hours.

Also, about paying my staff in a single monthly payment, I figure that if a Bookkeeper cannot budget their household to run on a single expected monthly payment, then they should not be a Bookkeeper. It is also a way to prequalify people who may have poor money management skills, poor credit, or not enough savings. They drop out immediately when they find out that they will only be paid once a month.

Lesson 2. Create a Strong Image and Establish Trust.

I want to talk to you about the importance of having a marketable business and how you can accomplish that on a tight budget. Your image plays a big role in how others perceive you, and if you project a strong one, you will have an easier time establishing trust early on in your customer relationships.

At Complete Controller, we recognized we needed to have an established office location as a way to build our street cred. Customers want to know you can be easily found, especially if you are working with their money. As we developed the company within what is now known as a cloud environment, we realized we didn't need to ever lease an office. So we adopted the virtual office model that many startups use to save money over leasing space.

We knew we wanted to lease from a virtual office provider ✗ that was more than just a service that provided a local office address, like a UPS store. To be true to our model, we needed a solution that had national reach and provided a true office environment for use when we needed it. We found a company that provided virtual offices all around the world. By using them, we not only had on-demand access to an actual office, conference room, and reception services, but we gained that "pick as you go" access at any of their locations around the world.

In March 2010, we established our first office in Southern California where we were headquartered. Without adopting a huge rent bill, we now had a place to meet with important people and a corporate address that was not my home. We soon realized the importance of this decision on our reputation. By allowing prospects to come to the office and sign the service agreement to become customers, we provided otherwise wary people with the assurance that "virtual" did not mean a lack of stability and standing in the community. I encourage you to do the same. It will do wonders for building rapport and trust with your customers right from the start.

By April 2013, we had established a virtual office in Seattle, Denver, and Atlanta. We chose them because we had a few customers, staff members, or firms that called those cities home. Now we had a way to further penetrate those markets through local listings and community outreach. We were able to list in local directories and become members of community associations and networks. In August 2014, we opened in Austin. Little did we know that we would fall in love with Austin during our outreach efforts and eventually move the corporation and build our first brick-and-mortar office in the great state of Texas.

By the way, we are only building that office because, as it turns out, sales, marketing, and business development people do better in a team environment. I suppose it's the ability to see someone else achieving that drives them to do the same. Now, we can afford to give them that place where they can foster healthy competition and take our sales process to the next level.

By staying true to our model and finding a solution that would solve the trust problem for prospects and colleagues, we have been able to run lean on overhead while still enjoying the fruits of geo-market penetration. Meanwhile, we gave our customers a place to drop off paperwork, look someone in the eyes, and rest assured that we are part of the community. As an aside, without fully staffed offices, we further support the elimination of a 9-to-5 construct. No one in our company commutes to work and sits in a boring cubicle, and no one is ever sitting in the office being paid to watch YouTube and file their nails.

Lesson 3. Take a Risk.

What do you do when you have no choice but to try something you have never done before? Of course, you do it. One of my closest mentors taught me that a business that is not growing is dying. I took this to heart when it came time to increase our customer base. While the decision to open virtual offices helped to overcome the barrier of marketability, it did not solve the barrier of customer acquisition. Marketing is establishing a brand presence, reputation, and voice. Sales is getting the ink on the contract, and that is a very different problem to solve. My inability to acquire customers in sufficient numbers was really a deficit of my own personality and skill.

For this to make sense, you have to know that I am an introvert. I get along great with people, but what fills me up is being alone with my projects, pets, garden, beach, a good book, you name it. Introduce people to the equation and you add a whole layer of unmanageable emotions and expectations that I would rather not interact with. Naturally, one of my flaws as an introvert is that I'm not good at follow-up or closing, both core functions of sales. I could meet you and talk about my company—my baby—all day long, because, of course, everyone can talk about their own business. But when someone said, "Here's my number, give me a call so I can learn more," it seemed great at the moment, but it wasn't going to happen. Truth be told, I would set their phone number on my desk and stare at it. I would literally come up with every reason why they wouldn't want to get a call from me at that very moment.

Closing a customer that was referred by a friend or colleague wasn't a problem. At the time, I had landed everyone in my portfolio through a referral. The problem was that I couldn't get those referrals coming in frequently enough to overcome attrition in the soft recession market. And without those referrals, I couldn't close. When I had to start the sale from scratch, I completely fumbled. I was afraid to make the phone calls, and it didn't help that I didn't have the language and background in sales. It just wasn't in my toolbox. I was afraid of it because it wasn't my strength.

My vulnerability, however, gave me a gift. Coming to terms that I was not a salesperson was the first step. Accepting that as my truth, I had to fill the gap. I was going to have to bite the bullet and bring somebody in to help with sales. Turns out, it was one of the best decisions I ever made.

In 2011 I met a guy at a friend's pool party, and we started talking about business. Then he started telling me about his sales experience, specifically how he could sell all these different things. Isn't it amazing how the universe provides? There I was, needing a solution to my sales problem, at a pool party talking it up with a guy who was telling me he could sell anything.

So, I invited him to come to my office and talk more. Remember, our virtual office was only used when paying prospects and customers wanted to meet. The daily work by me was done at my home office, which at that time was in my dining room. So, I ate the humble pie in the interest of finding a potential solution and invited him to meet with me.

I shared my vision with him and he was (and still is) my biggest cheerleader. After hearing about what I was doing he said, "You know what? This is awesome. This is more than a million-dollar company; it could be a billion-dollar company. If you let me sell for you, I will make it happen."

While I was excited, I was transparent with him and said, "Listen, this is not my area of expertise. I actually don't know anything about it. I have some friends with sales experience. They are the ones who told me to hire a cold caller to generate leads. I've done that, and I'm still not getting the results I need."

During our discussion it became clear to me that Drew was a perfect fit for my company. As we were talking things over, I was thinking he would be a great addition to my team, but I was wondering how I would be able to afford him. And then he said, as if anticipating my concern, "Listen. I'm not going to ask you for much right now, because I know you don't have a lot to give. But when you do, I want a piece of the action."

I was quick to take him up on his offer and said, "Oh my God, I absolutely, 100 percent will. Let's do this!"

Drew was a hotshot. He was very confident, which was concerning and impressive all at the same time. I thought, what if he knows something I don't know? What if he can actually do this thing? So, I went for it and hired him. I mean, what did I have to lose?

Up until then, business development and sales consisted of me going to networking events and having a part-time cold caller reach out to local businesses. The conversations were along the lines of, "Hey, just wondering if you need some help with your bookkeeping today? No? Okay, bye."

The first day on the job, Drew listened to the cold caller and afterward we sat down to talk about strategy. We talked about what we were currently doing, what he would change, what marketing efforts were needed, that sort of thing. And then he said to me, "Okay. The first thing is you've got to let me fire this guy."

If you've ever met Drew, you know how charismatic he is. He's got big energy. A real driving force. I knew in that first meeting that hiring him was a good call. He genuinely cared about my company and knew what was needed to help it succeed.

Drew shook things up that first day, and I immediately handed the sales process to him. I set him loose—without a lot of guidance—to do what he does. And he did a lot of hiring and training callers the way he wanted to train them and got the word out. It was amazing how he could get good talent to work in my garage on commission only. And when the team was able to get a prospect to the point where they were ready to close, I would then drive to meet the potential customer and make the deal.

I always say that we are a 100 percent virtual company. But really, back then, we focused on the California market because that's where we were headquartered. When it came time to close with a customer, I came with a paper contract, usually to their place of business. I would drive out and talk to them, and maybe they would close, and maybe they wouldn't. In the beginning, if the sales team got me to the point where there was an appointment, it was about 75/25 in favor of the prospect signing.

This was before we had digital contract management technology like HelloSign ✖ in place. I also didn't think customers were quite ready for cloud technology at the time. They didn't understand exactly what was going on. And while the sales team was able to give them a user demo and explain how we could do their bookkeeping virtually, the closing still needed that personal touch to get a signature on paper.

In the meantime, all the callers were working on commission. We were not paying hourly. It was just, "Hey, if you think you can get an appointment for Jennifer, then you get paid." I had paid that first cold caller, before Drew, by the week. So, once he was gone, I just turned around and used that money to pay Drew his base. Then, of course, he was also going to get commissions on every closing along with the promise of bigger things as we grew.

In every entrepreneur's journey, there are risks that they are willing to take because not taking them has already proven to be a failure. I had tried the other way, and it didn't work. I took the risk of hiring Drew and giving him free rein over the sales process in May 2011. That same quarter, the company nearly doubled its revenue over the prior quarter. Our growth trajectory has remained strong ever since, with a compounded annual growth rate of 38 percent, which is higher than typical for this industry.

The risk had provided a handsome return. If something isn't working in your business, don't hesitate to change it. Don't let ineffective people or processes bog you down and drain your wallet. Be nimble and willing to change, even when the problem you are solving is not in your area of expertise. Trust your instincts and take the risk.

Lesson 4. Know When to Make a Major Investment—And Do It!

In July 2011, I was able to take my first real paycheck from the company. It was tiny, but it was official: The business was paying me on the regular! By January 2012, it was clear the tide had shifted. I had righted our Franchise Tax Board debt and reinstated our good name. However, with growth comes growing obligations to shore up infrastructure and quality control. And in 2012, the company required major reinvestments.

By that February, we had outgrown our current technology and needed a new system. The cost would eat up our cash reserves and leave us lean, again.

Bootstrapping can sometimes feel like with every two steps forward, there is a step back. However, I took comfort in knowing that every time I invested in the company, I was stoking the flame for it to produce more.

Keeping in mind our promise to host customers' books and records, it was absolutely necessary to upgrade our system. It was no longer large and powerful enough to handle the customers that we were bringing in. We had to have a system that was reliable, always up, and capable of managing the hosting without slowing down to a point where it was disruptive and making us look bad.

My technology guy put the specs together on a more robust, upgraded system with a price tag of nearly $19,000. Ouch! Here's the double ouch—within nine months, we outgrew that system and needed yet another. You read that right. We outgrew the system just as we were getting our feet back under us.

Although we were in a colocation, a secure building offering cages for servers, badge-only access, climate control, and terabytes of internet bandwidth, our new machine didn't have the capacity to process the data uploads and downloads and store the amount of data we were processing. Another upgrade was imperative. This one was a rack system, not a box system, with a $35,000 price tag. It would give us the ability to expand our capacity quickly by simply adding to our rack as we grew. Our promise to provide always-up hosting was now more reliable than ever.

But the trade-off was that our bank account balance was meager. There is nothing scarier than building up a reserve only to empty the coffers on an investment that you soon find yourself having to replace. This experience made me particularly grateful that I had made a habit of reinvesting in the business from the start to ensure it had a prudent reserve on hand in case a "spend to survive" moment presented itself.

At last, our technology was running smoothly and we had a future growth strategy. It was a huge weight off our backs. We experienced less downtime, greater capability, and no more worries about whether we could take on more customers without breaking. The sales team felt the new energy and started to acquire customers like never before. And I'm happy to report that the investment paid off. From 2012 to 2013, we doubled our revenue!

Big investments can be scary. If they allow you to stay true to your vision and grow, do it anyway. Usually they come on the heels of a growth spurt, so you should have an increase in revenue before the need arises. The key is to always keep a prudent reserve. If we hadn't had one, we might have gone out of business, or at the very least, gone into debt. Keep three months of operating capital in a reserve account at all times. When you have to borrow from it, pay yourself back as quickly as possible, just like you would a bank loan.

Lesson 5. Keep the Faith.

THE MIRACLE CUSTOMER

You now have a pretty good idea of what my mid-2012 year looked like: tight on cash despite the growing customer base, knowing the business needed my full attention, taking home only a small paycheck, and struggling to keep the faith. With the subscription model, I always knew that my staff was covered, but the last person to get paid was me. I had next to nothing in my personal bank account.

I wondered if there would ever be enough for me to personally develop financial stability and wealth for my family. There was a day when my family caught me losing my composure. Losing my faith. They reassured me that, even if this was as good as it got, it would be good enough—and that we were blessed beyond measure. We stopped everything and said a prayer as a family, a prayer of gratitude. And then they told me that they did not think there was an ice cube's chance in hell that this was as good as it would get. They had seen me work tirelessly. They knew that I was surrounded by talented, dedicated, wonderful people and considered them like family (remember, the sales team was still working out of my garage). Thank goodness for family and friends who remind us that we are okay and smack us on the butt as we climb back into the ring.

In June 2012, I was starving for cash flow. The first new tech system had been built and we had just migrated everyone over in the first quarter. With troubleshooting and stabilizing, my tech guy was getting paid a lot more than I was. The company was going to be fine, but the chance of my getting paid on the fifteenth was slim to none.

Right then I was thinking, "I don't know what to do. I'm going to have to borrow some money or something." And then Drew comes dancing in.

"I've got a guy but you have to drive out there right now," he says. "He's going to pay you cash because that's all he has on him. And he's leaving to go out to his farm up in Northern California. He's not going to be back for a while. He's leaving tonight, so you have to go."

So, I gathered my things and ran out the door to meet him. He wasn't too far away, thank goodness. I sat down with this guy at his breakfast bar, in this house he had just closed escrow on. There wasn't a stitch of furniture in there except for the breakfast bar where we were sitting. My first thought was, "This is a little bit creepy. How is this going to work?" But as we talked I learned that he was an organic farmer. He also owned a construction company that ran backhoes and concrete cutting for other larger construction companies and commercial customers.

He said, "Listen. I've been so behind and I need things to be caught up. And I need to be put in good order for my accountant. He's breathing down my neck to get my bookkeeping. I am signing up two companies."

We talked about his businesses so that I could understand his needs and selected a service plan for each that would get the job done. After which he signed the agreement and gave me cash. I walked out of there with enough cash in my pocket so the business could give me my paycheck on the fifteenth. It was nothing short of a miracle.

I had so many of these little moments along the way. Signs from the universe at times when I was asking myself, "Is this working? Is it going to make it? Is it okay?" By just continuing to show up, the answer was always yes.

Remember that we talked about perseverance being one of the areas that presented barriers to growth for me? The lesson I learned time and again was that as long as I kept showing up, persevering even in the face of doubt, everything would fall into place. Keep the faith and expect miracles.

Lesson 6. Don't Count Your Chickens Before They Pay!

After that and other similar experiences, I became an expert closer. Drew's team was working so hard to get these appointments for me, and I did everything in my power to close them. The pressure was enormous.

I remember meeting with the owner-operator of a construction company in the San Diego area. I was based in Orange County, so San Diego was a good hour and a half drive for me. It had taken many, many calls, but we had finally landed an appointment, so the pressure was on.

I've learned that some people are not quick to close. They need to talk about it and talk about it some more and then need follow-up. And some perhaps just can't tell you no. The sales team had let me know that he was one of these people. If I didn't get him signed, we wouldn't get another chance.

When I got to San Diego, I brought out the agreement as we talked. By this time, I was comfortable with opening up that agreement, walking through it with a prospect, and handing them the pen. I went through the entire agreement with him, and we talked some more about what the services were going to look like and the next steps. I then handed him that pen and he signed on that dotted line. Except he didn't have his checkbook with him.

He had a credit card, and I chose not to take it. I didn't take his credit card because my model was to not to accept credit cards. Our merchant account was capable of accepting them, but my model was to processes customer subscription payments by electronic funds transfer. Taking the credit card would have been an exception.

I'll never know, if I had accepted that card, whether he would have, in fact, become a customer and eventually given us his bank account information, or if he just would have disputed the charge and disappeared into the ether. I called him multiple times and Drew called him multiple times, but the sales team was right; he never did wind up becoming a paying customer.

I do know that if I had given in to the handful of prospects over the years that wanted to pay by credit card, I would have paid more to date in merchant processing fees than we made in revenue the entire 2012 fiscal year.

So not worth it. I think I would rather use that money to buy a small yacht or jet instead! You have worked hard to develop your business model based on a vision. I definitely wanted to avoid doing collections. By sticking to my guns on the subscription electronic funds transfer model, I have avoided collections and chargebacks for thirteen years. Do not compromise your model out of desperation because you are worn out and beaten down, in response to peer pressure, or for any reason at all.

Lesson 7. Choose Corrective Measures Over Being Right.

When I started Complete Controller, I had been doing full cycle accounting for more than a decade, but I had never run a full-blown bookkeeping service. My learning curve was high, and I didn't know what I didn't know.

Traditionally, when you take on the controller or bookkeeper role for a business or household, you go to them, do a deep dive into their model and practices, and agree on timing that works for the customer to have you periodically visit to update the books. When you visit, one of the first things that happens is they hand you any mail of financial bearing that they received since you were last there, so you can sort and handle those items. I had designed Complete Controller similarly—the customer would scan and send us anything that came in the mail having to do with financial matters.

When serving self-storage facilities, we worked directly with the on-site staff for each location. They were scanning all of the bills that were coming to them through the mail, and we were handling payables, reconciling to the point of sale reports and daily deposits, and managing payroll.

We weren't counting on, however, any bills not coming to a site address. It turns out the company had a corporate office that owned these facilities and that staff had not been trained in our processes, because they managed their own corporate-level accounting. They assumed we would know when the property tax bills came in, probably because they viewed those as facility-specific. We are talking about huge pieces of property with a self-storage facility on them, in Southern California. If a bill that size doesn't get paid on time, there are stiff penalties in the thousands of dollars. Needless to say, one of those bills got missed. That was the trigger for them to say, "Oh, no. We have to take this back in-house."

I was mortified and miffed. How were we supposed to know they had facility-specific bills coming to the corporate office? I needed the customers more than anything and I wanted them to be happy. I wanted them to be Complete Controller success stories.

Unfortunately, they were not.

They said to me, "You should have known that those property tax bills were coming. You should have known the dates they were due."

On the one hand, I could say, "Hey, listen. I told you to send me all the bills, and I can't know about bills you didn't send me." Or I could take corrective measures to make sure something like that never happens again. As an accounting service, Complete Controller should know when the property tax bills are due, in the same way we know when corporate tax bills are due. We should also know to ask for them.

I had already created a checklist to help my Bookkeepers get through their monthly tasks, and now I realized that we needed checklists for much more than that. We needed one for onboarding, not just the technical side of it, but also the account management side of it. We needed to dig in early and find out what our customers' structure and needs would be, so we had to start asking the important questions in advance. We needed to be informed rather than surprised.

As a result of this learning experience, the onboarding checklist was born. Not only did we need to ask all of the right questions, we also needed to gather the necessary supporting documents. This opened a whole new side to our document-gathering and storage process. We no longer just stored the vendor bills that were sent to be paid or invoices and payroll ledgers to support our entries and last year's tax return. We started to ask for entity formation documents, insurance policies, vendor agreements, and anything that might have a critical date attached to it. We began to calendar not only the critical dates and deadlines in our internal process, but also our customers' critical dates so we could remind them when something important was coming due.

Customer, you are right.

Calendaring and checklists became a big part of each process, ensuring quality control through each stage of the customer's life, from sign-up and onboarding to servicing, reporting, reviews, and termination. Take it from me; create and follow those checklists. When something slips through the cracks and a customer complains or terminates service, learn from it, and create a new best practice and checklist item to prevent something like that from ever happening again.

Lesson 8. Document Relentlessly.

When my company launched in 2007, I was doing the work of developing the model based on my vision. Then I hired my first two Bookkeepers that year and built a period process checklist that guided them through the periodic work that needed to be done before we could prepare financial reports. I also put together materials that they could reference to see the scope of work for each customer based on their subscription service plan. Finally, I created a *Getting Started Guide* to help the customers understand their processes and deadlines in working with us. This guide also served the Bookkeepers, as it completed the picture of what our total process was for providing virtual accounting services.

Then we added the onboarding checklist and followed that with a customer information form so we could make sure that the information we were gathering from each customer upon signing was consistent. Next, we added a termination checklist so we could be sure we were doing everything we needed to do to return a functional, password-free QuickBooks file and intact paperless records to the customer.

The checklists I created were supporting our processes that any new Bookkeeper could follow to achieve success, but what about the techniques? It's one thing to tell people what you want done, but it's a whole other thing when you discover the most efficient, most elegant way to do that thing and share that knowledge with them.

In the beginning, I was constantly emailing my team about the new ways we would perform tasks better, faster, cleaner. Each time a customer-related problem showed up, a solution had to be built. I disciplined myself to ask, "How best can I solve this for anyone who ever has this problem in the future?" Then I shared the solution with my staff. My early directives looked something like this:

Hi Ladies —

I figured out how to _____ for Mr. Smith and here's how:

[Insert whatever I had figured out.]

Let's be sure to do it this way going forward. Let me know if you have any questions or suggestions that can make this better.

Every day it seemed like a new thing was happening that would change a process or procedure. I wanted it documented on a checklist, if applicable, and in an email so the whole team would know.

With growth came hiring. We needed more staff to meet the demand, but these new Bookkeepers hadn't been around to see all of my emails delineating our solutions and techniques. By now, we had about three years' worth of these communications. It became apparent that these emails needed to be distilled into a single searchable document.

So, I asked the most experienced person on the team to help with a special project. I went through my sent mail and forwarded every directive/solution email I could find. She combed through them, discarded obsolete directives that had since been improved or replaced, created topic sections, and compiled everything into a single document. The Bookkeeper Scope of Work was born.

Eventually, I promoted that same Bookkeeper to take over my duties as a Controller, and we created a separate scope of work to memorialize the processes for that role. As the company has grown and added roles, we have been careful to document relentlessly, which has saved us untold tens of thousands of dollars in efficiency gained from not having to relearn and reteach.

Documenting everything also achieves the goal of having everyone doing it the same way, the Complete Controller way. This is an area where many businesses are lacking. When a business is young, it is busy and things are changing every day. It may seem like a senseless use of time to document roles and tasks. I am challenging you to rethink that perception.

If you make documentation a habit, you will be nimble in the toughest of times, like when you lose a valuable staff member, need to expand rapidly, or become uncertain of what a particular staff member is doing with the hours you are paying them for. Also, documentation is critical to your ability to delegate efficiently. Without a succinct set of instructions, any staff member in any role will have to keep coming back to you to get direction, and you will be tempted to fall into that way of thinking that is so crippling to growth: It's quicker for me to just do it myself than to have someone else do it. Next thing you know, everything is reliant upon you, and you become the barrier to growth.

Lesson 9. Invest in Good Quality Control.

By 2012, I had started to come up against the extent of my knowledge, where I felt like I didn't know what I didn't know. Yet, I had plenty of people applying to work for us, and the sales team was building the customer base. We were starting to get customers at a pretty regular pace, and because of this, we could start predicting the number of new customers we would acquire each month.

With the customer acquisition problem solved, I next had to tackle customer retention. I needed to create a role that was solely responsible for actively developing further processes and techniques across all roles, making sure they were included in the scopes of work and the knowledge was spread across the teams. We needed to develop methods for ensuring the quality of our work, setting the bar to a height that would satisfy our most critical customers, the CPA/Experts.

Naturally, I was looking for somebody who could fill my knowledge gap, someone who knew what our target customers were going to want and could help us make sure our books were clean and tight. I was looking for a CPA. Meanwhile, I had to keep the budget under control. This would be my first investment in someone who would not be making the company money. We put out help wanted advertisements for Bookkeepers and I watched who came in, weighing the candidates for that Operations position we hadn't advertised.

The first candidate I considered was in Florida. She had a CPA after her name and seemed like she would do a pretty good job as a Bookkeeper. I wanted to find out. I hired her, thinking she might eventually be able to help with other things as well. Alas, I also overlooked some red flags, because I had dreams for her that I had no idea if she could fulfill. She was spotty in her communication, didn't seem to be Type A–organized, always seemed to be taken by surprise, and wasn't as thorough as I would like. Okay, I will admit, she was a hot mess. Thankfully, as soon as she started to miss our strict deadlines—those service promises to our customers—terminating her was easy.

I continued to watch the resumes roll in, trusting that the right person would come. Finally, another candidate with that CPA designation after her name appeared. Having been once bitten, I grilled her. She always came back with a level of measured professionalism that was impressive. She understood full cycle accounting, had supervised a small bookkeeping team, and prepared taxes based on that bookkeeping. By April 2012, we had started to use a bookkeeping skills test to weed out candidates that weren't high quality. That test had an 87 percent fail rate and she passed it. She really knew her stuff. Although she had applied for the Bookkeeper position because she liked the idea of working from home and only making a part-time commitment, I ended up talking to her about my other opening for a Chief Operating Officer (COO).

It wouldn't have as many hours as the bookkeeping role, but I was willing to pay a touch more and it would give her an opportunity to stretch some of those CPA muscles. She was excited about the opportunity and we were off to the races. Actually, it was a very slow start because we had to create the position from scratch.

Up until now, it was just me and the Bookkeepers on the financial side. I did have the one Bookkeeper who was learning the Controller role, which involved making sure the checklist tasks were completed, deadlines were met, and the books were reviewed for accuracy prior to reporting. But those books could only be as accurate as the extent of my knowledge.

We needed someone who knew what a set of books was supposed to look like so it would pass muster with the CPA community. We needed standardization in our reporting and year-end processes. We needed someone who felt confident with direct CPA communication. And we needed someone who could conduct periodic internal peer reviews.

One of the other compelling things about this candidate was that she came to us having worked on and off throughout her career. She had a son at home with autism. When she took the COO job, he was a teenager and getting into those years when he was having trouble in school. Sometimes she had to just leave and take care of him, making it difficult to hold down a more traditional job. But she wanted to stay sharp and work not only for herself, but for her family as well. I knew we could make meaning in her life as she would in ours.

Our new COO thoroughly reviewed our bookkeeping process. She immediately made some changes to how we kept the chart of accounts and equity sections. She also made sure that the trial balance was tying out to match last year's tax return and that we were properly reconciling payroll. These were things we hadn't thought of because we hadn't filed tax returns, so they weren't factors for us. She took over the role of documenting those changes for the team, and we developed a fun way to keep fresh changes in front of the appropriate staff through continuing education. Finally, she developed a process for performing internal peer review and systematically worked her way through every set of books we serviced.

Knowing that our quality now met CPA-level standards and needs, I was able to tackle that market with assurance. We went about shoring up our reputation with the CPA community, and I started pitching for them to bring me their entire book of business.

And then, not surprisingly, we got a whole other set of problems. More customers meant more onboarding work, more staff, greater accountability, and better training and load balancing. Eventually, you find yourself having challenges in areas where before you didn't even have areas. Entrepreneurs are used to wearing all of the hats, seeing around corners, and making smart decisions quickly, because we have the benefit of the vision and passion. That ability can give us a bit of a complex. We begin to think everything could be done better if it were done by us. But there comes a time when you must admit that there are things you don't know, tasks you will never be very good at, and others that you shouldn't be doing because your time is better spent elsewhere. Be willing to admit when you need to fill that gap. For me it was CPA-level expertise. I didn't have it, and I recognized that I needed it in order to solve the quality problem. What is yours? Be willing to invest in filling that gap.

Lesson 10. Expect Growing Pains.

Our growth was taking off and with that, more tools and supporting roles had to be put into place. Each role or tool supported core revenue-generating activities, but did not in and of themselves generate revenue. This is where we really felt the cash flow three-step: The moment we were two steps forward in earnings, one of these costs would put us back a step. I took solace, however, in knowing that we were building the foundation for our future. We did this by incorporating a Help Desk/technical support, skills testing, data entry and scanning, technical videos, and a work tracking system.

March 2012—Help Desk/Technical Support. Customers were coming on board in record numbers, and our system administrator, who still only worked part-time, couldn't field all of the calls or field them at times when it was convenient for our customers. We realized that we needed a Help Desk to assist our new customers and new staff members in getting connected to their cloud desktop. This was to be our front line. Each customer's first experience with Complete Controller after the sign-up or recruiting process was with the Help Desk and it had to be flawless. Thankfully, a company with exactly that skill had reached out to us to ask about bookkeeping support. We flipped the script and hired our first technical support call center to be our Help Desk.

April 2012—Skills Testing. Remember that skills test I had our new COO take when recruiting her? As recruitment increased, so did our need to sift quickly through the unqualified applicants. Some were easy to see from their resume and email responses, or lack thereof. But others presented well: They had the required certifications, experience, and degrees, and came up clean on the background check. Unfortunately, it was not until they were hired and paid to learn our techniques that we discovered their weaknesses. So we created a skills test that would allow us to know if potential staff members really knew what they needed to perform well on the job. Now that we have implemented this test, very few actually pass it. We currently have a 13 percent pass rate on our test—what an easy way to separate the wheat from the chaff. I highly encourage you to implement testing as an essential part of your own recruiting process. You will not regret it.

April 2012—Data Entry and Scanning. I never thought we would provide scanning and data entry services, but we came across a customer that needed a large amount of information entered on their books for a cleanup/catch-up scope, and they no longer had the associated bank account for easy import. This was before the prolific use of optical character recognition technology and import macros to handle these tasks, so we were stuck with manual entry. A staff member had worked with a neighborhood friend on some accounting projects in the past and had encouraged this friend to go through our recruiting process to see if she could get a job. The friend just barely failed the bookkeeping test. Luckily for her, we needed someone with accounting knowledge to help with the data entry project, so I thought we should give her a chance.

We created a new data entry role. Data entry services would be project-based rather than full cycle customer-based, and there was no guarantee of more work once each project was completed. This person jumped in and meticulously managed the first project. She followed our nomenclature for stored documents, broke down the scanned source documents, and entered every transaction on the books. By August, we were glad we already had her in place because a customer came on board that literally gave us banker boxes filled with receipts and invoices to piece together his accounting. She jumped right in, and he is still a customer today. Later, we reshaped our data entry and scanning services to be a revenue-generating role and it fits nicely with our core offerings. We also make data entry available to our bookkeeping teams to use for big projects at a direct expense to their efficiency. If the math works, they take advantage of that valuable resource to move through scopes more rapidly than they could do alone, which keeps the customer satisfied, even impressed, by the deft completion of a monumental task.

August 2012—Technical Videos. Even though we have checklists and scopes of work to manage our tasks and roles, some people are visual learners. They need to see you do a task to really grasp the technique. In the early days, I would show techniques to new employees through GoToMeeting. It had a recording feature that worked great because our new hires could revisit the recording later when they were putting that learning into practice.

Eventually, we had video snippets demonstrating all of our proprietary techniques, as well as others for work management topics like how to find your way around the Bookkeeper and customer desktops, and how to monitor your efficiency and determine your bonus for the period. All of the important stuff. While these were helpful, we wanted to formalize those snippets into a set of complete videos that new recruits could use alongside written materials to grasp the full picture of their role.

At first, we had someone come in and render them for us. Later, we purchased our own editing software and got busy creating and editing in-house. We wanted to set permission-based viewing privileges to protect our proprietary techniques, so we opted to use Vimeo as the delivery system 🛠. This gave us the ability to password-protect our videos, see who was revisiting them, and monitor progress.

September 2012—Work Tracking System. Remember my earlier mention of the work tracker? We initially sought out and put this tool in place because we needed a method to determine the average number of hours it took for our new staff members to complete their training, so we could set a maximum. This helped us to manage our initial investment. It also allowed us to add a clause to the staff agreement allowing us to recoup that cost from the staff member's final pay if they did not meet our standards for the role within the probationary time period.

That worked brilliantly, and we found other ways to use the work tracker as we developed the KPIs we wanted to monitor. Today we compare reported hours to tracked hours to keep everyone honest. It is all very transparent because we also use the work tracker to help our staff members monitor their efficiency. When we first established the tracker, however, we kept it as more of a secret weapon to catch the ne'er-do-wells that otherwise would try to pull one over on us.

In November 2012, in fact, we caught our first person overstating their hours. I had not been happy with this young man's performance to begin with, so I started looking closely at the time he spent to complete the work, thinking perhaps he's just phoning it in and has a lack of dedication to perfection. Looking at the time records, I saw that he was spending a lot of time on the work and still not meeting standards, so I wondered if it was a proficiency problem. The moment I compared those time records to the work tracker, however, all was clear: It was a dishonesty problem. When I confronted him with the evidence, I expected him to deny the validity of the work tracker or claim a mistake on his timekeeping. Instead, he had the gall to respond, "What do you think I should have done? There's no way to make a living on only hours worked."

Suffice it to say, he no longer works here, and we've gotten our money's worth and then some from this investment.

Lesson 11. Always Have a Second Hand in Negotiating.

When we were hit with all of the infrastructure and support needs—new tech, more new tech, Help Desk, work tracker, and building new departments to handle support and management roles—I was using the company's profit to pay for them, so it was essential to get the very best price.

A business owner often has to negotiate to pay below value to remain relevant and competitive. You might make it up to the vendor with promises of a long relationship, growth, revisiting the compensation subject at a later time, bonus opportunities, etc. But the bottom line is that you cannot pay full value, or you will soon be out of business. It is in negotiating to pay less that you win an edge over your competition. In the early years, we didn't have anyone on the team who had the skill to negotiate our purchases at a level that I felt gave the company a competitive advantage.

My most valuable player when it came to negotiations would be my head of sales. In fact, this is what earned Drew a position as a director within the company. I would go in and negotiate what I believed was going to be the best possible opportunity for the company. Then I'd run it past Drew. Inevitably, he'd be able to go in and cut off even more fat. Whether he was coming at it from a different standpoint or making the necessary calls to competing vendors, he always astounded me with the savings he gained for the company. What I discovered during this process was the importance of having that second voice in negotiations.

The potential vendor had already been dealing with me. They knew my needs and pain points. They knew I needed or wanted what they had. Candor allowed me to deep dive into the features and problem-solving ability of the service or tool they were selling, but it cut my advantage off at the knees. After they have worked so hard to understand my needs and develop the perfect solution, it compromised the relationship for me to then say, "Thank you. Now I need to pay you half as much as you're asking."

PRO TIP

A second voice in negotiations preserves the vendor relationship. The reality is, you are going to work with these vendors on a day-to-day basis and you actually already feel like you have a relationship with them because you have worked together to find a solution. Now, just before you intend to purchase the solution and bring it on board, you don't want to alienate the vendor. You also don't want to make them feel like you don't value their service or product. Negotiations must simply be a money matter, not an issue of value.

So, after I determined which vendor I wanted to work with, I'd set the ball so Drew could spike it. And did he! There were situations when I was dumbfounded by the deals we were able to get. Drew didn't have an emotional association to the deal. It wasn't his money. He didn't have a relationship with the vendor. In fact, he saw them as a salesperson, just like him. So for him, there was no way to lose. He went into the negotiations knowing that his boss had told him to get the best possible deal and his only motivation was to deliver. He would go in so low, that I would be embarrassed, but it totally worked. Not everyone has a Drew, but I highly encourage you to find one. This method has saved our company hundreds of thousands of dollars. And because of that, we take very good care of our Drew.

Who's your Drew? Even without staff members on your team who can fill this role, you should still have someone you can put in as your pinch hitter. Get the best pricing you can from your vendors. Then let them know that you cannot make any final decisions without so-and-so's sign-off because they are "in charge of the budget." Then hand the negotiations to them. Who fits that bill for you? Perhaps your attorney since they will be reviewing the contract anyway? Or maybe it's a colleague or spouse.

Lesson 12. Take Care of Your Business First.

I believe this is where we separate the men from the boys and the women from the girls. This is where you decide that pride—what you think others think of you—is less important than the survivability and strength of your business. My husband mentors young men, and he always tells them, "You don't have to spend money to spend time with someone special, and you don't have to impress anyone with how much you spend. If you really care about them, enough to care what they think, you just tell them that you are busy building your empire." That quickly weeds out the people who are with you because they think you can afford to show them a good time, and shows you quickly who respects your goals and achievements.

In Orange County, California, I saw a lot of otherwise brilliant businesses fail because their owners became distracted by the trappings of financial success. Or they landed startup funding and took a steady salary from the start, even before profits allowed. Then the business never realized a profit, and they were left with nothing.

I always tell my customers and protégés,

"Your business is your lifeblood. Take care of your business first, and the rest will come."

That's why I don't like it when the spouse handles the bookkeeping for a business. The spouse will naturally be loyal to the family unit, so their motivation is around making sure the family is secure, well-educated, and socially active. If given a choice between paying the mortgage or the staff, they would likely pay the mortgage, even though through proper use of the staff, the mortgage will be paid for years to come.

If they already have the trappings of success, it's worse—especially if they are leveraged with debt, like a house with a three-car garage, three vehicles (one recreational), private school and a college fund for the two kids, plus the pup that they rescued. Imagine the look on their faces if you tell them that the business needs to buckle down and it would be wise to rent out some rooms, sell the house, share a car, and go to public school for a couple of years, until the foundation is strong.

Don't screw up a perfectly good business because of pride. Think of your business as your baby, who will grow up strong and healthy and someday take care of you. As a baby, it needs attention, late nights, and food. It gets sick at the most inopportune times and requires more than a single skill set to raise it. It has growth spurts and setbacks. If you are reliable, consistent, and dedicated, it will thrive. If you stop caring for it and abandon it for the more pleasurable things in life, or if you expect it to take on more responsibility than it's ready for, it will buckle under the pressure.

When we were starting to get a strong customer influx and the tech was steady, I wanted to spend money on myself and my family. I could have starved the business to satisfy my wants. In doing so, however, I would have rendered it helpless to survive some of those backward steps it had to take to become foundationally strong. I have shared with you a few of my moments of despair, wondering when my family would ever enjoy the fruits of my labor. All I can say is it was worth it.

Today, the business is so foundationally strong, it fully scales. If I lost a couple hundred customers tomorrow, it wouldn't be the end of the world. I don't have unscalable layers of management and infrastructure because I couldn't afford to have them when I built the model and developed its strategies for success. I'm able to support my staff, negotiate the lowest possible price, with scalability, from my vendors, and then feed the profits right back into the company to make it a bigger, better, stronger, happier place to work.

What are your bells and whistles, and what sacrifices are you making to keep your business foundationally strong? This can be a tough and intensely personal question. It may seem like this lesson is about cash flow, but I think it's really more about courage.

Lesson 13. Don't Let Frustration Get the Best of You.

Have you ever heard the box kite story? It's the story of a boy who saw the most beautiful box kite he had ever seen displayed in a store window. He walked past the store every day and longed to make that kite his own. He spent months saving every dime so he could buy it. The day came when he bought the colorful kite. He was so excited that he rushed to the field, even though there was no wind that day. For many hours he tried to get it to fly, running up and down that field as fast as he could, trying to catch the wind until the sun hung low in the sky. Finally, in a fit of frustration and disappointment, he stomped the kite to pieces, without ever getting it off the ground.

I know you can feel the emotion in that story. And believe me, I get it. You are so excited. You have this cool thing you want to do. Then you get out there and it doesn't work the way you want it to because of whatever factor—the windless day. It's so easy to give up in frustration.

What I'm telling you is, don't smash your box kite. Don't give up the Boot-strap Boogie. It's a difficult path. You know this. No matter how tempting it may be to walk away, instead I challenge you to put on those high boots and start getting ready to wade through some sh*t. Because it is so worth it here on the other side.

Pen to Paper

Every business has its barriers to further growth. Whether your business has plateaued or is experiencing a growth spurt, healthy financial strategies will ensure its survivability and scalability into the future. Your barriers to growth and the challenges that arise from them are probably different from mine. Set yourself up for success by developing smart financial habits early on and ask yourself:

- ☑ What does your capitalization plan look like?

- ☑ What is your plan for keeping sufficient operating capital on reserve?

- ☑ When does the business become self-supporting?

- ☑ When does it begin supporting you?

- ☑ Are there things in your life that might prevent you from making the smart choice when your business needs you most?

PART FOUR

PEDIGREE IS A DOG FOOD

"Better degrees don't automatically translate into better skills and better jobs and better lives."

—ANDREAS SCHLEICHER

OVERCOMING PERSONAL BIAS

FIRST OFF, LET ME just say, higher education is fabulous. I'm very happy for people who take on the challenge of furthering their education. It takes time, resources, and a certain amount of drive, which demonstrates commitment. I respect that life path.

Earning a degree shows your ability to commit to a long-term goal—yet just because you are able to get that coveted credential doesn't necessarily mean you bring greater value to the company where you are employed. Truth be told, it doesn't matter how smart you are if you can't create value by sharing what you know with other people. It's like showing your work in math class. You might know the answer, but greater value can be achieved by showing others how you got there so they can understand your critical path and logic trail. It also helps you to see where you went wrong when you miss the mark. So, if you don't show your work, you don't make the grade.

I don't believe that the more letters you have after your name, the better you are. What I do believe is that

a person's value to a business is determined by how well they meet the goals of that business.

I'm more interested in whether a person can meet those goals with a high level of personal satisfaction, customer satisfaction, and to the betterment of the bottom line than how many degrees they have.

Complete Controller is a bookkeeping company. We are not performing sophisticated mergers and acquisitions, rocket science, or deep-water exploration. We are a company that values dedication, the ability to meet deadlines, accomplishment-driven ambition, and empathy. All of these are treasured assets, and to me, much more valuable than the ability to write a dissertation. Therefore, you won't be surprised when I tell you that *I strongly believe that it's important to abandon traditional methods around hiring practices.*

As an employer, look at finding talent in other ways to save on how much you're spending for that talent and also to empower people who will be loyal to you because you gave them an opportunity that perhaps they couldn't get elsewhere.

Think of it this way: You have two $100 dollar bills. The first one has been kicked around the block seven times, has gum on it, and is crinkled and dirty. The other one is fresh and crisp off the press, and it hasn't been anywhere. Which one is worth more to you?

They are worth the same, of course. You may prefer to have the unmarred bill in your wallet, but I would encourage you to take the one that has been around the block. And here's why.

The Power of Pedigree

The power of pedigree is something I struggled with early on. I don't have a bunch of letters after my name, and a part of me in the early years thought if I did, I could have more influence. I thought with more degrees, I could market myself better and be more well received. It turned out I had self-imposed limitations due to my own personal bias.

In reality, I *was* well received. It was only my inner dialogue that subscribed to the very outdated belief that a reputation for excellence was best born from higher education. Why did I value that more than the street-smart individual from the School of Hard Knocks?

I knew that I had to get over this because I wasn't going back to college. I was passionate about making Complete Controller succeed, and there was barely enough time in the day to manage all the pieces as it was. I knew I could do a good job and I could surround myself with people who knew the things I did not. At first, I thought that meant hiring people with more credentials. I put those people in positions of leadership, hoping to create a framework for success. As it turned out, they were only the scaffolding we needed to get to where we are now, not permanent fixtures.

The virtual nature of my company afforded me access to people who might not have had the opportunity to be in the traditional workforce and at a competitive rate. I didn't want people who were looking for a clock in, clock out job. I wanted people who were interested in getting work done and getting paid for the work they were doing. Our flexible schedule attracted people who wanted the freedom to pursue other interests and passions. They valued not being stuck somewhere for eight hours.

The result was a talent pool of people with skill, diligence, and a zest for life. They insisted on balancing their life and filling it with meaningful experiences, rejecting traditional model rigidity. It wasn't pedigree that mattered most after all—it was passion.

My company's organizational pyramid is upside down. The sole job of the people at the executive level is to support our staff and the customers above them to the best of their ability. The responsibility of success and failure falls on our leaders. If we experience a failure, we look to ourselves first to ask, "What could we have done to better support the people involved?" We call mistakes "discoveries." That helps us to remember that they are opportunities for learning how to do it better next time. I believe it is that culture that makes us nimble innovators.

In the pages ahead, I'll talk about how Complete Controller finds, hires, and trains our employees. This will give you a peek behind our staffing curtain, in case you want to incorporate any of these (or similar) methods when you hire and train your own staff.

Our Hiring Practices

THE MAGIC OF CRAIGSLIST

Online help wanted ads have always served us well. Right from the very beginning, we put our advertisements on Craigslist under the part-time work section. I never wanted to give the illusion that I was going to be able to promise anybody full-time work. My big fear was that someone would have it in their head that I had promised them a full-time position, and we would learn about the misunderstanding only after they had taken the job, we had invested in them, and they were assigned to customer relationships.

So, we made it clear. We put up an ad for part-time work in the part-time section in the Orange County area in the beginning. That's where I was located, so it made sense. Then it dawned on me—why am I only hiring in the Orange County area? We are virtual. I don't need to *see* my Bookkeepers, just like I don't need to *see* my customers. This realization came to me around the same time we started signing up customers virtually—without bringing them the contract in person. We had customers in Hawaii and other states. We emailed them their service agreements, which they signed and sent it back to us, and that process was working. I decided that if we could do it with customers, we could do it with our staff.

That was a bonus because there are many areas of the nation where the cost of living is lower than Southern California. Thank heaven for that, because if we all had to keep up with Southern California wages, we'd all be out of business.

Since our pay structure is the same for everyone regardless of where they are located, candidates in areas with a lower cost of living find our offer more enticing. We often find excellent staff members in towns and rural spots where opportunities to make the amount we are paying do not even exist.

MY FIRST LESSONS IN PEDIGREE

In those early days, I was open to the idea of hiring people fresh out of college and teaching them my processes, thinking they'd be malleable and teachable and I'd be able to scoop them up, provide them mentorship, and give them an opportunity.

That turned out to be a bad idea.

I hired a couple of newly minted college graduates. They had good grades, came through a clean background check, and even passed the bookkeeping test. But, *and this is an important but*, they did not have the experience that was needed to work with small business customers.

We know small businesses are special, right? In school, you're learning the basics. Yes, there are internships, but they are generally in a corporate setting where tasks are departmentalized and strong controls are in place. As an aside, it bears mentioning that many of my colleagues have interns working in various positions in their companies. Interns are generally free, and they are great for unskilled task-work or positions that do not require seasoning. Meanwhile, we decided that the professional services we were delivering required a seasoned hand.

 Pedigree Spotlight: Small Business Experience a Plus

Give me a moment to explain why small business experience is so important. Fresh grads might be able to produce a balance sheet, close the books, and even reconcile a bank account, but they don't know how to have the important conversations that empower our customers with financial literacy. That's because a small business requires a different set of skills than you learn in college. Small business owners are generally good at what they do, but not always good at the business side of their business. They often require help with business processes and financial forecasting. That type of help is difficult to provide if you have not seen how other small businesses operate or if you have not worked with the many services and software that support those operations. Because financial literacy and empowerment is such a big part of my vision, we have learned that if a candidate has worked for a small business before, they will be a much better fit with us.

OUR MAGIC FORMULA

We knew we had to change the way we were looking for talent and realized we had done better with the staff we had hired early on, so we looked at their characteristics. They all had small business experience and had worked at a CPA firm or under a CPA for several years helping during tax season. Several of them had started and run their own small business, supported their spouse or family with a small business, or had been involved with several small businesses as the consultant or bookkeeper before coming to us. They could speak the language our customers needed to hear and had enough experience to bring something valuable to the table. So, we changed it up. We now require candidates to have small business experience, preferably in multiple industries. That small change opened up a new set of resumes to us.

We started attracting people who had had their own bookkeeping business as a solopreneur. This was perfect because these candidates were highly skilled as bookkeepers but typically did not like doing collections or being responsible for customer acquisition. Complete Controller provided the opportunity to focus on what they loved, working with customers.

Bingo! We landed on our magic formula.

Once we figured this out, we started to place ads all across the country, not just in university towns. As we brought on talent, I realized that the more I spread my Bookkeepers out geographically, the more coverage I had for my customers.

It was great to have a Bookkeeper on the East Coast handling West Coast construction customers, for example, because construction companies start their day at 6:00 a.m. By 7:00 a.m. their teams are dispatched and getting to their first calls. Then the day shift cuts off at 3:00 p.m. An East Coast Bookkeeper gives them the coverage they need, when they need it. Our fine dining restaurants may not start business until lunch or dinner service and have deliveries throughout the afternoon and evening. An East Coast restaurant can get great coverage from a West Coast Bookkeeper. We now had the flexibility to load balance our staff while keeping in mind when they preferred to work and when their customers would need them most.

In addition to multi-industry small business experience, we also require our candidates to be QuickBooks ProAdvisors. We've actually required that from day one. Why? Because I was a ProAdvisor way before I started the company and I understood, that unless a person had that certification, they didn't really have a deep enough knowledge of the functionality of the QuickBooks software to be efficient and effective at the level that I wanted them to be.

Like me, you will have some hits and misses with your staffing. After you have hired some and start to notice trends, learn from them. In the mistakes and the successes, you will create your own magic formula. Ask yourself: Are there certifications that should be required for the role they are applying to? And is it better for candidates to bring experience to the position or arrive as a blank slate that you can write on?

OUR APPLICATION PROCESS

Creating an Online Ad

When creating an online employment ad, you need to be specific about the role you are looking to fill and include any requirements for the position. This seems like a no-brainer, but many employers get lazy here or don't want to reveal too much about the job up front for fear that they will eliminate potential prospects. Perhaps they are coming from a place of desperation rather than intent. They *need* someone and they are already setting themselves up to make a pick that might not be the best fit.

Instead, think of each step in the recruiting process as a filter that will gather the valuable prospects and let the others fall through. Also, make sure you save the ad somewhere so you can use it again. Remember when we talked about documenting relentlessly? Take the time to build your template for future ads and really lay out the job parameters. For example, we include the following qualifications in our job ads:

- ☑ QuickBooks ProAdvisor certification

- ☑ Small business experience, preferably in multiple industries

☑ A four-year accounting degree or commensurate experience working directly under a CPA or a CFO who will vouch for you

☑ Ability to work remotely

☑ A phone with data capabilities

☑ High-speed internet (because let's face it, my whole business is based on efficiency. If staff don't have high-speed internet, they will be pissed off and so will I.)

Reviewing Resumes

When we receive an application, we first review the resume to see if the applicant meets all of our requirements. While doing so, we are particularly impressed if we see these specific qualifications:

☑ **Experience as a solopreneur.** As I have shared, we love solopreneurs! It always piques our interest when we see that someone ran their own bookkeeping business because we know that they've had exposure to small business issues and understand what makes a bookkeeping business tick. That will be valuable to our customers and our company.

☑ **Transparency with information.** We look to see if they have included information about their past employers—typically their names and phone numbers. We look because the people who leave out that information have a reason, while those who include it are open and transparent. We want people we can trust since they will be dealing with our customers' confidential information. If they are honest and transparent on their resume, chances are they will be honest and transparent with us and our customers.

Separating the Wheat from the Chaff

When we like what we see on a resume, we ask the candidate to review our website and provide us with five pieces of feedback regarding what they learned and how they feel about working for a company with our model. We give them a deadline for this task because we want to know if they are willing to invest the time to research our company or if they are just spitting out a bunch of resumes. Their feedback helps us know if the information on our website represents us properly, and it tells us important things about the candidate. If they respond immediately, we know where this job search is in their life's priorities. If their responses are insightful, we know they can digest and think critically about information. If they meet the deadline we gave them, we know they noticed it and it mattered to them. And we can see firsthand if their research and communication skills are up to par.

In particular, we look for—

☑ **Thorough research skills.** We can tell by the feedback we receive who reads only the home page and who actually takes the time to scope out the rest of the site.

☑ **Excellent communication.** As a virtual company, 85 percent of our communication with customers is through email and text. So, if a person cannot email clearly, chances are they will not do well. Knowing that candidates can communicate in a succinct and professional manner with gratitude and humility is a big deal for us. When they share their insights about our company in writing, we watch how they organize and present the information. Is it a long strung-out paragraph with lots of commas? Is it a bulleted list? Do they use numbers? Do they use full sentences? Are their thoughts communicated clearly or muddled and disorganized? Do they have a strong command of the English language?

Today, we have the perfect person looking through the resumes and those feedback emails that reveal so much about the candidates. She's also the publisher and editor of our company blog and she's meticulous. With no emotional connection, she is able to gauge their communication skills and effectively spot promising candidates to move forward in the process.

PRO TIP

We recognized early on that it's inefficient to have one person per-form only a single role within the company. As the company grew, we started to see new roles emerging that weren't full-time at first. For example, we have had a Bookkeeper straddle the role of Programs and Training tech along with her bookkeeping portfolio for a couple of years now. She loves getting the extra hours and the change of pace. Why hire a whole new person when we have the people with the skill, talent, and willingness on our team already? So look for ways to use your staff's talents in multiple areas that are relevant. Just be careful not to dilute those staff members by giving them tasks that aren't utilizing their core talents and skills.

The Dreaded Skills Test

If we like a candidate's resume and feedback, we give them our skills test. It covers accounting functions and QuickBooks knowledge, and tests more than just knowing where to go in the software. It tests a person's accounting prowess. Candidates need to know some of the basics right off the bat. The process of recruiting and training staff is expensive and time-consuming, so the sooner we know if they really understand accounting, the better. Sched-uled and completed online, the test is multiple choice with no reference materials and timed at forty minutes.

The kicker is that each candidate only gets one chance to log in and take the test. We warn them about this ahead of time. We tell them to make sure they have a strong internet connection and give them a phone number to call if they run into any technical problems. There are no second chances! We made this a best practice because people got in there and realized they didn't know all the answers. So, they'd flip through the test and try to figure out what the questions were going to be, then they'd come to us and say they had some sort of technical problem or emergency and wanted to retest later. What they didn't know is that we could see their progress through the test. We learned our lesson from this and now make no exceptions.

The applicants who make it to our talent pool are the cream of the crop. I don't think it would be a stretch to say that they are some of the top book-keepers in the country. Candidates have to get 70 percent or better on the skills test to earn an interview. We've determined over the years that on average only 13 percent earn that passing score. We're picky about who we hire, and you should be, too.

If they fail the test . . .

If a candidate scored high but didn't pass, and we liked everything else they submitted, it's not quite over for them. If at that time we happen to be in need of data entry-level support, for example, we may offer them the opportunity to take that position. Because recruiting is so costly, I encourage you to look at entry-level positions that can be filled by candidates that just barely miss the cut for a higher-level position. In my experience, these staff members are grateful, loyal, and motivated to improve their skills and expand their opportunities.

And if they pass . . .

A passing score gets the candidate on our calendar for a verbal interview. In the early days, before testing and process-driven recruiting, qualified applicants would go straight to the interview process, which I would do, and whoever impressed me got the job. Fortunately, I am no longer involved in the recruiting process. I save that for our Account Services department.

This department oversees recruiting and staff contracts and is managed by our CFO. Our CFO likes to handle the initial interviews personally. She has this knack for being able to create a safe place where people feel comfortable sharing their experiences. Her tendency is to like people until they show her otherwise, which is a good quality to have. If they don't impress her, then they definitely won't cut it at Complete Controller. But if she likes them and thinks they are viable, they get an interview with one or more of our managers.

We feel it's important for candidates to interview with our management team, since that is who will be reviewing their work and supporting them if they are hired. While our CFO might ask questions about a candidate's work history, philosophy, or problem-solving ability, our managers—in our case, Controllers—typically ask task-oriented questions. If the candidate can't answer these nitty-gritty questions, the Controller probably isn't going to want that person on their team. And if a Controller isn't interested in having a candidate on their team, then that candidate is not getting the job. Period.

If a candidate impresses the Controller, however, we move on to the background check—which is our CYA. It tells us if a candidate has any civil judgments or criminal activity, plus where they have lived and when. Our insurance company and I are in agreement that we should pass up anyone who does not have a clean background check. We are working with people's finances, after all.

If their check comes back clean, the now qualified recruit is added to our talent pool. Rarely do our talent pool members wait for long to begin working. We created the talent pool to prevent hiring from a place of desperation. Anyone who has recruited knows that there are times of feast and times of famine. The talent pool allows us to store up those great candidates in times of feast, so we do not become desperate and tempted to just hire anyone in times of famine.

Pen to Paper

Finding the right talent is a process. As with any process, if you standardize it and repeat it, you will save time and be nimble when adjustments are needed. Your exercise for this chapter is to write employment ads for each role in your company. To do this:

☑ Be clear about your expectations and requirements for each role and do not overpromise.

☑ Think about the filters you want to run your recruits through. What are the steps needed to fulfill each role?

☑ Once you have your top candidates, what skills should be tested?

☑ How will you test and score each candidate?

☑ Who should interview them, and what types of questions will they ask?

ONBOARDING STAFF

ONCE YOU HAVE ENGAGED your new recruits, you will need to onboard them. Onboarding involves much more than gathering employment documents and issuing an email address and desktop. It's important to have a succinct process in place so new staff have a good experience right from the start. Remember, often a new recruit will still have active opportunities that were fostered during their job search. A bad onboarding experience can cause a late offer from your competition to look tantalizing.

At Complete Controller, once we decide a new staff member is needed, we select someone from the talent pool and funnel that candidate into the onboarding process. If more than one Bookkeeper is in the talent pool, the Controller will often look at industry experience and make the pick they think will best augment their team. A contract and a nondisclosure agreement need to be signed, and identity verification has to happen, then they get to meet with the supervising Controller who selected them.

The Controller guides the onboarding journey, providing wisdom and encouragement and training materials. A new Bookkeeper's successful journey through training rests on the Controller. If the Bookkeeper is lost, it's up to the Controller to get them on track. If the Bookkeeper is not reading the materials, watching the videos, or turning in the accompanying work on time, it's up to the Controller to take notice and terminate them before the company invests any more time.

Orientation

Since our business is virtual, our training is too. It all starts with a desktop orientation during which the staff member sets up their email and phone line. During this orientation, they are pointed to the scope of work for their role, our *Practice Standards* booklet, technical videos, and accompanying outlines. The scope of work provides a step-by-step walkthrough for each task involved in their role, including how to get started, processes for fulfilling the work, information about the cloud environment, common troubleshooting issues, and customer service techniques. By following the scope, the new staff member is primed for success.

The scope of work is a key document for any new staff member and will continue to be a reference as they mature in their role. Especially in a virtual workplace, staff can feel unsupported and confused if they are not provided with a concise set of instructions that help them understand their role and how it interacts with other roles within the company. The scope sets the expectations for the staff member and for us as a company, making it clear what must be done, how it should be delivered, and when. It gives the new recruit vision, direction, and a sense of purpose, and without it, we would find ourselves spending each day giving them minute instructions for what needs to be done.

I always tell new recruits, "You're going to want to get yourself a cup of hot chocolate and curl up on the couch for the first run through your scope of work. Take your time because just knowing what's in it is half the battle."

They may not remember every detail, but just knowing a topic is discussed in the scope is all they need to run a search and find whatever deadline or technique they have a question about when it comes up later. It's basically our outline of how we deliver excellence.

Coupled with our *Practice Standards* and technical videos, our scopes of work also address a variety of issues such as deadlines, ethics, and standards of care for the customers' privacy and security, as well as what we do and what we never do. We also address time records, which is exciting and important because that's how they get paid. We tell them when to expect payment for their services and where to record their hours, paying special attention to training hours and the expectation that they will not exceed the maximum.

We make it clear the number of hours we anticipate it will take them to learn the Complete Controller techniques. They are welcome to spend additional time honing their skills on their own time as professional development.

PRO TIP

I highly encourage companies to set a not-to-exceed number when it comes to training hours. This is the first major investment you are making in a person and it should be equitable for the business as well as fair to the new recruit. Be up front about your expectations and you will quickly weed out those who don't care or don't pay attention.

Visual Learning

The position we hire for most frequently is that of Bookkeeper. Since no one advances within our company without first being a Bookkeeper, that is the role for which we have created the most support. One of the first instructions in the Bookkeeper scope of work points them to technical videos because not everyone learns best by reading and a combination of the two gives us the greatest chance of success. When using videos to teach, I suggest you provide a way to engage the learner to discover if they understood the main points and give them the opportunity to ask questions. Our videos are accompanied by outlines on which Bookkeepers can take notes as they watch. As the Bookkeeper progresses through the video series, those outline notes are required to be submitted to their Controller. That's how we know they are making progress in their training and can catch anyone who has become stagnant.

Controllers are communicating with their Bookkeepers regularly during the training period to ask how it is going and if they have any questions. Ideally, our Bookkeepers will be responsive to that outreach and engaged in the process. The outlines not only clue us in to whether they are progressing, but they also provide a place to ask about any topic or point that needs clarification. This sets the tone for sharing knowledge and collaborating with their manager. It reinforces the relationship, which is what we want. The staff member needs to know they can go to their manager and get the support they need and that the manager is accessible, willing, and able to work with them to make sure they succeed.

Our orientation period typically lasts from thirty to sixty days. We give them about fourteen hours to get their feet wet, digging into the materials. Once they have worked their way through, and before customer work is assigned, there is another test. Yes, another test! This test checks to see what they learned in the videos and scope of work. We want to know that our new staff members really understand their role. The test is an open-book, untimed series of questions. All of the answers can be found in the scope of work so our learner has a chance to use their search skills.

What we foster here is resourcefulness—we want new staff members to go find the answers if they don't know. While it starts off with searching the scope of work to answer test questions, we hope this skill extends to include other resources like professional knowledge bases, Google, or other forums to solve everyday problems that aren't addressed in the scope of work. We want to encourage solution-finding. If a staff member runs into a snag and isn't sure what to do based on the information available in their scope of work, they should do a little research and find out what others have done, then bring those solutions to their manager. Who knows? They may present a solution their manager didn't know about that has the potential to become our new norm. If the manager wants more input, they will put it out to our other managers to see what they've done. In this way,

we breed a culture of knowledge sharing, so if someone comes across the best, most efficient way to handle a particular thing, it gets shared, and if it's better than what we were doing before, it becomes part of our technique and is recorded in the scope of work.

This is what I mean when I say that our Bookkeepers are given autonomy, but they are not alone. They have the support of our shared knowledge and our ear when they come up with a new and better way. We are listening and we are sharing, constantly.

After a Bookkeeper completes the open-book test, their Controller starts to fold in work—usually starting with a customer who has a basic service plan. The Controller will assign a few tasks and then check to see if the work was completed correctly. The Bookkeeper will get feedback so they know if something needs to be fixed. Once a Bookkeeper is doing those tasks correctly, they will get a few more until they are able to take on another customer and so on and so forth. Now, the customer work experience begins, but the training never stops. Regardless of the industry you are in, you can follow a similar process of train, test, repeat to bring out the best in your staff and your business.

Continuing Education

In the spirit of learning and staying current on our best practices, every month, we put out questions to our entire staff that make them dive back into their scopes of work. Our Controllers are required to answer a couple more questions than the Bookkeepers, because they need to stay sharp not only on their scope of work but that of the staff members they are supporting. This exercise gives us an opportunity to have our team relearn any processes that we found lacking during our internal quality control checks; to point out any new, changed, or seasonal processes as we near critical dates in the year; and to remember techniques that aren't used all of the time. It also helps to keep our staff in the scope of work and at their best.

Our industry deals in a lot of technical work so we are constantly updating and pointing the team back to their scopes of work. Your industry may be such that it could benefit from a different type of continuing education. You might encourage them to stay current by taking online classes. You could also offer something fun like a book club on a topic specific to your industry to encourage discussion on trends and best practices with staff during a virtual meeting.

It's a great way to stay current and in touch, regardless of their location. Whatever it is, the investment in your staff's learning will be noticed in their work product, knowledge contributions, and job satisfaction.

Timekeeping

Timekeeping is crucial to the success of any business and even more so when value pricing is part of the model. I believe a timesheet should be more than just a place to record hours worked. It should empower the staff members using it to know how they are performing on a day-to-day basis against their goal. So, the first thing you will need to do is set a performance goal. For us, that goal is an efficiency level of 40 percent of the customer portfolio value they serve. Our staff members know they must meet that goal, or their performance will come under scrutiny and they may be terminated. Meanwhile, if they exceed the goal, they are rewarded with a profit-share–based bonus that is designed to be greater in direct relation to more efficient performance.

Obviously, we are rewarding efficiency, and by giving them a tool to monitor it constantly throughout the period, we empower them to succeed. Our timesheet not only measures efficiency, it actually calculates the bonus that they will receive that period at their current rate. By fiddling with the tool, they can quickly see that a better efficiency rate results in a bigger bonus because it increases the portfolio's profit. After a few periods of being efficient and meeting our standards, a Bookkeeper learns that we like to stack our most efficient team members with more customers, which increases their total portfolio value and, ultimately, their bonus.

While efficiency is everything to a service firm that uses value pricing, it is nothing without accuracy, timeliness, and customer satisfaction. Earlier, we talked about the KPIs that tell us if a Bookkeeper is failing to maintain our standards in any of those areas. If they make a mistake that costs them a perfect score, they lose a portion of their bonus in response. So, they have to be efficient as a baseline in order to keep their job and earn bonuses. And failure to meet our standards will cause them to forfeit part of their bonus. Thus, our staff are always striving for a perfect score. We do this because

properly structured compensation can be an invaluable tool for incentivizing your staff to produce the outcomes you desire, and a well-designed timekeeping tool can be used to give them control over their destiny.

Pen to Paper

Onboarding new staff and providing them with the tools for success within your company will set the tone for your ongoing relationship. By setting expectations, laying out concise role definitions, and giving them peer support, you can ensure they do not keep coming to you for minute directions. By setting performance goals and practical ways to measure those goals, you will reduce waste and increase the desire to achieve.

Ask yourself these questions:

- ☑ What are the tools that you want to provide to new staff members? Start with the basics: email address, phone number, business cards, etc.

- ☑ What social tools will you encourage new staff to use so they can become evangelists for your company or participate in team-building?

- ☑ What tools will you use to augment your written materials? Written scopes of work and practice standards are important tools for success, and we will dive deeper into how to construct these in Part Five, "The Art of Delegation."

- ☑ What processes will you have in place to test your staff's ongoing knowledge in their role?

11

CULTIVATE SUCCESS AND WEED OUT FAILURE

WHAT IF YOU GO through the screening process and then hire and train an employee, only to find out that they are not efficient? Inevitably, this will happen. Believe me when I say that the sooner you know, the better off you and your new staff member will be. The longer you allow inefficiencies to go unchecked, the more costly they become and the more difficult they are to remedy.

At the beginning of each period, we calculate each staff member's maximum hours for that period. For us, the maximum hours equal 40 percent of that Bookkeeper's client portfolio value divided by their hourly rate. For you, it may be something different. We check their timesheets weekly to see the progress toward that maximum. If a staff member is expending a large number of hours in the first week or two of the period, leaving little to no time for work during the last half of the month, it's a red flag. By watching weekly, we avoid getting all the way to payday before realizing that we have a problem.

Now that we know, you may be wondering what do we do about it? We know that they would not have landed the job if they didn't have the experience, skill, and training to do so. So we focus on how to help them succeed. There are two resolvable areas that can rob a staff member of their efficiency to such an extent that they will fail: a lack of taskwork streamlining and performing extra work without charging for it.

Task-work Streamlining

After you have been working in a role for a while, you learn certain tricks for streamlining tasks or multitasking that are huge timesavers. We share many of these in the scope of work, but some are best taught to help resolve an area where the manager determines their staff member is struggling. Perhaps it's guiding the setup of dual monitors with multiple logins to maximize workspace and task performance, or it could be teaching them how to download all of the attachments from a single email in one fell swoop, rather than individually.

Every role and industry will have its own set of task-work challenges. The point is that managers aren't just there to check the boxes for staff training. They are also there to mentor and to pass along knowledge that they have accrued, since they have been in the new staff member's shoes and have done it before. Streamlining does not always involve a skilled task; sometimes it has to do with best practices for working from home or working virtually. A manager cannot know until they ask.

We like to have the staff member walk us through their typical day and let us know where they are getting hung up. We often use screen-share to have them show us how they are tackling a task that has them frustrated. By doing this, we are able to quickly see how they might do it better, faster, and smarter and offer tips on how they can improve. In the spirit of empowerment, we look to ourselves to see if we have set our new staff member up for success.

Extras on the Side

The biggest efficiency thief is the performance of tasks that are not included in a customer's service plan and failing to charge additional hours for the work. Those of you with a value-priced business model will suffer the most from this type of activity. The minute a staff member provides a service that is not included in the plan and does not get approval for an hourly custom request, they are adding time at their hourly rate to a portfolio value that is unchanged. Not only is this detrimental to their efficiency, it is damaging to the customer relationship.

We have had Bookkeepers who thought that doing the customer a "small favor" on the side would build rapport, when instead they were actually setting that customer up for unreasonable expectations. Once additional services are provided free of charge, the customer comes to expect it and becomes less cooperative in approving future add-on work. Even worse, if that staff member leaves the company, when the customer is reassigned, the trust bond is that much harder to establish if both the customer and the new staff member discover that there is an imbalance in the amount paid for services that must be rectified.

Our Controllers make a point of knowing what services are being provided to each customer and they can support their Bookkeepers with techniques for avoiding add-on work without approval. If they see that a Bookkeeper is struggling or the customer is being pushy or avoiding approvals for work, they can connect the customer with Account Services to rectify the disparity.

Truth be told, I would rather lose a customer that does not value my Bookkeeper's time enough to pay for it. It's up to the company to fight that battle so our Bookkeepers can have peaceful and profitable relationships with the customers they serve. It is our responsibility to create a clear scope of work and a strong construct within which everyone can succeed.

So, if somebody is failing, it's on us, until it's not anymore. While we relate to mistakes as discoveries and we support our motivated staff members to work through them and grow, if I see that someone isn't learning from their discoveries, I'm the first to let them go and open up that slot for someone else to have a chance at success.

Hiring from Within and Training for Advancement

NOT EVERYONE CAN LEAD

It can be tempting to look outside of the company for new talent, but growing people within the company yields higher efficiency, greater loyalty, and better job satisfaction. I strongly believe that if you hire someone who hasn't been through all the roles in your company to manage those who have, it creates a disconnect.

I speak from experience. This practice creates a kind of lofty culture where management becomes the God above all and the sayer of what should be done. It's not coming from a place of understanding what your staff is doing on a day-to-day basis. There's less compassion.

> *There's a special kind of person who's really good at what they do and wants to share that with others. They want to empower. That is a good leader.*

The person who facilitates empowerment. You know the person. When you get off the phone, you feel smarter for having had a conversation with them. You don't feel ashamed. You don't feel belittled. You don't feel like they are better than you or didn't have time for you. You feel grateful that they took the time to explain something and now you are better for it.

It is important to remember that those people don't always have extra letters after their name. The first person that I appointed to an executive-level position to run our operations was hired to fulfill the goal of bringing our quality control up to CPA standards. I should have kept her focused on that goal using KPIs. Instead, I put her in a leadership role, and it almost cost me my company. Don't get me wrong; she implemented key structures into our bookkeeping process that were necessary for our service to be complete and valuable to the CPA/Experts we wanted to impress. I believe that we needed her to be a part of our journey. My mistake was allowing her to become a layer of management that separated me from my staff in a way that I never intended.

She joined the team in October 2012. After about five years, she had brought all of the value she was going to bring to the company. I say this because it was around that time that I saw a marked decrease in strategic communication from her. Follow-up from her slowed and was sometimes nonexistent, and my staff were no longer excited to have management meetings and didn't participate with the vigor and joy they once had. This should have been my clue. Instead, I persevered for another year and a half in an awkward dance of me trying to spark excitement about innovation and strategic participation and her being uncommunicative, resistant, and slow to start.

During a conversation about her compensation, she mentioned that she was a CPA with a master's in finance, and it was at that point I knew that she valued her pedigree more than the company did. She had gone to graduate school while she was with us, and while our business model supported that effort, she loved her job. But once she earned those extra credentials, she lost her ability to be satisfied serving our business model, vision, or purpose. Soon after that conversation, she resigned to take another position—perhaps one that needed her master's degree and was willing to pay for it.

Here's what I learned after she left. Staff members across all roles in the company came forward to tell me that while they respected her knowledge and strict attention to practice standards, when they had occasion to seek her support, they often felt as if they were wasting her time, an inconvenience. Worst of all were those who said she made them feel stupid. This about a leader in a company that purports to advance empowerment through sharing knowledge and creating a supportive, collaborative environment? I was horrified. The bottom line: She was smart, but she lacked the ability to strengthen others through strong leadership.

Unbeknownst to me, the company was being fed a daily diet of condescension and inaccessibility. Remember my reference to your business being your child? My child was starving. Those in her inner circle were hearing her constant complaints and resistance to any suggestions for improvement. Some were even being told that they should leave the company to find work where they would be better appreciated. Because that's how she felt.

Thank heaven for the autonomy part of our model. Our team members were used to being self-sufficient and enjoyed the flexibility and satisfaction their jobs provided. They performed well because that mattered to them. They sought support from other team members and didn't let anything keep them from success. Today, the person directing the operations of our company is someone who has held every role. She has the battle scars to prove it. She understands and, most importantly, she empowers our staff with her knowledge. She is a true leader.

PRO TIP

Watch for people who are willing to jump in and get the job done, no matter what that job is. They embrace change if it creates efficiencies and increases accuracy. They want to dig in and learn more when something new comes along. They will learn for the purpose of practical application rather than recognition by others, but that does not mean that they do not need recognition. They don't expect it, but they thrive and grow more when recognition is given. Give them the ability to suggest changes, run with their ideas, and report the results. You will find your leaders.

NOT EVERYONE IS CUT OUT FOR MANAGEMENT

Every successful company has some type of hierarchy. I subscribe to the practice of promoting from within and rewarding those who excel. Our advancement is structured so that motivated and talented staff members can work their way up through each role in the company, so no one becomes a manager who doesn't have an understanding of what is involved with each of the different roles. To advance to the role of Controller, for example, you have to be a Bookkeeper first. That means our Controllers know all of the processes that the Bookkeepers have to go through. Because of their experience, they can spot when something is not getting done, empathize with staff, and support them when challenges arise.

While our Controllers are excellent Bookkeepers, not all excellent Bookkeepers can become Controllers. Let me explain.

A mistake that I think a lot of business founders make—including me—is promoting somebody into management who's really good at what they do.

Just because someone is really good at what they do, does not mean they are really good at managing people.

My first Controller took over the role from me. I picked her because I felt she had the best grasp on the Complete Controller way, she had been with me for a while, and she had high-level accounting experience in a diversified portfolio. I pitched her the idea of taking on a Controller role with some of the other Bookkeepers, while I would continue in the Controller role for her. She said yes.

After this, whenever we added enough Bookkeepers to require another Controller, we would promote the best Bookkeeper with the most diverse experience. As a Controller, they would begin reviewing their Bookkeepers' books at closing, guiding the training process for new Bookkeepers, diving into complex problems, and onboarding new customers into the portfolio.

It worked great! Until it didn't. A couple of Bookkeepers who were promoted to Controller floundered the minute they had a Bookkeeper reporting to them. They got frustrated with the varying levels of skill each Bookkeeper had. Some wanted only Bookkeepers who could work alone right from the start, and others wanted to manage every detail of every task to make sure it was up to snuff. Bookkeeper after Bookkeeper would let them down and need to be terminated.

We recruited really strong Bookkeepers who jumped through all of our hoops and seemed to be great candidates, but they just weren't succeeding under these Controllers. So, we were going through Bookkeepers like crazy. When a Bookkeeper failed, the Controller just ended up doing the work. It was frustrating for the new Controller, it was frustrating for the Bookkeeper who had failed, and it was frustrating the company's ability to grow. We couldn't understand what was happening.

A Better Succession Strategy

What we needed was an in-between, a better succession strategy. A good succession strategy provides the opportunity for ambitious team members to experience advancement without jeopardizing their current position. All too often companies promote only for failure to mean termination or an embarrassing demotion. We needed to create a safe place for a Bookkeeper who is interested in becoming a Controller to stick their toe in the pool and find out if it's the right temperature before diving in. It was also important to stop promoting people just because we needed to and start doing it because they were ready.

First, we created a qualification matrix that was more than just "You're a great Bookkeeper." We measured KPIs in these areas: efficiency, aptitude, timeliness, reporting accuracy, and customer satisfaction, because those attributes matter to us. Then we looked only at Bookkeepers who had expressed a desire to become a Controller. Some Bookkeepers are happy as clams in their role with a large portfolio of settled customers. They know what to expect from day to day and have total control over their destiny. Being a Controller is not at all interesting to them.

For those who make the grade, we offer the position of Executive Bookkeeper and begin to introduce them to essential parts of the Controller role. To start, we have them shadow some onboarding calls and listen to the discussions that take place with new customers. When they are ready, we have them facilitate a discussion with a new customer, while being shadowed by their Controller, of course.

That experience alone is enough for some to decide that they do not want to be a Controller. They would much rather get the customer when they are already warm, perform the tasks that need to be done throughout the period, develop open communication, streamline processes, build trust, and become more efficient as they go. Constantly introducing new customers to the service, tackling new and changing problems, and developing relationships with new CPA/Experts is not their idea of fun, fulfilling work. They learn that about themselves and can go back to being Bookkeepers with no effect to their pay or portfolio.

The Executive Bookkeepers who enjoy these interactions, however, may decide to move forward and learn more about what it takes to succeed as a Controller. They got a taste and they are excited.

At Complete Controller, mentorship is not only encouraged, it's required. As the Executive Bookkeepers go through their training, their Controllers guide the process and mentor them on how to onboard customers and eventually how to hire and train their own Bookkeepers. We also subscribe to the culture of giving it away to keep it. The first customers a new Executive Bookkeeper passes along to their new Bookkeepers come from their Controller's own portfolio. Our Controllers are compensated in part based on the size of their portfolio. So, to give away a customer to empower their Executive Bookkeeper's advancement is a true act of selflessness.

After Executive Bookkeepers become comfortable with onboarding customers, the next phase is to hire someone under them. For some, this is an eye-opening experience. While they may enjoy the new challenges and interaction of customer onboarding, some realize very quickly that they don't want to deal with Bookkeepers contacting them all the time with questions and texting them at all hours, sometimes five minutes before a deadline. They're not up for creating the necessary bond with the Bookkeepers and becoming a mentor. Maybe they find themselves unwilling to have the tough conversations about what it takes to succeed. Or they decide they really don't like people all that much and that they'd rather stay where they are. They can remain as Executive Bookkeepers assisting their Controller in onboarding work, getting the satisfaction of wearing the white hat for new customers and solving all of their problems. Plus, they can continue to serve their bookkeeping portfolio.

For others, this is the beginning of a new chapter: working with new Bookkeepers to develop the skills they need to take on the bookkeeping work and shifting customers to them until bookkeeping is no longer a part of the daily workflow. By the time Executive Bookkeepers hire and train their second Bookkeeper, they get to take the title of Controller, which entitles them to a raise based on the new responsibilities they will be taking on.

Pen to Paper

Once you have hired and trained staff members, the challenge becomes how to keep them on track and give them opportunities for advancement. You will begin to see leaders emerge from the pack. Ask yourself the following:

- ☑ How do you spot them?

- ☑ What key performance indicators tell you that they have the potential to manage or lead?

- ☑ What are the opportunities for advancement in your company?

- ☑ Is there a plan for succession that allows them to try the role before giving up the safety of their current position? If not, take steps to create one.

- ☑ What happens if they fail?

12

ANOTHER LESSON
IN PEDIGREE

I WANT TO TELL you a story about something I call a hostage situation. It can creep up on you when you aren't diligent about documentation and cross-training. It steals your leverage and your sunshine. And it never ends well. Remember my tech guy who developed the architecture of our first and subsequent tech systems? I really respected him. He was smart and had experience that was valuable to my company. The systems that he was running in his full-time day job provided a training ground for the ones he built for us. He also had a plethora of credentials after his name and, while that was impressive, most important to me was that he was solution-oriented and nimble.

When I floated an idea, he thrived on finding a solution. He made my vision come to life. I dubbed him the Magician, and for many years, he made more than I did on Complete Controller. In 2010 and 2011, he agreed to defer payment on his invoices to free up capital for growth. We made payments but weren't entirely caught up until late 2012. He eventually got paid for every hour billed, but the fact that he was willing to put the business survival before his own financial gain proved to me that he was in it for more than just a gig. He saw the vision that this could be something great.

Then came the tech meltdown. You remember that we had outgrown our system and needed to overhaul our configuration right on the tail of a huge investment in new technology. He showed up and made it work. We migrated and the fire drills started to die down. We got back to the daily grind and one very important component was pushed to the sidelines—system documentation.

We had evolved more quickly than we could document. As the business owner, I wanted to make sure every process was recorded in some way and that we understood the process and the reason behind the process. In the case of technology, it was even more than that. While prior systems had been accompanied by emergency protocols, system architecture information, backup, restoral standard operating procedures (SOPs), and more, this one had nothing. I trusted that my tech guy would come through in a crisis, but what if he were hit by a bus?

As the company matured, we dreamed together. We started to have company retreats and encouraged our Controllers to share their hopes and fears. We discussed innovation opportunities and future goals. My tech guy, my Director of Client Relations, and I worked on a strategic plan for the company, and we saw how our dreams aligned and how we could achieve them.

Can you guess what one of my hopes and fears was? I wanted and needed the system documentation to be in place. I asked for it and the task of creating it was added to the strategic plan, but nothing happened.

And then in 2015, he quit. He wanted more; he wanted me to stop dangling the carrot and make him a partner as we had discussed. By now his full-time job had changed and he was working out of the country and didn't need the headache of working for us during his free time, unless I was willing to make it worth his while.

To keep him, I gave him shares of the company so he would have a fiduciary duty to it. His shares would produce some minor additional income, but primarily they were assurance that if we were acquired or brought in venture capital to expand, he would be included and enriched for his involvement. We also laid out a contract that defined my expectations for his new role as Chief Technology Officer (CTO) and made it clear that it would be different than the system administration work he was currently doing.

Everyone agreed to start tackling the items on the strategic plan that related to their roles, and we were off to the races.

Let's face it: Complete Controller is a marriage of service and technology. We do the hosting. We do the integrations. And we rely heavily on our platform in order to perform and monitor work. Our technology is a huge part of our solution. The Help Desk gets people connected to our platform. The system administrator runs it and keeps it running. I was counting on my CTO to create standard operating procedures for those roles and ready us for disaster recovery. But that was not what happened.

In actuality, he continued to administer the system. He tried and failed a couple of times to find people who could sufficiently fill the role of system administrator. But he wasn't having much luck. I soon realized that hiring wasn't his top priority. He had his day job, tech innovations, and support issues, and as more things landed on him, this reduced the amount of time he devoted to hiring and developing documentation to train a new staff member. Rather than reprioritizing documentation to the thing he did above all else, he let it fall to the bottom of the list.

Everyone has that part of their job that they don't like—the part they do because they have to, not because they have any passion or desire to do it. I believe that was the case with the system documentation. If you haven't trained someone to handle a role, then you have to step in and handle it yourself. Because he wasn't dedicating the time and energy necessary to getting the documentation down and then training someone in that role, he continued to find himself needing to perform that role.

You cannot delegate a role
if you cannot create the framework to
train someone else to do it.

We even had a few conversations along the way that were a foreshadowing of what was to come. He said things like, "The system manual is going to be like a dissertation!" And I remember thinking to myself, "That might work for the tech world, but I know from my own training and operations purposes that my scopes of work don't look like that." Who wants to read a dissertation? Yuck!

 PRO TIP

People will show you and tell you who they are early on. The key is to watch and listen. If the relationship is inequitable, you may start to turn off those instincts because to acknowledge them means to change, and you can't see a path for change that doesn't rock the boat. Denial will just get you in deeper. Better to tackle it head-on, and if they can't handle you shining the light, asking pointed questions, and setting expectations, they will misbehave, and if you are lucky, they will leave before you have to terminate them.

In 2018 I hired my brother as our web administrator to totally revamp our website, blog, and web media. A big innovation was incorporating the sign-up process into the website so customers could get a quote and sign up for services online. When the work was completed and only ongoing maintenance was required, I began to look at him as an untapped tech asset and a potential candidate for the system administrator role. He had previously done that work for a satellite college campus and knew enough about the technology to be teachable. I presented the idea to my CTO, and he said he was on board.

But again, nothing happened.

Eventually, my CTO did design a succession plan, which included how to train a new system administrator. But when the time came to hold meetings to push that training forward, he lagged. During a training process, clear communication and regular follow-up is essential. Momentum is a big influencer to training success. Briefings and work reviews are typical. Unfortunately, none of this happened. While he thought the succession plan would take a couple of months to work through and expressed an availability to invest that time, he abruptly left the company without completing it.

He later commented that the person we were bringing up in the role had a fraction of his experience. To a leader, that is a tantalizing opportunity to foster growth in a protégé. It is also an opportunity to pay less for the position as the person is learning and developing that experience. It was revealing that he didn't see it that way. Some people do not have the instinct to empower and mentor. Perhaps they fear that perception of their own value will be lessened by teaching someone with less experience how to perform the very work they do.

Here we had a person who was highly educated—a great visionary and administrator, until he had to manage others to do the work. All the pedigree in the world couldn't give him the skill and desire to empower others to succeed and create the tools to support that success. As you reflect on this story, ask yourself: Do you have a hostage situation? Is anyone refusing to document and cross-train their position for fear that they may be replaced or otherwise no longer valued?

Recognize and Maximize Value

It is important to bring people onto the team that have competencies you do not. Even though you may not have the same skills, you can still quantify their value to your company by developing goals and measuring KPIs for their role. As they show promise in a particular area, foster that success and leverage it to the benefit of the business.

PRO TIP

In negotiating the deal for a new hire's talents, build it on a framework of only paying for work that produces revenue, reduces costs, or improves efficiency.

MEASURE YOUR LEADERS

If you are putting a person into a leadership position, define the expectations for how they will lead. Our leadership expectations are simple:

- ☑ Mentor the staff.

- ☑ Support vital functions within the company.

- ☑ Monitor and report on KPIs.

- ☑ Apply the vision to new innovation.

Our leaders are constantly looking for ways to reduce friction, improve quality, reduce risk, and enrich the team. Is your leadership team doing this? Are they doing it well? Ask yourself these questions and make changes accordingly. Don't be distracted by an Ivy League education or high-level credentials. Sure, they're great. We have many CPAs and MBAs work for us. What's most important is whether they can fulfill the role within your business model effectively. That's what you need to find out. And all the pedigree in the world can't tell you that.

KNOW YOUR CORE COMPETENCIES

In a small business, it is common for a single staff member to wear multiple hats. This practice can save you a lot of money and allow the staff member to experience multiple options for advancement, but you must be careful to not put duties on their plate that detract or distract from their performance.

 Pedigree Spotlight: Maximizing Core Strengths

Say you have a hotshot sales guy. He is particularly good at developing profitable relationships and getting solid referrals that convert into paying customers. He's so good at it that you have him train new salespeople as the business hires them, because you want some of that talent and skill to rub off. You ask him to create the training materials and run the training and then report on who he thinks will be successful.

Unfortunately, you just cut that hotshot sales guy's value by distracting him with efforts that are not centric to his core value. Instead, you should do everything you can do to keep him focused on his core value and talent. Yes, he will need to record activity in the CRM so others can follow up and his actions can be measured, and yes, he will need to record his mileage and take the extra thirty seconds to take a picture of the meal receipt for a lunch he just purchased in the field. You need him to perform that 10 percent of his job that he doesn't like, because it allows you to track his activity, measure and monitor performance, and comply with the rules of good business.

But you do not need to make him train new staff. He would be a great person for the trainer to interview and get feedback from when designing the training, or ask to give a talk about his experience, but he is not using his core value and talent when he is creating the training materials. So,

keep people in their core competencies and don't let management off the hook. That said, have backup and cross-train so you aren't left with any gaps.

Although several people on our team straddle two roles, each role complements their core competencies or strengths. But how do you know what your team's core strengths are? My favorite tool for this is the previously mentioned CliftonStrengths assessment. It helps us discover individual strengths based on the premise that improving weaknesses is less efficient and effective than building on strengths. Because I have tested my management team, I can tell you the following:

☑ Who will get the ball to the end zone if a task needs to be completed.

☑ Who is best to dig into the details and streamline a complex structure or protocol.

☑ Who will patiently process a problem and find an equitable resolution.

☑ Who will champion for a new idea and get everyone on board.

This is valuable information because when you are playing to a person's strengths, they are most likely to succeed and that turns out well for both of you!

CROSS-TRAIN

As our company grew, we made it a requirement that all management roles cross-trained their duties to at least one (usually more) other person in the company before they could take a true out-of-pocket vacation. Then they would take their vacation, and we used that time as an opportunity for discovery, finding all of the things no one knew how to do. Today, we embed cross-training into our roles and constantly ask ourselves, "Who knows how to do this if I'm gone?"

Some might think that cross-training is a luxury of larger companies, but I think it is most valuable to small businesses, which can be hobbled by losing a role for any substantial period of time. Don't think about cross-training an entire role. Break it into bite-size pieces. Look at how your scope of work for a role is divided and train several people, giving each the division that best plays to their core competencies.

SHARE THE VISION

As we discussed in Chapter 9, one of the first things we do during the recruiting process is have potential recruits go to the website and provide us with five reasons the company would be a good fit for them. Their first impression of our company is how we present ourselves to the public.

After being here for a while, staff members can get so into the nitty-gritty that they forget what is being presented to the customer. They forget what the company looks like from the outside looking in. Or perhaps a lot has changed because they have been here for a good chunk of time. The website is a great place for them to gather current information about how we are marketing ourselves as a company and understand our value propositions. Sometimes we will pop a question on their continuing education that makes them take a fresh look at the website.

Particularly important to companies with a virtual model is to illustrate to their staff members who the company actually is. That helps them to have the language they need to work confidently with customers. Keeping everyone on the same page about new products, new collaborations, and new messaging is key to our cohesion as a company. Common language when discussing services and propositions is so important because, when a customer hears you say the same things that someone else in the company has said, that builds trust.

HAVE SOME FUN

We also are very present on social media. As a virtual company, having a strong online presence gives us a platform to spark conversation among our target demographics. We are on Facebook, LinkedIn, and Twitter, and we encourage our staff to engage in those communities with us. Your staff can be your biggest social media evangelists. Each of our staff members is encouraged to have a LinkedIn page, keep it up to date, and add Complete Controller as a place of work. We also love for them to follow our company page and engage with all our social channels by liking, sharing, and commenting. Our goal is to keep the energy fun and active, so we have created a contest and crown a new social superstar each week.

We have internal messaging capabilities on our cloud and every time a staff member celebrates their birthday, instead of cake and a song, we release a ticker tape to let the whole team know. Yes, it's embarrassing and their birthday landing page shares fun and silly information about them, but it is a small way for us all to feel more connected. In the cloud, team members don't get to see each other every day. So,

it's even more important for virtual businesses
to find ways to create opportunities for camaraderie.

My advice is that you make a point of sharing and acknowledging birthdays, babies, and puppy dogs, because they are of the utmost importance to us all.

Pen to Paper

A person's value to your business usually includes a combination of their skill set, experience, personality, and core competencies. It is important to boil that value down and ask yourself the following:

- ☑ Does this person produce revenue, reduce costs, or improve efficiency for my business? If not, what can I do to remedy this?

- ☑ Do they understand the vision for the business and can they express the value propositions? If not, ask yourself: Where did we drop the ball, and how can we help them learn this and prevent future employees from failing to understand?

- ☑ Are you providing an opportunity for their personality to shine in an unstructured environment? If not, how can you?

- ☑ Are they having any fun? If not, cultivate some fun into your work, such as having contests and team-building events.

- ☑ Cross-training and documentation are essential to avoiding a hostage situation or being left with a gap in your business function. Find out where your vulnerabilities are and ask who is essential and who else can do their job?

PART FIVE

THE ART
OF
DELEGATION

*"If you want to do a few small things right,
do them yourself. If you want to do great things and
make a big impact, learn to delegate."*
—JOHN C. MAXWELL

13

BEFORE YOU
PASS THE BATON

HERE WE ARE. AT the place where I am going to divulge some of the practices and procedures that allow my virtual business to run like a well-oiled machine. When you're first starting out, you may be the one who does it all. But as your company grows, you will be adding employees and giving them specific tasks. Being able to delegate is crucial. But there's more to it than just saying, "Here you go. Get this to the client by Friday." I can tell you right now, learning how to delegate properly is at the heart of our success. We didn't have it figured out overnight. It was more of a slow, painful learning process. The good news is I'm here to save you some of those heartaches by sharing what I've learned over the years.

First off, it's critical for companies and department heads to understand that, if you're going to delegate work, the best way to create a scalable model is to do it in a way in which you can measure milestones and the performance of that work, without having to look at every little detail.

Mistakes happen when people delegate because they don't know what's happening anymore.

Many managers address that blind spot by requiring daily briefings or project updates, just to give them insight into what's happening. But what about the other side of that equation? Does the staff know what's expected? Is their scope of work clear and concise? Has their purpose been defined in a way that allows them to self-manage during those moments that aren't covered in the scope of work? If not, they will need to keep coming back to their manager to find out what to do next.

Yes, that is a form of delegation, one in which staff are constantly keeping you updated and you're constantly feeding them stuff to do. But that method is too highly managed and, as a result, inefficient. As you know, in any company with fixed value pricing, efficiency is key. Our Bookkeepers, for example, earn bonuses for being efficient. We have strict deadlines. So, if we ran our company by delegating the way I just described, it would be difficult to maintain consistent and predictable profit margins.

Micromanagement is not necessarily a bad word. It is an indicator that there is a breakdown between how much feedback the manager needs and how much they are getting or how quickly they are getting it. Micromanagement happens when KPIs are not feeding back to the manager, allowing them to see that tasks and processes have been completed or have met certain standards.

Without seeing the right KPIs come through in a timely manner, a manager has no way of knowing if the team member is performing and that compels the manager to ask at every turn. To streamline things, you can fix that feedback loop by instituting circle back processes and tools that deliver KPIs automatically, which will give you instant relief from feeling the need to micromanage.

BS (Before Standardization)

In the very beginning, I did what a lot of managers do, email directives to my team. I would say something like, "Hey, we discovered a better way to do this thing. Now, I want everyone to do it this way from here going forward. And hey, somebody had a question about how to do A, B, or C, so here's an instruction set below. I'm sharing this with everybody so you can all reference it."

As you can imagine, there were a lot of these emails over a stretch of time as I was developing my business model. My early model had the customers (or whoever represented my customer at the self-storage facilities) scan their bills and paperwork as they got them in the mail. Then my team and I would sift through all of those documents and determine what was payable and what was not and post the transactions that had already been paid to the correct payment account or petty cash, while posting the others to accounts payable. Then we would get statements from vendors and we'd compare and see if we had any missing bills and ask for any that hadn't been submitted. We'd fill in those gaps and send a bills due report to the customer for approval, notifying them of their cash flow. They would approve the bills they wanted to pay based on that information. The daily transactions that were hitting the bank account and credit card were all being reconciled, and we were making sure that periodic entries for depreciation and amortizations were posting correctly, checking that the financial statements were true and accurate, and asking for clarifications from the customer when needed.

This was our process. And we were hashing it all out over email. Do you see any problems with that?

Pretty soon, we realized we needed to create a system for doing things since there were multiple people working on different projects. There were constant changes at first. For example, we wanted our files to be named a certain way. The power of nomenclature! It's a small thing, but we needed all our naming to be uniform across all virtual filing cabinets so they were easily searchable, which would lead to greater efficiency and audit readiness.

Sometimes customers would send files over without a name—and then what do you do? I wrote an email telling my staff that if a customer sends us a file without a name or with an incorrect name, that's okay, we can accept it, but we need to charge them for a custom request to rename it. We'll warn them three times and after three warnings, we'll let them know we are just going to rename the file and charge them for it at the end of the month.

While file naming may be a small part of our process, it had a ripple effect on the rest of our processes. If we didn't set succinct guidelines for our customers and staff, we were going to pay for it in additional time and work. We had to create a standard process and then document it, so it could be used as a guide going forward.

Build to Scale

If you ever hope to scale your business, you have to remove yourself and your future managers from becoming bottlenecks to the process flow.

The only way to do this is to document your processes for each role, allowing others to reference it as they do the work. In our case, I realized very quickly that we were going to have a problem with scaling if we didn't record all of our processes and procedures in real time as they were evolving, captured in a living document. This discovery emerged right as I was bringing our first Controller up from the Bookkeeper ranks.

When she came into the role, we created the initial version of that living document by grabbing all of those email directives and pasting them into a scope of work in some fashion of logical order. That became the Bookkeeper Scope of Work. Then we started on the Controller Scope of Work.

As with the Bookkeeper scope, the Controller scope was constantly evolving. As she tried to implement the techniques I had laid out, she would say things like, "This works or this doesn't work. This isn't clear and I have no idea what you are talking about. What do you want me to do here?" It was helpful to receive this feedback.

And sure enough, as I received her feedback, I started to realize all the things that I didn't say because it was just in my head. If it's not on paper, no one else is going to know how to do it. Consequently, I found myself updating the scopes of work several times a week at first.

PRO TIP

Creating and updating documentation is the hard work that many businesses do not take the time to do. They make the excuse that their process isn't standardized yet, so they will wait to document it when they get it perfect. Don't give in to that thinking. Start now and evolve rather than waiting until the evolution is complete to start. I'll let you in on a secret, in case you don't already know: The evolution is never complete!

One of my concerns was that we were actually changing things up too much and my staff would become weary. But I had to set that aside because the changes that we were making were in response to customer or staff behavior. And, as it turns out, those changes were welcomed because we were solving problems. What I learned is that while you don't want to be constantly changing the process on people and just dictating it from the mountaintop, if you have an evolving document, people start to understand that a process has changed because something has happened and we are avoiding potential future problems.

And as we got bigger, we started to present it that way. We would send an email or alert them to a recent change during our monthly continuing education and say, "Hey, there's been a change to the scope of work because we ran into this problem. And this is how we decided to solve it." Or, "We introduced this new tool, and this is how we want to use it." I found that if people knew the *why*, they were more apt to accept and implement the new directive.

The scopes were living word documents, served up in PDF format to my staff. Each role had access to the correlating scope but not those for other roles. Eventually, however, we had to go to greater lengths to protect the scopes. We started publishing them as web documents, using FlowPaper Zine 🛠, a PDF flipbook viewer that makes it much more difficult to just copy and paste the whole darn thing. After all, *these scopes were becoming our secret sauce, the keys to our kingdom, our intellectual property.*

As I started to delegate each of the roles I used to perform to other people, I had to create a scope of work to guide their process. Sometimes a role did not require a full-time investment of hours, and that's where my strategy was born to have people wear multiple hats, so long as each role played to their strengths. I would approach the team members who I thought would enjoy and excel at a role and say, "I'm willing to pay you this rate to do these things in addition to what you are already doing." And it worked. My staff appreciated the opportunity. And as we evolved and became more sophisticated, we started to refine our processes.

Streamlining and Evolving

Streamlining and evolving go hand in hand. One leads to the other, perpetuating a cycle of continuous improvement. For example, as we evolved and began to refine our processes, we decided the best person to onboard the customer was probably not the Bookkeeper. Originally, the Bookkeeper scope contained pretty much everything you needed to know: how to onboard a customer, how to do their cleanup, how to perform the periodic and seasonal bookkeeping tasks, and how to terminate a customer. The Controller Scope of Work explained how the Controller supervised the Bookkeeper. It became apparent that interrupting the Bookkeeper, wherever they were in their daily, weekly, monthly, and yearly schedule, was a total bummer because we had taught them a process that was running like a well-oiled machine. The Bookkeepers are our doers. They're clicking and clacking, and then all of a sudden we're going to throw a wrench in their game by having them onboard a customer? Additionally, the Controller role didn't have a lot of hours because it was purely supervisory, so we were doomed to always have people straddling two roles in order to make a good living. Then we had an idea: What if we have the Controllers do the new customer onboarding process instead?

We liked that idea. So, we pulled all the onboarding information out of the Bookkeeper scope and stuck it in the Controller scope. Now, all that the Bookkeepers had to do when they were introduced to a new customer was work with their Controller to define the necessary tasks, establish ongoing communication with the customer, manage the cleanup/catch-up scope, and jump into the periodic work. Think about your own company and who your doers are. Do they have any tasks that could be reassigned to someone else to help you streamline your processes and become more efficient?

BUILD IN ACCOUNTABILITY

As we separated out the tasks that each role would complete, we started to create this symbiosis between the roles. All of the scopes would become interdependent, so nothing had complete autonomy. In my line of work, you have to have some kind of handoff. You can't have the same person taking in a bill, recording, and approving it, and then also making a payment and reconciling the bank statement. We know that is a perfect recipe for embezzlement. In accounting controls, we are used to the back and forth of interdependence that creates necessary checks and balances. So, we applied that concept here.

In my case, when we split up the Controller and Bookkeeper roles, we made sure each would play off of the other so both the Controller and Bookkeeper would be held accountable. Then, as we added other roles, we made sure to do the same.

Pen to Paper

Once you have developed your business model and laid out the roles that will be necessary to support it, you are ready to define the process for fulfillment. Fulfillment is all of the stuff that happens in between receiving information from your customer and delivering a product or service back to them. It is typically internal but may require interfacing with external solutions or people. In the next few Pen to Paper exercises, you will pull together what you need to develop scopes of work by role for your staff to follow. Start by gathering the information you already have. Look at emails, business development notes you have taken along the way, and instruction sets from your vendors. Gather them all in one place, separated by role.

CHAPTER 14

PASSING THE BATON

Follow the Flow

NOW I WANT TO take you through our internal fulfillment process as a customer moves from onboarding to periodic service, through quality control checks, and finally to termination so you can get a feel for how the baton is passed. Role interdependence is the key to accountability and ensures the baton keeps moving, allowing us to maintain continuity while handling myriad tasks in the background. Notice that each new role is introduced to the flow by way of a trigger—either a baton pass directly from another role or a calendared event. As you develop or fine-tune your own fulfillment process, you may discover that you have fewer, more, or different roles and tasks than what we outline here. Our journey is meant to get your creative juices flowing so you can discover your own process.

ACCOUNT SERVICES

Our fulfillment process starts with Account Services as soon as a signed service agreement is received. It's a great place to start because it builds trust with the customer and gives them a point of contact besides the sales team, who can answer questions about cost. You may have a similar department where you choose to begin.

Account Services will verify that the service agreement is properly completed then call the customer to confirm the service level they signed up for. During this call, they let the customer know they can scale their service level up or down as their needs change. They also discuss the first amount that will be drafted from the customer's bank account so there are no surprises.

During this stage they are filing the service agreement, extracting the customer briefing to be passed along to the Accounting team, entering a recurring invoice for the customer into our billing system, setting up a custom Complete Controller email address @talk2cc for the customer to use for Accounting team communications, establishing a LastPass folder for the entity, and notifying Operations Tech of the customer's internal identification so they can begin preparing for a new customer onboarding to our cloud.

OPERATIONS TECH

Once Account Services completes their part, an Operations Tech staff member sends the customer a welcome email with instructions on how to contact our Help Desk and get connected and then sends the customer briefing to our Director of Operations so an Accounting team, which consists of a Bookkeeper and Controller, can be assigned. Based on that assignment, the technician will set the customer and Accounting team desktops with the necessary permissions to access the QuickBooks file, virtual filing cabinet (where all pertinent documents are stored) ✖, and any add-on applications we or the customer may be using.

All credentials are placed in the customer's LastPass folder, and an onboarding phase checklist and customer information form are placed on the desktop for customer reference. Finally, they authenticate the customer through our phone app and notify Operations that the customer is ready for their launch meeting.

OPERATIONS

Operations will follow the customer throughout their life with Complete Controller, starting with the launch appointment, which is attended by Operations, the customer, and the Accounting team. This is where they review the customer briefing, talk about the services the customer will be receiving, and discuss the current health of the QuickBooks file and any applications that are part of the customer's process that may need to be integrated or accessible. If a cleanup or catch-up scope is determined, that is discussed.

As credentials or software are gathered for each account access, they are saved to the customer's LastPass where they are protected and the Bookkeeper can use them when needed without disturbing the customer any more than absolutely necessary.

ACCOUNTING TEAM

Having defined any add-on scopes during the launch meeting, the Accounting team then puts those in writing for the customer and obtains the appropriate approvals before beginning to serve the customer's needs per their service plan.

Now, a rigorous information gathering process begins. The Accounting team asks the customer to complete our customer information form and to provide specific documents like past tax returns, business licenses, and loan agreements. Basically, we'll ask for anything (even things the customer might not think of, like property tax statements) that affects their accounting. When all of the necessary documents are gathered, access to all sources of accounting data are secured, and cleanup/catch-up scopes are completed, Operations is brought in to review the health of the books and records in what is to be the first of many internal financial reviews.

OPERATIONS AND CONTROLLER

The financial review that ensues after the Accounting team has completed all onboarding tasks is a deep dive into the customer's books and records to determine if they are an accurate and complete reflection of the customer's financial activities. Operations may have questions and the Controller provides insight. After fixing any issues, the Controller reaches out to their customer to have a financial review meeting with them.

ACCOUNTING TEAM AND CUSTOMER

The customer's financial review with their Accounting team marks the end of the onboarding phase. During this meeting, the Accounting team reviews the onboarding checklist with the customer, and they discuss any needs, concerns, and remaining items that require attention. An email is sent to Account Services and Client Relations to mark the end of onboarding.

Typically, a customer's CPA/Expert (tax preparer) is not involved until after this meeting, because we don't want them popping in to look at the books while we are still in the onboarding phase and cannot vouch for accuracy. But there are times when we need their eyes on something before we get to this point. If not, we will always reach out to them once onboarding is completed.

CPA/EXPERTS

Our CPA/Experts are extremely valuable when we are dealing with complex books and multiple entities. We do not purport to be tax experts on any front, and we want to follow the guidance of our customers' experts to reduce our risk exposure and provide excellent service to our customers.

Because of this, we insist that every customer has a CPA/Expert relationship. While you may not have a specific need for CPAs, it is very likely you will need to rely on some level of subject matter expertise in your own business. Take it from me:

A little transparency and collaboration with an expert team will go a long way.

Our insistence on this alone has served us well.

ACCOUNT SERVICES AND CLIENT RELATIONS

Regardless of whether we tapped our customer's CPA/Expert for input before or after completing onboarding, Account Services and Client Relations are notified when the customer has completed their financial review meeting and is off the onboarding platform.

For Account Services, this is a trigger to reach out to the customer's CPA/Expert and make sure they have access to the customer's books, records, and Accounting team. If the customer was not a referral from the CPA/Expert, this may be their first impression of Complete Controller, so Account Services uses this opportunity to ask them if we can be doing something more to improve their experience and introduces them via email to our CEO who connects with them on LinkedIn.

Client Relations uses this notification as an assurance that the customer is well on their way. They reach out to see how the onboarding experience went and if they get a rave response, they will ask the customer to provide us with an online review of their experience. If the answer is yes, they send a "Share the Love" email with links to make five-star reviews.

ACCOUNTING TEAM

Now the Accounting team steps back in to run point on the customer account. The Bookkeeper manages daily needs, including things like transaction downloads, soft reconciliations, payroll, gathering receipts and W-9s, preparing billings, and whatever else the customer desires.

They place work-in-process into their customer's Action Items folder, and when the tasks are complete, they file it in the virtual filing cabinet. At the end of each billing period, they reconcile the accounts, run any unclear transactions by the customer for clarification, and set a closing appointment with their Controller to review the period work. After the work is reviewed and any corrections are made, a report package goes out to the customer.

OPERATIONS: REPORT PACKAGE REVIEW

Report packages are copied to Operations so they can be reviewed for quality. This review ensures our deliverable is accurate, timely, and complete. Whether you have an Operations department or not, you will want to have a process in place to ensure quality control. Operations reports its findings to the Controllers and Account Services, so mistakes will be addressed and bonuses calculated properly and rewarded at the end of the period if all reporting guidelines have been met. Remember, those bonuses are incentives that help us maintain consistent and quality service for our customers.

OPERATIONS: INTERNAL PEER REVIEW

One quarter after a customer is onboarded—and quarterly after that—operations performs an internal peer review. The peer review puts a triple check on those books and records, looking for anomalies that the Accounting team may have missed because they are so used to being in the transactional and periodic tasks.

It's easy for an Accounting team that is not subject to peer review to miss documenting a task or a nuance that is obvious to them because of their immersion in the customer work. Or it might be tempting for them to become lax in their record keeping, on the justification that they will do it later in the year in one fell swoop. Our peer review eliminates these possibilities and identifies areas where the Accounting team may need more support either internally or from the CPA/Expert. After the initial peer review, we schedule quarterly reviews to provide ongoing checks on our Accounting teams' quality of work.

CONTROLLERS

Our Controllers reach out to each customer at least quarterly. This keeps the conversation going about the things that were discussed during onboarding and anything that has happened since. It's an opportunity to let our customers know that we can perform more advanced services if they need them. It also solidifies the relationship with the customer and that can come in handy when a customer needs to confide in the Controller.

To further encourage that bond, Controllers also send out quarterly feedback emails asking their customers how things are going. The Bookkeeper is not included on this email, but Operations is blind copied, just so they know it went out. The objective is to create a safe place for the customer to ask questions or discuss a concern about their Bookkeeper or services, and to find resolution without affecting the trust bond they have built with their Bookkeeper.

ACCOUNTING TEAM AND OPERATIONS

The Accounting team and Operations work hand in hand to get through year-end, which starts in October with a nudge to the customer to review their 1099 report and gather missing W-9s for the year.

The Controller sends an email asking to meet before year-end to discuss hopes and plans for the new year. This is our opportunity to offer and facilitate typical year-end happenings like preparing a budget, making a payroll service switch, or changing entities.

When the t's are crossed and i's are dotted, the Controllers reach out to Operations to perform a pretax review, which ensures that the books can be used to prepare a tax return for the customer. Once this review is completed, Operations gives the Accounting team the nod to notify the customer's CPA/Expert that the books are ready for tax prep and that we are here to answer questions, change stuff around, or otherwise serve their needs.

ACCOUNT SERVICES

When a customer terminates the relationship, everyone pitches in. The Accounting team is usually the first to know. They will email Account Services, who confirms the termination with the customer and conducts a verbal debriefing to understand why they are leaving, where they are going from here, how we could have better met their needs, and what their experience was with Complete Controller.

Account Services then stops the recurring billing after collecting the final amount due from the customer. Operations performs a final internal financial review to make sure everything is in good order, prepares a backup of the file, removes users, and prepares and drops a copy of the virtual filing cabinet to the customer. The customer is then marked inactive in the database and CRM, and their desktop is removed from our cloud.

Create the Framework

I realize that the process just described contains a lot of detail. While it illustrates the dependence of one role on another, believe me when I say that it doesn't come close to describing every task necessary to our fulfillment process. In order to keep track of our progress, we were going to need some checklists to provide a framework for the work as it was passed between roles. You will too. Because while the scope of work will state your technique—the when, how, and why—checklists will allow you to keep track of what has been done and who has the baton at any given time.

The processes described in this chapter alone require no fewer than eight supporting checklists, they are:

- ☑ Client Information
- ☑ Onboarding
- ☑ Periodic Processes
- ☑ Customer Reporting
- ☑ Report Package Reviews
- ☑ Quarterly Reviews
- ☑ Year-End Closing
- ☑ Termination

Our checklists guide the succession of each task or phase and are generally touched by multiple roles for completion. So, the checklists not only guide the role that is currently performing tasks, they also allow subsequent roles to see the progress and anticipate their upcoming involvement.

Meanwhile, the scopes of work, which we will cover in the next chapter, articulate when, how, and why we perform those tasks by role. They are broken down that way so that someone in the Bookkeeper role isn't privy to the entirety of the Controller role. This keeps some of the magic behind the curtain, protecting our intellectual property until a person advances to fulfill a new role. Not all roles fall within the accounting track, so no one is ever trained in all roles, and in this way, we keep our secret sauce truly secret.

PRO TIP

If a given task is a complex, multistep process, we provide a standard operating procedure (SOP) to support the scope of work and the checklist. We don't want a complex SOP in our scope of work because it will make it bulky. When using checklists and SOPs, the key is to mention them in the scope of work and tell the reader where they are located so they can be used as reference documents and support tools through the completion of any task or phase. The reader can then return to the scope for their next piece of work.

Keep in mind you will want to make your own checklists based on the way you model your business, the type and number of roles you have, and what you want your customer journey to look like. For example, if you are in publishing, you will want different checklists for your editors, proofreaders, designers, and project managers to use in support of that internal customer fulfillment journey.

Today, our checklists are incorporated into a database where we make them available to the appropriate team members as needed. In doing this, we were able to reduce redundancies, allow team members to have access to some areas while protecting others from changes, maintain an audit trail to see what changes were made by whom, and even keep some information from being seen by selected roles. Using a database also allows us to query reports about our customer base as a whole. While we moved to this more sophisticated method a few years ago, for a very long time, our checklists were in Excel.

PRO TIP

It is not necessary to spend the money to implement a database until your customer base becomes too large for you to extract patterns easily from within QuickBooks or Excel. Make checklists easy to change so they can evolve even when your scopes of work do not. Sometimes a quick addition to a checklist or SOP is all that is needed.

It is up to you to provide the framework for your business to become autonomous. Think back to your school days. Most classes were accompanied by a textbook, workbook, and lab. If the lab is the practical application of the learning, then that is your fulfillment. The textbook and workbooks provide the framework for the fulfillment process. This is truly the most difficult part of the business-building process. I promise you that it is worth it, for without it, you will be caught in a constant feedback loop, unable to measure performance or quality.

Pen to Paper

 For this chapter activity, I'd like you to create a flowchart of your internal fulfillment process:

- ☑ Break each process down by role.

- ☑ Make sure the baton is never dropped by building in role interdependence at critical times, using deadlines and communications.

Ask yourself the following questions:

- ☑ What will trigger the next role to know it's their turn to pick up the baton?

- ☑ How will the next role know if the past one has completed their job?

- ☑ What checklists, CRMs, or other tools will you use to guide the task-work?

15

PREPARING
A SCOPE OF WORK

HAVING SCOPES OF WORK for each role in your business can help you streamline your workflow while providing your staff with clear expectations and guidance. A good scope of work can do the following:

- ☑ Provide delegation without bottlenecking at management.

- ☑ Offer purpose and direction to new staff.

- ☑ Eliminate the need for relearning the same lessons.

- ☑ Allow for efficient training and retraining.

- ☑ Support continuing evolution of processes.

- ☑ Establish expectations.

- ☑ Empower staff with formula for success.

- ☑ Force interdependence for better flow and quality.

- ☑ Keep the magic behind the curtain.

- ☑ Allow for easy change out of supporting checklists and SOPs.

We have scopes of work for each role in our company that hold all of our practices and methods for that role. Each has a table of contents because we want to empower our staff to find the information they need quickly and easily. Extra time spent searching means our staff becomes extra *inefficient* and we want to avoid that.

I have provided high-level snippets of our current tables of contents for each scope in the next chapter. These scopes are the backbone of our company and are meant to serve as guides as you begin outlining what will become your own scopes of work.

The Building Blocks

If you have been completing the Pen to Paper sections that follow each chapter in Part Five, you should be ready to begin putting your scopes of work together. It's been my experience that one obstacle for many companies trying to tackle this monumental project is knowing where to start. It's easy to get overwhelmed and paralyzed. I have provided a roadmap for you to follow. Your process may differ, but for those of you that just need to get started, this can launch your effort.

STEP 1.
CREATE A DOCUMENT FOR THE SCOPE OF WORK.
START THE DOCUMENT BY STATING THE ROLE AND
ITS PURPOSE.

I always start my scopes of work with a clear definition of the role's purpose within the company. Creating an early understanding of purpose allows the reader to embrace the way they will make meaning by performing the role. In each scope, you will want to clearly describe the impact of what each person will do and how their work will empower the people around them, internally (within the company) and externally (your customers). This will help you know what to look for as you perform the next step.

STEP 2.
GO THROUGH YOUR EMAILS TO SEE WHAT RELATES TO THE ROLE YOU ARE SCOPING.

I already told you that my MO when I first started was to email a bunch of directives to my staff, and then we took those directives and put them in a document. This is a common practice and can be a good place to start.

To do this, go back through your sent mail and forward to yourself anything that pertains to the role you are building and include the role in the subject line. This way, you will not upset your audit trail of sent mail, but you will be able to gather what you need into one place—storing the emails into folders by role. Also, go through your inbox and subfolders, looking for items that would make good SOPs or impact the role in some way. Even if you only wind up with five emails, this is the perfect place to springboard the development of your scope of work.

STEP 3.
CUT AND PASTE THAT INFORMATION INTO THE DOCUMENT.

Our first scope of work was for the Bookkeeper role. We cut and pasted information from our emails directly into the document without regard for structure or formatting. Our only concern at that time was that we included loosely related information about particular elements of that role all in one document.

STEP 4.
START TO ORGANIZE TOPICS IN A WAY THAT MAKES SENSE TO YOU AND YOUR TEAM.

As you are pasting information into the document, you will start to see topics emerge. We arranged our topics starting with the things each new hire to the role needed to know, then moved on to identifying a customer's needs based on their service plan, followed by the tasks that role needed to complete along a timeline. And we wrapped it all up with troubleshooting and hints.

STEP 5.
CREATE AN OUTLINE. BUT DON'T WRITE A DISSERTATION!

Once you have decided what topics you have and know in what order you want to put them, create an outline. Kind of like the table of contents. Remember, nothing is permanent. You can rearrange easily at this point, so if it makes better sense in a different order, change it.

STEP 6.
FILL IN THE GAPS.

As you go through the outline-building process, you will inevitably think of topics that need to be included. Add them to your outline so you won't forget them. Then move forward until you have a rudimentary but somewhat comprehensive outline of what will be in that scope of work.

STEP 7.
CLEARLY STATE YOUR DIRECTIVES AND INSTRUCTIONS.

Now begin writing your topic sections. Just make the outline topic your title and start writing about that subject. If you have pasted information, this is when you fold it in. Cross-reference your flowchart to make sure you are building in that interdependency. Be thorough and try not to leave anything out. At the same time, know that you will probably leave things out inadvertently, so don't be too hard on yourself. Remember, this is a living document that will change over time. So, each time you remember something else, go ahead and add it.

STEP 8.
MAKE IT EASY TO READ.

After you have bulked up your topics with all of the information you want to convey, go back through and make your writing succinct and clear. It's best if you have someone else do this part, preferably someone who has worked the role you are creating a scope of work to support. They will quickly find redundancies, conflicting instructions, and missing steps. If you will be both writer and editor, I recommend you space out the time between both tasks to create some objective distance.

STEP 9. BE WELCOMING!

This last step may make you laugh, but I'm serious with this advice. People are working for your company. Your scope of work should embody your company's personality and voice. At the very least, it should be warm and friendly and demonstrate that you are glad they are on your team.

PRO TIP

When you create your scopes of work, write them the way you *wish* the work to be done, not the way you actually do the work. This is your chance to improve quality and efficiency as you delegate. While you may have cut corners to save time or invested more time than expected to perfect a task method, set the bar for your staff right where you want it to be.

Scopes of work will allow you to standardize the processes used in each role. Standardization will allow you to measure performance. Measuring performance will allow you to know where in your business to focus, when to invest more for greater success, and when to let go. From a staff standpoint, the scopes will provide a point of reference, help your employees understand accountability, and empower them to take ownership of their role. People quickly embrace the idea that they are filling a particular need, and without them, that very important work doesn't get done.

The Glue That Holds It Together

EVERYTHING IS CONNECTED

Something that you'll want to foster up front is how interdependency brings context to each role. By doing this, you and your employees can see the bigger picture and understand how important each person is in the process. Understanding interdependency and planning for it will be crucial when you are writing your scopes of work and creating your processes and procedures, since you'll take into account how the work moves back and forth between various roles.

It's also important to

encourage your staff to understand the process in their scope of work and to pay attention to their role as it relates to other roles. This holds each person to a level of accountability that is missing when they just have complete independence.

Instead, the interdependence of roles creates an environment that is transparent and has baked-in accountability.

It is human nature to perform more optimally if you know someone is waiting to take the baton. This brings out the best in your team and encourages them to throw up the white flag quickly if they need support. This is also a great filter for new hires. If they do not feel the pressure of personal responsibility to meet an expected deadline because someone is waiting for the baton, chances are they will not do well on the job.

Recently, we had a new Bookkeeper show us her true colors soon after she was hired. She had prepared a few sets of books for closing and had her closing appointment with her Controller. All that was left was for her to complete the tie-up work in the post-meeting email and get reports out to the customers and their distribution list by the fifteenth of the month. On the fifteenth, the Controller waited to see the reports come through, and waited, until almost to the deadline. Then she reached out to see if the Bookkeeper needed support.

It turns out the Bookkeeper, who failed to recognize or appreciate the interdependence of her work, was at a softball game. She said she had planned to get them ready the night before but hadn't gotten to it, so she would do them the next day. The next day was after the deadline. This meant extra work and a mad rush for the Controller, who had to get those reports out to our customers by the promised deadline. Whereas the Bookkeeper didn't have to do anything the next day except look for a new job.

WHEN THERE'S A BREAKDOWN

While scopes of work are helpful and necessary, they are not foolproof. In a virtual organization, communication breakdowns like the preceding example can be fatal. Think about it, if you can't walk over and see that someone is working or even present, you have to get that assurance in some other way.

The best way to see if work is getting done remotely is to monitor the communication that accompanies the work. It is a great indicator of activity. That is why the Controllers in our company monitor the talk2cc email inboxes that are used for customer communications. It may mean they have to jump in and take over a task or fill in for a Bookkeeper. But even when they aren't taking over, seeing the responsive and helpful communication between Bookkeepers and customers is reassuring. It also helps to ferret out frustrations before they grow into unresolvable issues. If they are privy to a conversation that is beginning to sour, they can reach out to the Bookkeeper on the side to support them in how to best handle it so it doesn't get out of hand.

Another way we monitor activity is with the work tracker. We aren't really looking at every click a Bookkeeper makes throughout the day. A deep dive into click-by-click activity rarely happens unless we are trying to determine the root of a particular task level problem. Instead, we use the work tracker to monitor time spent and spot inefficiencies or absences. The work tracker is used to view the forest more often than the trees.

Direct communication among your staff is essential. Especially when something is happening that needs to be addressed. With us, this usually looks like a quick text by someone asking if the other is available to talk, followed by a phone call to discuss the matter. In our work environment, it is more about being responsive than being always available. A quick text back letting someone know when you can talk is often just as good as being available in the moment, as long as you can talk sometime that day or sooner based on urgency.

Because communication is so important, we take it very seriously. But we don't want to terminate anyone the very first time they miss a deadline or a chance at communication. As you recall, those first deadlines are met while the Bookkeeper is still in training, so quick action to address shortfalls will usually result in a permanent lesson learned. This process is especially important with new hires, as it will send home the magnitude of the error. In these instances, we have a meeting to discover if, in fact, we let them down by being unclear about our expectations.

A meeting to debrief a missed deadline or communication will explore the following questions:

- ☑ Where did the breakdown occur?

- ☑ Was it a failure by the initiating person, or a failure of the scope of work to communicate clearly?

- ☑ Was it just an accident? For example, maybe they didn't hit "Reply All" and instead only hit "Reply" and didn't notice that the other person was no longer on the chain.

- ☑ Was it purposeful?

- ☑ If it was purposeful, why was the strategy not communicated to those who needed to know?

By debriefing in this way, some important things happen:

- ☑ They realize that it is important and we noticed.

- ☑ They know that to do it again will be fatal.

- ☑ We get insight into their logic trail.

- ☑ We get to spot unclear direction in our communication or scopes.

> *As you delegate, telling*
> *people what is expected of them is*
> *the best way to empower them.*

Then, giving them the tools to do what's expected goes hand in hand. Don't let issues and challenges get swept under the rug. Be swift to figure out what is derailing the process. Use it as an opportunity to grow and change so you can make meaning from what is happening.

SEEKING SUPPORT

When delegating to an employee, that person may need more support. Maybe they are up against a deadline because they are struggling to figure out how to get something done. While we encourage critical thinking and problem solving, in the spirit of efficiency, I also want my staff to quickly seek support if they can't figure out how to handle a given task. I encourage you to invite the same of your staff.

Typically, in our world, support will be around technique because information about deadlines, tools, and expectations are clearly stated in our scopes of work. Regardless, when we need to figure something out, we encourage our staff to ask themselves the following:

☑ Is it in the scope of work?

☑ Is it on the QuickBooks ProAdvisor knowledge base?

☑ Is it on Google?

☑ How does my supervisor do it?

If a new hire is going directly to their supervisor for every little thing without first trying to use the resources at hand, the relationship will be short-lived. Remember that our Controllers have all fulfilled the Bookkeeper role, so they know what is covered in that scope of work, the checklists, and SOPs, and they will simply tell the Bookkeeper to look there.

If the Bookkeeper has done their research and is just hung up on a detail or a question of what method the company prefers, the Controller will be quick to respond. When it comes to methodology, visual training is usually the best. Controllers will hop onto a web meeting ⚒ with their Bookkeeper and guide the process.

COMMUNICATE TO CYA

Have you ever had a telephone conversation with a company representative only to receive follow-up communication that did not clearly discuss the contents of your call? Or worse, totally got it wrong? Although verbal communication is the most personal and is highly encouraged when building trust with your team or your customers, it is also the loosest form of communication. Things are sometimes said that later are put into question, and acting on only a verbal instruction can be very risky business.

Our company has a protocol of following all verbal communication of substance with a CYA email. You put in writing what you discussed so there will not be a question about it later, and it provides an opportunity for the other party to confirm or correct your understanding of the conversation. Here's an example:

It was great to talk with you today, Mrs. Jones. I am excited that you will be bringing your personal books on board with our service so that we can get them caught up and ready for taxes. I have included Account Services on this email as they can help with establishing a service agreement for that work and getting you launched. We talked about trying to get it all done by the upcoming extension deadline. While we will push for that result once we have you signed up and onboarded, the sooner you get the ball rolling, the better. And still there are no guarantees only because I haven't seen those books yet and do not know how close they are to being tax ready. Looking forward to seeing those on my desk soon!

With this conversation documented in writing, Mrs. Jones cannot call three weeks from now and chide the Bookkeeper for not advancing the onboarding of her personal books that they talked about. Nor can she say that the Bookkeeper promised her they would be done by the tax extension deadline if she signed up.

Even the smallest agreements and instructions require a CYA email. Here's another example:

Glad we had a chance to connect today, Mr. Williams. Per our conversation, I will initiate an ACH payment to the electric company for $143.15 as soon as I receive your approval through SmartAP. Please watch for the approval request email and approve that payment as soon as possible to avoid any further delays. When I have completed the transaction, I will email you to confirm so you know it has been done.

Now Mr. Williams knows he must approve the payment before it will be sent via ACH as he requested. Even though he already said he wanted it paid.

And in case you're wondering, voicemails also require a CYA email. After you leave a message, you'll want to follow up with a CYA email, and text them if they have previously told you that it is a great way to reach them. You are persistent because they are busy, and it's your job to stay on their radar.

Here's an example of an email we would send after leaving a voice message:

> Hi, Ms. Miller. I just left you a voicemail. I'm trying to connect with you to get clarity on a few transactions to vendors you have never used before. Just want to make sure I get the posting correct. I sent them on your Ask My Client report last week and have attached it here again for your reference. I'm hoping to get your answers before I put your report package together tomorrow.

Encouraging consistent, clear, and open communication among staff members and customers will help you to build trust in a virtual environment where meetings don't happen in conference rooms. It also lets you create a reference point for any important dealings that can be revisited if someone is questioning your intent or understanding. We have a rule that sent mail is never deleted and all talk2cc customer communication email boxes are archived long after the customer's termination. Just to be safe, to CYA.

COMMUNICATE TO BUILD TRUST

Because communication within a virtual environment is so critical, another email protocol that is paramount to successful delegation begins as soon as an Accounting team receives a new customer. We assign our customers their own custom email address with which to communicate with their team. Some businesses will use a Slack channel or other similar method. The point is to have a central place where all customer communication is held. We instruct our Bookkeepers to set the custom email accounts up on their mobile phone as soon as a customer is assigned to them. Because that email is the customer's direct line to their Accounting team. The best way for a Bookkeeper to keep a finger on the pulse of their customers is to monitor those boxes throughout the day.

We're living in the 24/7 age, and Complete Controller is a virtual company.

We want our Bookkeepers to be in close contact with their customers. We also know that our Bookkeepers can be highly efficient if they master the art of knowing when something is important and when it can be done later, so we teach them to communicate in a way that supports their work balance strategy.

The key is to be quick to let your customers know that you have the ball firmly in your hands so they don't have to think about it anymore. This is huge. And it has been a large part of our success.

Say, I'm a customer and I'm sending something important over to my Bookkeeper, like I'm supposed to, and I'm very excited. Then I come up with a question, so I send another email to my Bookkeeper. Suppose I'm a weekly customer so my Bookkeeper is not really going in and checking my books, updating them, and managing all of my incoming work, except for one day per week. Communication-wise, I know I can reach out to her whenever I want. So, I email. But I don't hear back.

It's okay if I don't hear back for a couple of hours because I'm a weekly customer. But if I don't hear back until the next day or later that week, I'm thinking about my question for a long time. It's twisting and turning in the back of my mind. I'm wondering if she has even gotten all of the other emails I've been sending over or if she has read them. Now, I'm starting to write the story in my head and it's not sounding good. The trust bond is eroding.

I know I have a contact card and I can look at her signature block and call her. So, I do. And she says, "Yes, I got your emails. Everything is good. I work on your account on Wednesdays. I'll be sure to get back to you."

I get my answer. It's all right. But then I start to think, well geez, if every time I send a question, I'm not going to hear back until Wednesday, that's not going to work for me!

I think you can see where this is going. The question I am going to pose to you is what could this Bookkeeper do differently that would set the customer at ease and set them both up for a successful relationship?

Since the Bookkeeper is monitoring the emails on her phone and the customer is sending over bills and other documents that she knows she will see on the unpaid bills report, there is no need to send a response to those transactional communications. Just so customers can rest assured that their emails got through to us, we have a little auto-responder that ticks back and says, "Thank you for sending us information. It's been received."

But, if just as she's heading into yoga, that Bookkeeper sees the customer has sent over a non-urgent question, she can just quickly email back and say, "Hi, Mr. Smith, I got your question. I will definitely take a look at that and circle back to you. I'm going to be in your books on Wednesday. Would that be okay with you?"

Then what happens? Mr. Smith now knows his Bookkeeper is super-responsive and knows what's going on with his account. She cares. He also realizes that what he needs is more urgent than he's showing. So he says, "Oh geez. You know what, Wednesday isn't going to work for me because I'm getting a new mortgage on my home and I have to get it ASAP."

And that Bookkeeper can say, "No problem, Mr. Smith, I'll make sure that I get that to you as soon as I'm back in front of my desk. I anticipate you will have it by two o'clock this afternoon. How does that work?"

At this point, Mr. Smith knows he will get an answer in time for his deadline and he can move on to other important business. He also knows his Bookkeeper is not currently at her desk, and the very fact that she responded makes him grateful that his peace of mind is that important to her. She is now free to enjoy her yoga class, grab some groceries, pick up her son from preschool, go home, get things settled, and then sit down in front of her computer to get that work done. Or if it's a quick thing for her, she might log in on her tablet while waiting for her son's school to let out and have it over sooner than anticipated.

The important thing is that the customer is reassured that the Bookkeeper knows his needs and will competently deliver. He thinks she is the greatest and when she delivers on that promise, the trust bond is reinforced.

On the flip side . . .

If communication is of paramount importance to the relationship, what do you do when a customer is being nonresponsive?

If this is going to happen, it typically first happens during onboarding, which gets the account off to a bad start. We want to avoid that at all costs so we have a method that does a nice job of nipping it in the bud.

Here's how it goes with us:

When an Operations or Accounting team member reaches out via phone followed by a CYA email and doesn't hear back, that staff member reaches out again via phone followed by another CYA email, which includes a forward of the original CYA email, this time copying Client Relations. Client Relations is the sales team. These are the folks who had the original relationship with the customer during the sign-up process. If the customer wasn't signed up by a Client Relations representative, the email includes Account Services in the carbon copy line. The copied party does nothing at this point—their inclusion simply applies some peer pressure.

If there is no response after doing these things, the staff member reaches out a third time via phone followed by a CYA email, which includes a forward of the first two outreaches, and again copies Client Relations or Account Services. By now, that chain is getting pretty long and the copied party has enough evidence to reach out and shake the tree. The call might go something like, "Hey, Mr. Davis, did you see that your Controller is trying to get in touch with you? Should I patch them into the call right now?" This usually does the trick.

As we are developing our processes, we are always looking for ways to lean on each other to improve accountability and provide support without it looking like an escalation from the customer's perspective. We want them to know that we recognize they are busy; that is probably why they hired us! Meanwhile, we insist on providing them with accurate and timely service, and to do that, they need to fulfill their responsibilities in the relationship.

STANDARDIZE AND PERSONALIZE

Do you ever find yourself writing the same email over and over to customers or staff members at certain points in your fulfillment process? If so, use snippets and templates to standardize your communications. Many of our tasks require email communication and we have now developed company-approved templates by role for just about every repetitive communication that we perform.

Preparing templates is a great opportunity to create standardization across your teams and conformity in your language and branding. Every communication is an opportunity to put the company in front of the customer as an entity that is making meaning in their lives.

In a virtual world, we have to balance standardization, which increases efficiency, with personalization, which increases loyalty.

To personalize standardized communication, you might have each team member include a button to their LinkedIn profile in the signature block.

Or you can make it lighthearted by having them share something fun about themselves:

> Jennifer Brazer
> CEO & Founder | Complete Controller
> "I love rocky road ice cream and black Labradors."

Do you feel like you can relate to me better now? The point is to humanize the sender and give them some pizzazz of their own. It's endearing, and it works.

PRO TIP

If you use social links, make sure you do regular quality control checks to ensure that each staff member has a professional picture up on LinkedIn and that they are associated with your company as a place of work. By the way, this is a great way to keep an eye on their social pages to watch for pattern changes that may clue you in that they are planning to jump ship.

If you have already started to create your scopes of work, take a moment and feel proud. You have accomplished something that very few small businesses ever achieve. The truth is, small businesses cannot scale without this vital piece. They will always stay small and dependent upon their visionary to guide every process. If scopes of work are the building blocks and checklists are the framework, then your staff are the masons and communication is the glue. You must have all of this to build a strong structure. Provide your staff with a role and give them the tools to support that role and understand their importance in the business model. Care for them by noticing problem areas quickly and discussing them thoroughly and openly. Teach them how to communicate to build trust and lasting relationships with customers and the rest of the team.

Pen to Paper

This is where the rubber hits the road. Don't wait to build your scopes of work. Do them now and make them living documents that will evolve as you and your business learn and grow. I recommend that you cross-reference your saved materials by role and your flowchart of internal processes. When building your scopes of work, remember to ask yourself these questions:

- ☑ What is your vision and purpose for each role?

- ☑ What topics will you outline for each role as it touches your company's fulfillment process?

- ☑ Did you cover the important stuff like how to get paid, where to find templates and checklists that will be needed to complete certain tasks, and what resources are available to reach out for help? If not, go back and add these in.

- ☑ Did you incorporate each baton pass or trigger into the process and identify when to expect others to be involved in the flow?

THE
SECRET SAUCE

IN THE PREVIOUS CHAPTER I laid out the basic steps you can take to develop scopes of work for your business. As you can probably tell, I consider the scope of work to be one of the most important documents you can create—in fact, I call it the "secret sauce" because it's so essential and unique to each business. Now, I'm going to show you a high-level view into some of our company scopes of work. As you review the purpose, nature, and high-level contents of each scope, I hope you will begin to form ideas that you can use in your company. While our scopes are broken down by role, we have one document that is critical to every member of the team, our practice standards.

Practice Standards

This uniform document addresses our practice level standards, and it is among the first tools that we give to all new hires.

PRO TIP

I highly encourage all companies to have a published practice standards document. It will help your staff members know how to address issues such as conflict of interest, understand the company's stance on risk management, and give them a place to learn about the corporate level culture of your company.

Here are some snippets from ours to give you ideas:

> Complete Controller strives to provide a safe, supportive, and productive environment in which our work can be performed accurately and efficiently. Our practice standards help to create that environment. It is important for each of our team members to be familiar with these standards and follow them carefully.
>
> Our team is our greatest asset and we are always available to discuss concerns and support you in any way we can. Please do not hesitate to ask if you require assistance in understanding or attaining these standards.

The standards we cover include the following:

- ☑ Avoiding Practice Conflicts
- ☑ Insurance Practices
- ☑ Confidentiality Practices
- ☑ Efficiency Practices
- ☑ Work Tracking Practices
- ☑ Timekeeping Practices
- ☑ Certification Practices
- ☑ Practice of Environmental Responsibility
- ☑ Practice of Personal Responsibility

BOOKKEEPER SCOPE OF WORK

This scope of work covers everything our Bookkeepers need to know from a technique perspective. We like to be clear on what they can expect in this document and want to make them feel welcome right off the bat. Here are snippets from the intro and conclusion:

> Through training and conformity to Complete Controller standards, we can make meaning for our customers by bringing them a reliable, friendly, and quality service. We can create a fulfilling and nurturing work environment that leaves cubicles and commutes far behind. We are the future of accounting!
>
> We are blessed to have such a talented team and honored to have you be a part of this journey. We hope you find Complete Controller to be a fulfilling and supportive place to build your career.

The scope starts by walking them through training and then moves into the when, how, and why of each process in our periodic accounting services. The ninety-four-page scope of work covers the following topics:

- ☑ Who We Are
- ☑ Getting Started with Desktop Orientation
- ☑ Bookkeeper Training
- ☑ Bookkeeper Functions
- ☑ Managing Workload
- ☑ Communication Guidelines
- ☑ Accounts Receivable
- ☑ Accounts Payable
- ☑ Payroll Banking
- ☑ Balance Sheet Account Management
- ☑ Closing Periods
- ☑ Hosted Environment

CONTROLLER SCOPE OF WORK

The Controller Scope of Work is a different beast altogether. It addresses two very important relationships: the Bookkeeper and the customer. Controllers have additional tools and templates at their disposal, and the scope familiarizes them with those and how and when to use them. The scope tells them everything they need to know about how to select, monitor, mentor, measure, and report on the performance of their Bookkeepers. It also addresses the customer relationship and what they need to do on a regular basis to maintain the trust bond, which includes quarterly outreach calls and feedback emails to check on satisfaction without the Bookkeeper in the loop, and methods for initiating conversations about a customer's processes, tech stack, custom reporting, and performance. Here are some snippets discussing this role's purpose:

> As you embark on your journey into the Controller position, it is important to remember our corporate structure: Our customers are on top! Our Bookkeepers are supported by our Controllers who are supported by our Operations team who serves them. This means the Controller position is one of support, guidance, and encouragement. A Bookkeeper should never be afraid to reach out to their Controller for any reason.
>
> As a Controller and integral part of the team, it is important to have your input on how these procedures and policies are being implemented and updated as Complete Controller grows. Please notify Operations if you find that a process is missing from this scope or in any way conflicts with the Bookkeeper scope.

This seventy-five-page scope covers the following topics:

- ☑ Controller Basics and Functions
- ☑ Bookkeeper Training and Oversight
- ☑ Customer Training and Oversight
- ☑ Review of Financials Requested by Customer

☑ Quarterly Strategy Sessions

☑ Year-End Procedures

☑ Protocol for Troubleshooting

☑ Helpful Hints

OPERATIONS SCOPE OF WORK

The Operations department is our quality control. It handles our internal peer reviews and manages the critical first phase of our new customer onboarding, which includes making customer assignments to keep the workload balanced. Operations also handles user experience standardization, which includes the desktop environment, new product adoption, and quality control for our deliverables through the Operations Tech role. For the Operations team, continuity of all components is critical. The department also manages programs and training, which centers on updating our scopes, videos, outlines, training tests, templates, checklists, SOPs, and producing continuing education.

Finally, the Operations team handles ongoing process and procedure changes and accounting methodology. We figured it was a natural extension to the programs and training work. They decide what we do when the tax law changes and how we communicate those changes to the team and our customers. And those changes are typically communicated through continuing education.

The thirty-one-page scope of work covers all of the details involved in these components. Here are some snippets from our introduction and conclusion:

> The Operations team is critical to our delivery of a consistent and quality service and work product. Our work environment and reputation within the market is impacted by the oversight of companywide protocol, and it is a precise and efficient protocol that allows Complete Controller to offer such great value to businesses and individuals nationwide.

Operations is a very important part of our quality control and customer satisfaction. You are the first person new customers work with, and you support the Controllers throughout the life of their customers. We are honored to have you on the team.

These are the topics we cover:

- ☑ Tools
- ☑ Timekeeping
- ☑ Onboarding New Customers
- ☑ Establishing the QuickBooks File
- ☑ Finalizing Onboarding
- ☑ Financial Reviews
- ☑ Quality Control

ACCOUNT SERVICES SCOPE OF WORK

Account Services is the glue that holds our model together. While our Director of Operations runs all the departments mentioned, the buck stops at our CFO in this department and those within its purview. Account Services manages recruiting, onboarding new staff, paying staff, and terminating them. The team receives new customers from Client Relations or directly from internal growth and CPA/Expert referrals, and handles customer service, billing, service plan changes, terminations, and suspensions. Finally, the department manages our resource partnerships (read: alt. rev.). Here are some snippets from this thirty-three-page scope of work:

The Account Services role is critical to the health and strength of our company. It is the very foundation upon which we grow and prosper. The recruitment of qualified members to our team, monitoring of efficiency and profitability, and deft management of customer contracts result in stability. The whole team is counting on Complete

Controller to be a stable provider of revenue to them and their families—it is your goal to make sure we can fulfill that purpose.

Account Services is a trusted role that carries with it a great deal of responsibility. I know you will thrive! Always watch for ways to make our accounting more accurate, timely, and efficient and point out weaknesses so we can rest assured that the company is solid.

Here are the topics we cover:

- ☑ Account Services Setup
- ☑ Recruiting
- ☑ Onboarding New Staff
- ☑ Paying Staff
- ☑ Customer Subscription Management
- ☑ Tax Preparer Desktops and Outreach
- ☑ Commissions and Resource Partners

CLIENT RELATIONS SCOPE OF WORK

The Client Relations department is our front line. They are our soldiers. Supported by marketing and business development efforts, they manage lead generation through outbound calls, resource partner events, sponsorships, trade shows, and CPA firm presentations. They also manage inbound calls from referrals and web traffic.

In this thirty-two-page scope, we welcome them and address the importance of their role:

The Client Relations role is critical to the successful growth and retention of satisfied customers. Honest discussion about our services, pricing, and limitations is the foundation upon which you will create strong relationships. Complete Controller provides a much-needed service in today's market, and we have found that most potential users and referral sources find our solution to be intuitive and very well priced. We are counting on you to present it with integrity and professionalism so that our impeccable brand can be represented face to face across the nation.

We are very excited to have you on the team. You have been selected because we believe you are uniquely skilled to represent our brand in the market. Remember, if in doubt, ask. Always underpromise and overdeliver.

The scope covers the following topics:

- ☑ Establishing and Maintaining Relationships
- ☑ Pricing
- ☑ Important Definitions
- ☑ Getting Paid

MARKETING AND BUSINESS DEVELOPMENT SCOPE OF WORK

This role supports the Client Relations team and the company brand by producing compelling and actionable content for interaction with our audience. They are responsible for producing our blog, managing our social media and web presence, introducing new products and services, teaming up with affiliates to support community events, and empowering our community through education. Here is a snippet from the introduction:

Marketing and Business Development is responsible for the presentation of our brand to the public. We are counting on you to make bookkeeping and record keeping stimulating and fun. Make bookkeeping cool! Find the angle, introduce new ideas, and above all else, maintain brand continuity and a message of empowerment and gratitude.

The scope covers these topics:

- ☑ Process and Procedures
- ☑ Analytics
- ☑ Social Media
- ☑ Directory Listings and Profiles
- ☑ Blog Articles
- ☑ Press
- ☑ Website
- ☑ Trade Shows
- ☑ Email Campaigns
- ☑ Business Development

While your company roles will differ from ours, I hope this chapter has provided enough examples to spark ideas for how you can build scopes of work for your business and create your very own secret sauce.

Pen to Paper

By showing you examples from our scopes of work, my hope is that I have freed you from traditional models and provided permission for you to make this critical documentation just what you want it to be. Your scopes of work are not dissertations; they are an expression of your business model by role. They should reflect your personality, purpose, and gratitude for those embarking on that role you are defining. Your staff members will follow your lead; if you are casual, they will be too. If you are witty, they will feel free to be as well. You set the tone.

Once you have drafts of your scopes of work, read them through and ask yourself the following:

☑ Where are the gaps?

☑ Do you start or end each scope with an expression of gratitude and respect?

☑ What is your desired tone/voice for these documents?

☑ Is the tone you selected an expression of your business messaging and brand?

☑ How do you convey your message and brand to your team, even those who may never meet you?

PART SIX

KILLER
KPIS

*"If you can't measure it,
you can't improve it."*

—PETER DRUCKER

CHAPTER 17

MEASURING PERFORMANCE

WHEN GROWING YOUR BUSINESS, you want to build a team that is vibrant and motivated. To do so, you will need to help them understand their value to the company. In knowing their value, they can feel a sense of purpose and belonging that you cannot instill in them any other way.

I like to define this value by using KPIs, or key performance indicators. I think they are the bees' knees. The hard data from these performance indicators tells us what works and what doesn't, which enables us to fine-tune our processes. But first, we have to know what to measure and how.

What Is a KPI?

A KPI is a valuable measure of performance that can be used company-wide, by department, by role, by staff member, and even by task. You must have a tool, however, that allows you to monitor the data that the KPI is measuring. Once you have your business model, create processes and detail tasks with the scopes of work and SOPs. Then create checklists and introduce other tools to help you monitor the status and completion of those tasks. The final piece of the business operations puzzle is developing and measuring KPIs. Determining which KPIs should be measured and how can be a collaborative process.

You can work with your staff to determine the goals for each role and decide which KPIs best measure a person's effectiveness in achieving those goals.

It's ideal to have KPI data reported to you automatically. If you have to go get it, you might not, or you might gather the data at a time that differs slightly from the previous iteration, thereby skewing your results. When you automate the delivery of KPIs, you truly become the master of the universe that is your company or department.

KPIs are especially important to virtual businesses because we do not have the ability to walk through the office and feel the pulse of things. We can't get a feel for how many people are taking frequent breaks, or whether there is a buzz or silence in the sales department. So, we need KPIs to feel the pulse for us. Larger businesses are used to using numbers to make every decision, because they have the same problem of not being in touch with every department and every staff member to feel out the situation.

> *Developing KPIs and learning to use them to fuel your business decisions will get you one step closer to having the ability to scale your business if the market loves what you are doing.*

In the pages ahead, I'm going to show you how my company measures KPIs for each of our departments. Get ready, because we're going deep into the nitty-gritty.

KPIs by Department

Without KPIs, it is difficult to stay on track with set goals because it's hard to measure the performance that is necessary for you to achieve those goals. You can probably tell when you have reached a goal, but do you know what it took to get there? The same goes for your staff. You want to keep them engaged and empower them to succeed. To do this, you have to give them the goal and the measuring stick to see how they are performing against that goal. Most people want to reach their goals just out of personal satisfaction, but when a goal is exceeded, it's always nice to sweeten the experience with a bonus. And we do that quite a bit around here.

As I walk through each role and discuss their related KPIs, I want you to think about what KPIs you will use for the roles in your own business model. Steal some from me, take what you like and change them up to meet your needs. At the beginning of each role, I will list the KPIs we monitor by stating what we are measuring, the related KPI, and the tool for measurement. After the list, I will deep dive into each and explain why that KPI or effort is important to our business.

CLIENT RELATIONS (SALES)

We're starting with Client Relations because it is the first department that touches our customers. Led by our Director of Client Relations, who has several representatives who report to him, Client Relations is responsible for generating and cultivating relationships that will result in customer acquisition. Notice how the KPIs produce a funnel. We know there will be greater numbers at the top and those numbers will decrease as the various levels get us closer to our goal.

Lead Generation—KPI: Number of cold calls made per day by target market to small-to-midsize enterprises (SMEs) and CPA/Experts. **Tool:** Phone Logs

Warm Leads—KPI: Number of new email addresses received during the cold call process per day. **Tool:** CRM

Hot Leads—KPI: Number of user demonstrations performed per day. **Tool:** CRM

Early Advances—KPI: Number of people downloading our financial toolkit phone app during the cold call or follow-up process per day. **Tool:** CRM

Follow-ups—KPI: Number of contact actions made to a given contact over its lifespan. **Tool:** CRM

CPA/Expert Track Closing Advances—KPI: Number of CPA firm presentations performed. **Tool:** CRM **Goal:** CPA referral received!

SME Track Closing Advances—KPI: Number of service agreements prepared. **Tool:** CRM | HelloSign **Goal:** Signed service agreement received!

I strongly recommend that you implement a customer relationship management or CRM system to measure KPIs for your sales department if you have one. It will help you tremendously. There are free options in the market that will get you far enough to be effective. If you are on the fence, I suggest you take the plunge even if you are still developing your sales process. That way, you can get your KPIs delivered to you on a silver platter, rather than having to dig for them. Who wants to do that?

Lead Generation

Lead generation is a big part of sales. One of the primary KPIs we look for during lead generation is the number of cold calls made per day. Cold calls are made to both SMEs and CPA/Experts.

We operate under the belief that lead generation is a numbers game. It's simple math. The more calls you make, the more chances you're going to get somebody who actually answers the phone. The more people who answer, the more chances somebody will listen long enough to hear the words, "Complete Controller," which is branding. And the more people who listen and engage, the better your chances of discovering one who is interested in our services.

Warm Leads

Acquiring emails is the next rung on the lead generation ladder. Once we get an email, that person turns into a warm lead. It might be a lukewarm lead, where somebody is *kind of* interested in the *idea* of Complete Controller and how we *might* do something for them. But at least they gave us their email and now we can begin an email drip relationship with them.

Hot Leads

After the phone calls and emails, we are measuring user demos performed. A user demo allows us to demonstrate our company's features, identify the prospect's pain points, and participate in active listening while we express our value proposition. This develops the initial relationship with our prospective customer and everyone sees the value we offer when they go through that experience. It also gives us an opportunity to connect and collaborate online and helps us quickly dispel concerns about working virtually.

Follow-up

Follow-ups are the necessary outreach to get an advance toward our goals for each target segment. Just as with cold calls, it is a numbers game. In this case we measure the number of touches we count as we work to keep the relationship alive.

We have callers who can make two hundred calls a day. Does that mean they are the best? It depends upon whether they are a cold caller or a closer. Callers make their goals by dialing. They want to get someone on the phone who expresses enough interest to give us their email or engage in a user demo. Then it goes to the closer. Closers make their goals by fielding incoming calls from interested prospects and doing the follow-up that moves us toward the advance.

Because we have a reward system in place, every person on the Client Relations team is trying to break records. Their goal is to surpass where the bar is set and then outperform the other bar besters.

 KPI Spotlight: Recognizing Sales Skill

The following aren't necessarily measurable KPIs but are worth mentioning if you are planning to build or monitor a sales team. Watch call frequency when you bring in a candidate for the caller role. See if they are pausing, even fifteen seconds, in between calls. If that happens, you will know it's not a good fit.

Wait! Why?

They are wasting time. What that tells us is that they don't understand that it's a numbers game.

Another thing to watch for is script deviation. This is important because the script is carefully crafted to express your value and messaging. Give your callers a cheat sheet so they know what they are supposed to be saying. Have them start with fifty calls. You will know by the time they have finished those (or long before they finish) if they will work out.

We've had salespeople who were successful at cold calling for us who didn't know the first thing about bookkeeping when they started. It's not about the industry. It's about making the numbers, using the script, being an active listener, and having a good voice. Voice is important. A phone sale person has to have a voice that is trustworthy. If their voice is too high pitched or too monotone, then it's not going to work.

Early in his sales career, our Director of Client Relations trained with Lee Hammerman, a known call center genius. Drew was phone selling and his employer was monitoring his calls because he was outperforming the rest of the callers by such a distinct margin, they feared he might be lying to the customers to get the sale. The results of their monitoring revealed that he was not lying. In fact, it didn't seem to matter much what he was saying to the customers, he got the sale because they trusted his voice. Drew tells his team, "You have to sing to them."

Another important skill for sales is active listening. If one of our salespeople has someone on the user demo, we check to see if the person conducting the call is participating and being a good active listener. An example that we always give our sales team is "The Hamburger." If someone tells you they had a hamburger at lunch, an active listener won't just go, "Oh, that's nice."

Instead, they would say something like this: "Oh my God. I love hamburgers. Did you get cheese on it? Was it juicy? Did it drip all over the place? I love it when it drips all over the place! Did you order fries? Were they super salty and, like, really good fries, or those crappy soggy ones?"

You catch my drift. A good salesperson will connect to the customer's experience and let them know they care. If you can feel their pain, if you can relate to them, then you are going to create trust. And that trust is huge because, at the end of the day, if people don't trust us, they are not going to hand over their business or household finances!

Closing Advances

Here, we have two KPIs as they relate to CPA/Experts. The first is the number of firm-level presentations we can secure. We set a meeting and have a team of two go into the accounting firm, bring lunch, and give an in-depth user demo in person. This is the ultimate golden ring when it comes to building the CPA/Expert relationship. Because once we meet with them, their next action is to make the first referral. A first referral is when a member of that CPA/Expert firm sends us one of their customers to serve. This is the beginning of a long and fruitful relationship!

For SMEs the follow-up is direct and has one goal in mind — to get signed service agreements in the door. If you have good callers that are mining a prospects and a steady flow of incoming leads, then a closer should be able to close all day long. We require all of our closers to read *The Perfect Close* by James Muir. It teaches how to advance the sale by bringing value. If you bring more value (than competitive offerings) at a lower cost—and we truly believe that we do—then you will acquire customers.

MARKETING

While sales gives us prospects and customers that sign on the dotted line, marketing nurtures our brand awareness, positions us in the market as compared to other solutions, and spreads the word about what we do and why we do it, our value proposition. Here is a list of our marketing KPIs that are fed to us through a variety of tools:

Social Media KPIs

Facebook and Twitter—KPI: Number of posts, new followers, recommendations, and engagements per week. **Tools**: CRM | Facebook Stats

LinkedIn— KPI: Number of posts, staff engagements, people looking, and increase in network size. **Tools**: CRM | LinkedIn Stats

Cell Phone App—KPI: Number of new app users. **Tool**: App Dashboard

Email Drip Campaigns—KPI: Number of new list members, unsubscribes, opens, time to open per send. **Tool**: CRM

Blog Articles—KPI: Number of published articles, number of blog reader visits. **Tools**: WordPress | FullStory

Website Sources—KPI: Number of visitors to our website by source per week—Yelp, Facebook, LinkedIn, Google My Business, product pages, local landing pages, blog. **Tools**: Full Story | Google Search Console

Business Development—KPI: Number of outreaches, number of referrals per week. **Tool**: Account Services Weekly Report

Share the Love—KPI: Number of reviews, recommendations, testimonials received per month. **Tools**: Facebook | Google My Business | Yelp

---

Social Media

Facebook and Twitter

Admittedly, we have more of a presence on Facebook than Twitter. But as you just saw, the KPIs we track are the same.

On these platforms, we focus our messaging to that which encourages and educates the entrepreneur. Let's face it, entrepreneurs need it! They are putting their all into their companies and they need somebody who is going to make them a little bit smarter or give them that encouragement to dust themselves off after a fall and get back on the horse.

Encouragement is easy. Just a few kind words can brighten anyone's outlook. How do we educate? We create share posts about business strategy, budgeting, taxes, just about anything financial, and we point them to helpful resources, including articles. We might link to one of our blog articles or to another source that is sharing valuable information. I'm all about sharing—I don't care who writes the articles. Our audience can decide whether to read it. The key is to create a vibe that makes people want to be part of your community.

On Facebook, we look at the number of click-throughs to our website, the number of new followers acquired (followers are better than likes on Facebook), and the number of recommendations. On Twitter, we are watching the number of followers, retweets, and mentions.

LinkedIn

We have a Complete Controller company page on LinkedIn and it is through this presence and that of our team members that we reach colleagues, CPA/ Experts, and C-level members of the industries we commonly serve. Using this as a more professional forum, we use it to discuss our products and innovations, industry-specific value propositions, and trends. This is also where we celebrate our preferred vendors and value chain partners, introducing them to our community and highlighting their value.

PRO TIP

As the owner of Complete Controller, I use LinkedIn instead of business cards when I'm traveling or speaking at an event. LinkedIn provides a QR code on your profile. When you meet someone, all you have to do is go on your profile in mobile and click the tiny QR code icon that is next to the search bar. That will bring up your QR code and a QR scanner to scan someone else's. What's cool about this is you don't have to give out your personal cell phone number to connect with colleagues and other valuable contacts. This works just as well because when you click each other's QR codes, you instantaneously connect, allowing you to then use private messaging to communicate further. If you haven't taken advantage of the LinkedIn QR code, I highly recommend it.

Customize your social media content to the audience you are targeting through that platform and use the platforms that best reach your audiences.

As a virtual company, people will know you by your social presence. Since you don't have a brick-and-mortar building on Main Street with the green awning for customers to recognize, you have to give them some other way to relate that can be delivered in the virtual world. Whether it's a bold color palette or an unexpected mascot, get creative. It's about getting the audience's attention long enough for them to see and hear your messaging and learn a little bit about your company. If you aren't creative, find someone who is and let them flex their muscles to get you noticed.

MyBookkeeper App

If you want people to give you their contact information so that you can market directly to them, you have to give them something valuable. We have many ways that we do this. The most prominent is our MyBookkeeper phone app, which is a financial toolkit that we give away for free to anyone who wants to download it. The app includes a handy mileage tracker, financial calculators, a receipt manager, an expense report maker, IRS documentation, QuickBooks training videos, Federal Trade Commission fraud alerts, a place to write a review or refer a friend, a feed of our blog articles, and a link to our website, of course. To get it, the only thing you have to do is give us your name and email address so we can add you to our email drip campaign. We use the app giveaway frequently at trade shows as an engagement strategy.

Recently, we have made some improvements that allow us to authenticate our customers through the app and give them access to approve their bill payments and access their paperless filing cabinet right there on their phone. It's turned out to be a nifty tool that has lasting value.

I highly recommend that you look at what can be offered to your audience in exchange for greater engagement. Some companies produce webinars, how-to videos, or quick references. Ask yourself what will hook your audience, and then choose your tools accordingly.

Email Drip Campaigns

We have a few different email drip campaigns, which are emails that are sent to our various recipient lists on specific dates about predetermined topics. The first one, called "relationship touch," is launched for anyone who engages with Complete Controller in any way whatsoever. This could be a cold lead that signed up to receive communication from us on the website, someone who chatted, reached out for a sales appointment, or downloaded our mobile app ⚒.

It starts with an email that says, "Hey, great to see you! Hope that you want to hear from us from time to time. If you don't, please unsubscribe." After that, we touch them typically on a monthly basis with some witty or interesting piece of information just to remind them that we are here. We don't want to overwhelm somebody's inbox. On this campaign, we count new list subscriptions and unsubscribes. We want to see if we are adding more than are leaving. Of course, we monitor the size of our list and how many emails are opened, so we can see how many people are actually reading our message.

Another email drip campaign we run is the 'CEO campaign', which tracks emails that I send to my staff. I send these important company-wide emails to announce new innovation, hand out kudos, and give encouragement during tough times. This is how I talk with my team. For these, I am not only looking to see how many people opened these emails, I am also looking to see how quickly they are opened. This tells me if my team is paying attention and if they are engaged with what's happening in the company.

PRO TIP

You can tell if somebody is no longer engaged and loyal to your company by how quickly they open emails from the CEO.

It's really interesting to monitor these KPIs and keep an eye on how much staff engagement you are seeing on LinkedIn and Facebook. It can help you get a feel for what is happening internally. It's one way I check the Complete Controller pulse. I've actually asked a manager to reach out to a staff member because I saw their engagement dropping, just to take their temperature, and discovered that they were planning to take a new job.

Finally, we have our "customer path" campaign for new customers. When someone becomes a new customer, they get that important first email to launch their onboarding, but then they also receive other emails from us that walk them through their path as a customer, so to speak. These emails share our philosophies to help customers get to know the company better and bring attention to the resources that are available to them. For instance, one of the emails tells them about our B1G1 initiative, which means Buy One Give One. It tells them that because they've become a customer, we're buying meals for the homeless in New York City. It shares our philosophy of "give it away to keep it."

Again, we are looking at the open rates of these emails and unsubscribes. We want to know their engagement level right from the beginning. If we bring on a brand-new customer, put them on a drip campaign, and then they unsubscribe on the second email, that tells us they are either annoyed by our emails and we'd better fix them or they are not really engaged. It gives us a bit of insight. Truth be told, we rarely get an unsubscribe on the customer path.

How do you stay in touch with your audience, whether staff, customers, or just interested parties who want to receive your content? Email is one way you can actively approach your readers rather than waiting for them to seek you out. I would caution you to use email only when you have a purpose. Even in our relationship touch campaign, we deliver value by leveraging holidays and critical dates as conversation starters. Think about providing the reader with an interactive quiz or give something away that is useful, like we do with the MyBookeeper phone app. Many CRMs will have an email campaign function. You do not have to spend a lot to use this tool for purposeful communication that will keep your company fresh in their minds.

Website and Blog

Our website is our knowledge hub, and we are constantly looking at where it ranks and how it's performing. Not only does our website tell visitors about who we are and what we do, including our service plans, it also allows them to sign up for our services on their own, without a salesperson. Some people have the philosophy that going through a salesperson will sway them in one direction or another. We want to give them autonomy, and it gives us another way to get business!

When people come to us, we want to know how they found us. So we track the sources of our leads, whether that be from Yelp, Google My Business, LinkedIn, Facebook, or a search engine. We also observe where they are going, which could be a local landing page, industry page, product pages, or most often, blog articles.

Understanding web analytics will tell you how your visitors behave and what is meaningful to them.

Knowing how people use your website will allow you to market and brand yourself accordingly. One of the most highly trafficked areas of our site is our blog. As I write this, we have an average of five thousand visitors a week and more than 85 percent of them come to us through a blog article. You already know that an important philosophy at Complete Controller is to empower others. Always. We strive to empower other business owners, other accountants, staff members, and innovative product developers. Empowering others is how you keep success in your life. I view it as a fabulous gift you are giving yourself.

We apply this philosophy to our blog. Our topics are based on top Google searches and are designed to be educational. In promoting financial literacy in all areas of our readers' lives, we may mention products we think are stellar and acknowledge other services and people in our industry who are doing a great job. The articles are not Complete Controller-centric marketing pieces. We want people to read our posts, learn something, and then make their own decisions.

Business Development

Business development is all about managing our relationships with value chain and resource partners. Here, we look at whether we are massaging those relationships both up and down the chain. We look at how many referrals we make and how many we receive.

Our value chain partners serve and target customers that are demographically different from ours. These relationships are valuable as our customers flourish and grow because their needs become more demanding or evolve to needs we cannot support. We define our sweet spot as any SME with fewer than thirty-five staff members. Of course, it varies a bit by industry, but that's our general target. We know that when a company gets over thirty-five staff members, they will seriously need to begin thinking about having in-house accounting staff. This doesn't mean that we cannot still serve as an oversight and compliance layer and handle some of the mundane grunt work, but they will be moving toward having an in-house person manage the financial departments more closely than we can do virtually. Typically, that means they will need a more robust software to match. They may also have a need for better benefits and insurance options and access to capital. All of these are needs our value chain and resource partners can address.

Business development is a free and easy way for you to expand your business reach. It is simply leveraging relationships that you already have in order to establish new ones. Think of all the people you work with, the groups you participate in, and associations you have joined and look for reasons to reach out to them. Ask what they think of a new idea or offer a free sample or trial. Or just talk about how you can work together. You will be amazed at who winds up making a referral to you months down the road, just because you thought to check in with them today.

Share the Love

This entails collecting reviews and recommendations on our social sites. Every person on our staff is encouraged to engage in helping us get more recommendations. We make it easy, because we want to avoid any awkwardness that can come along with asking. If someone says something kind or gives us positive feedback, we have a great "Share the Love" email template that has quick links to our Google, Yelp, or Facebook review pages. When our staff member catches a customer loving on us, they can tell the customer how great it would be to get a review and send the email. We have made it easy to increase our chances that the staff member and the customer will act. The positive review is then celebrated as it is posted across all of our social media. Why not make the best of a good thing, right?

TECHNOLOGY ADMINISTRATION

This role relates to the system administrator and web administrator positions, and encompasses the maintenance and development of our technology, which, as a virtual company, is at the heart of our success. Here is what we are watching:

Website Health—KPI: Number of rage clicks per week, number of errors present on the site, speed of site responsiveness. **Tools**: FullStory | CRM Site Analytics

System Health—KPI: Available memory as a percentage of total memory, uptime, number of open tickets, ticket response time. **Tools**: New Relic | SpiceWorks

Help Desk Accessibility—KPI: Number of calls routed to voicemail, number of calls answered. **Tool**: Help Desk Tickets

Help Desk Responsiveness—KPI: Amount of time lapsed before call is returned. **Tool**: Help Desk Tickets

Website Health

I talked earlier about how we monitor all activity on our website. We actually have a website monitoring ✖ tool that allows us to see what's happening in real time. Using it, we can literally watch a user on the site and see their mouse (which usually follows their eyes even when they aren't clicking on anything) or touch screen activity. It's incredible. This means, if somebody is on mobile, we know where their finger is touching the screen. We know when they are pausing, when they are scrolling, and exactly what they are seeing as they do it. It helps us to understand user behavior, what they are drawn to on our website, and what frustrates them.

We have occasionally freaked out a visitor by initiating a chat with them when we saw that they were copying the content from our site. We reached out to say, "We see that you are copying the content from our website. Would it be beneficial to have a meeting so we can share our value proposition with you?" One time we discovered it was a CPA firm that was preparing for our upcoming presentation—that was cool!—and they thought we were pretty cool that we caught them.

We see user frustration by measuring rage clicks. This is when a person clicks multiple times on something because they expect it to be a link or button and it isn't, or the link or button is broken. We track the number of seconds it takes for the website to respond. Responsiveness or lack thereof is almost always due to broken code or some conflict in the code. While it's trying to resolve the issue in the background, the user experiences a lag. Our website monitoring tool will tell us what code is running as the lag is occurring so we can home in on those conflicts and keep the site operating quickly.

I mentioned in our marketing section that we look at our website referral sources. When we do this, we look at where people come from and what they visit on our site. When someone lands on our product pages, sometimes they get there through the shortcut on their Complete Controller cloud desktop, and sometimes they come from a social post or product advertisement. Knowing where they came from helps us know how to approach them to talk about their interest in the product they were checking out. Each of our product pages has a form that visitors can fill out to get an outreach from us to discuss the product or service they want to know more about. Here's a great feature of web monitoring—we can see when someone has partially filled out a form and then changed their mind, or got distracted, and never hit "Submit." We call it form abandonment. When we see this, we like to reach out gently to offer assistance. Any time we engage with them, even about a partially completed form, brings value. I highly recommend using a website monitoring tool to refine responsiveness, help you understand your target demographic, identify problem areas, and deliver KPIs to you on a scheduled basis.

System Monitoring

At any point in time we can see how many users we have on our cloud system, how many of those users are active, for how long, and how many were logged off due to inactivity. We have the ability to log off users, send them messages, and disable programs that they are running. We also have a tool that helps us track the amount of memory we have available, the amount of memory we've used, and the amount of uptime we experience over any given period. It's programmed to notify us if spikes or outages occur so we can maintain an optimal cloud environment for our staff and customers.

For the longest time, we would manage our technology needs by sending an email to our system administrator when something wasn't right. Now, we have a ticketing system, and it has truly changed our world. Current status and ticket updates go to the submitter via email. We can see what types of tickets are being submitted, how long it takes for Operations Tech or the system administrator to respond, and how long until each ticket is resolved. Have you ever had a tech problem and felt like finding out the status was impossible? If so, you may want a ticketing system. The best part about the one we use is that it's free. That appeals to the bootstrapper in me!

If you're interested in learning more about our technology monitoring tools or ticketing system, we share those and the many other tools mentioned in this book in the Appendix.

Help Desk

The most important characteristic of a successful Help Desk is that it is available when you need it. We want to make sure we are demonstrating our value of being accessible and responsive, so we track the number of calls answered directly. Our goal is to have 100 percent of calls answered directly. Unfortunately, that is not realistic. The best we can hope for is 85 percent with a less than fifteen-minute call back time for those who leave a voicemail.

BOOKKEEPERS

We have talked about our Bookkeepers quite a bit because they are our front line when it comes to the fulfillment of client work. Depending on the type of business you are developing, your front line may be legal associates, stylists, editors, social media managers . . . you get the idea. Although what they do will be different from a bookkeeper's work, you can find appropriate KPIs to monitor the effectiveness of your front line team because KPIs aren't necessarily industry-specific. Some of these we've already touched upon, but I think it's worth putting them all in one place for reference because they are key to ensuring the overall quality of service we provide to our customers.

Responsiveness—KPI: Time to respond to actionable outreach by email or phone, Controller and customer rating of their experience with the Bookkeeper. **Tools**: Email Oversight | Feedback Email

Deadlines—KPI: Number of deadlines missed in a period. **Tool**: Baton Pass

Deliverables—KPI: Number of report packages that are delivered complete, accurate, and timely. **Tool**: Operations Review

Time Management

KPI: Deviation between timesheet hours reported and work tracker hours recorded. **Tools**: Timesheet | Work Tracker

KPI: Number of hours available for the period based on portfolio value, number of hours expended in period to date. **Tools**: Controller Allocations | Work Tracker

KPI: Percentage of efficiency. **Tools**: Controller Allocations | Timesheet

Task-work—KPI: How often there is a shortfall in the completion of taskwork. **Tool**: Controller Checklist

Responsiveness

The first thing we monitor is responsiveness. It is measured by how quickly the Bookkeeper gets back to a customer. Our goal is to be immediately responsive. This means we get back to them within a couple of hours, even if we don't have the answer they need. This is an important value we hold about customer relationships—by being responsive, our customer can rest their worried mind that the Bookkeeper has the request in their hands. Sometimes there just isn't a tool in place to effectively measure a KPI, and we have to resort to human monitoring. This is the case here.

Another way we keep our finger on this pulse is by gathering feedback received from the customer and Controller in response to our quarterly feedback email or otherwise. In this case, no news is good news.

Deadlines

Deadlines have to be at 100 percent. There can't be a failure to meet deadlines. Ever. There is a little wiggle room with responsiveness because we understand that life happens. A Bookkeeper might be stuck in traffic or their child is at the urgent care because he just broke his arm, we get it. But they can't ever miss a deadline. Period.

Deliverables

In our business, periodic report packages are the deliverables to the customer. Monitored by Operations, these reports need to be complete, accurate, and timely. A member of our Operations team reviews each package manually, to ensure perfection, and points out anything that is not in line with our standards. Shortfalls cost the Bookkeepers portions of their bonus, so this is serious business.

Time Management

Every week, our Controllers prepare what we call the Bookkeeper Report Card. Here, we are looking at the list of Bookkeepers in a Controller's portfolio. We look at each Bookkeeper's portfolio value, which sums up to Controller portfolio value. We compare each Bookkeeper's period-to-date hours per their timesheet to their corresponding work tracker hours for the same period. Any deviations must be less than 5 percent and are investigated immediately.

The total number of period hours for each Bookkeeper are measured against the number of hours expended to date. We are checking to see if they are eating up their allocated hours early in the period and are in peril of being inefficient toward the end. Spotting inefficiencies early and offering support is a key to our success.

The Controllers monitor and compile this data from several sources and write up the report cards weekly, sending them to our executive team. If our CFO notices that something is off, she will dig in for the cause and address it head-on. This weekly process ensures that we never get more than a week into any given period without noticing if somebody is going sideways. It keeps the Controllers' fingers on the pulse of what is happening with their Bookkeepers.

Task-work

Achieving standardization requires a high level of quality control, which can be challenging when the business offers a service, as opposed to selling widgets. To make sure each Bookkeeper performs the necessary maintenance task-work for their customers each period, our Controllers review their entire portfolio using a checklist. This checklist deals with a Bookkeeper's overall performance related to incremental deadlines, document filing, email maintenance, etc. Failure to complete items in each section of this checklist results in partial reductions to the Bookkeeper's bonuses. However, by staying aware of each Bookkeeper's accomplishments and deficiencies, the Controller can provide better support to their team. For instance, if a Bookkeeper is efficient but struggling to complete all of their taskwork, perhaps they should not be assigned any new customers until they become proficient. These are decisions that can't be made by simply looking at one KPI, such as efficiency. Our use of the checklist tool gives us the ability to see the bigger picture.

CONTROLLERS

Controllers are our managers. They train, supervise, and support the bookkeeping staff on their team. They are also responsible for creating a trust bond with the customer so they can be the go-to person if problems arise. We have designed their KPIs to directly impact their compensation at an even greater level than we do with our Bookkeepers. It is truly an art to make compensation directly related to KPIs. The more you can do this, the better you will be able to spot problems as they arise and not pay for problem work.

Bookkeeper Efficiency—KPI: Number of Bookkeepers who did not achieve 40 percent efficiency. **Tool**: Bookkeeper Timesheet

Quality Control—KPI: Number of quality control items detected during quarterly review of customer work, number that remained unresolved by next quarterly review. **Tool**: Operations Review

Customer Satisfaction—KPI: Number of customer complaints to departments other than the Accounting team. **Tool**: Feedback Emails

Checklist Completion—KPI: Period checklist completed. **Tool**: Account Services Review

Deliverables—KPI: Number of report packages delivered complete, accurate, and timely. **Tool**: Operations Review

Onboarding—KPI: Number of onboardings completed in period, number of onboardings in process, number of days to complete onboarding by customer. **Tools**: Timesheet | Onboarding Update

Bookkeeper Efficiency

Poor efficiency is an indicator of a lack of training and support. If this happens, the Controller loses a portion of their bonus for that Bookkeeper's entire portfolio. That is a big hit. We want Controllers to be thoroughly training their Bookkeepers and swiftly recognizing and cutting those who cannot make the grade.

Bookkeeper efficiency is calculated on a total portfolio basis, not a customer-by-customer basis. The reason for this is because some service plans have more of a profit margin built into them. Our plans are priced based on what the market will bear, which is a value perception strategy. They are not based on how many hours it takes to do the work. How do we bridge that gap for our staff members? We give them a nice mix of customers, which cushions their portfolio value and allows them to achieve a better overall efficiency than a customer-by-customer basis could.

Quality Control

Following the financial review that marks the completion of a customer's onboarding, Operations schedules quarterly quality control checks of the work. These checks are meant to uncover problems with standardization and mistakes with the application of accurate and approved bookkeeping practices. When problems are detected, they are noted on a checklist and the Controller is expected to promptly jump in and fix them or get more support or knowledge if applicable. Failure to fix a detected quality control issue by the next quarterly review results in that Controller forfeiting their bonus for that customer for an entire quarter.

Customer Satisfaction

The first piece we look at when measuring customer satisfaction is complaints. If any have been received, we first look to whom the customer expressed their dissatisfaction. If they bypassed the Accounting team and went to Account Services, Client Relations, the Director of Operations, or me, we know the Controller has not successfully built a strong trust bond with that customer. It takes time and effort to establish a trust bond, and the earlier in the relationship the trust can be established, the better. During the onboarding phase is preferable. If a customer circumvents both the Controller and the Bookkeeper to complain, it is a sign that the customer does not feel comfortable enough with their team to go directly to them for problem resolution. This circumvention in itself will cause a Controller to lose a portion of their bonus for that customer.

A great tool for gathering customer satisfaction information is the quarterly feedback email sent by the Controller. The email bypasses the Bookkeeper and asks direct questions about their performance. It's amazing how much information your customers will give you if you only ask and provide a safe place for them to do it.

Transparency is key to good management.
No relationship can grow and bloom in the dark.

It is our job as business owners to bring everything out into the light so our business can thrive and flourish.

Let me add that the greatest indicator of excellent performance by an Accounting team is a customer adding more entities to our service. There is no greater compliment and we make sure to recognize the good work the team did to cause that action. Look for opportunities to incentivize the outcomes you want and be strict about removing incentives when goals are not met. It will save your business money and encourage excellence.

Checklist Completion

The Controller checklist mentioned in our Bookkeeper KPI section is so important to the achievement of complete, accurate, and timely work that we incentivize our Controller for carefully performing this critical quality control check. Shortfalls will result in loss of partial Bookkeeper bonuses, so this is a way for the Controller to directly affect the compensation of Bookkeepers who aren't doing their job, as well as the ones who are.

Deliverables

Both Controller and Bookkeeper bonuses are affected in part by the complete, accurate, and timely completion of the critical report package deliverable. For Bookkeepers, we measure only their report packages. For Controllers, we measure the state of all report packages produced by every Bookkeeper under their supervision. The two roles share the impact of improper reporting, as both will lose portions of their bonus if perfection is not achieved.

Onboarding

This is another important KPI for Controllers because when a new customer completes their onboarding, the value of their service plan is added to the Controller and Bookkeeper portfolios. The more valuable the portfolio under management is, the bigger the bonus potential. That bump in value is why it is in the best interest of both roles to ensure each onboarding is completed in a timely manner. There is nothing more debilitating to a customer experience than a stagnant onboarding. So, we incentivize the Controller to avoid that unwanted outcome.

Recruiting

Let's face it, for many businesses, the recruiting process is a shot in the dark. It can be expensive to recruit and train new staff only to find they aren't everything you hoped for. We track a few KPIs here that can be applied to any active recruiting timeframe to help alleviate some of the guesswork and make us more successful.

> **Ad Effectiveness—KPI**: Number of ads running divided by the number of candidates receiving an invitation to test. **Tool**: Recruiting Email
>
> **Test Effectiveness—KPI**: Number of candidates taking the test divided by the number passing the test. **Tool**: Accounting Skills Test
>
> **Offer Effectiveness—KPI**: Number of qualified candidates receiving an offer divided by the number placed under contract. **Tool**: Recruiting Oversight
>
> **Staff Availability—KPI**: Number of staff in the talent pool. **Tool**: Recruiting Oversight

Ad Effectiveness

If people are seeing your ad but the candidates responding are not qualified, you have a problem with ad effectiveness. To narrow the field, you need to be more specific about the job requirements. If you aren't receiving enough responses, take a look at your posting. Is it compelling? If not, spice it up. Tell them more about the role they will be filling, its purpose, the expected skill set, and the company itself.

Test Effectiveness

Next, review your test. Are people passing? Of the people who pass, do they have a command of the knowledge that you need them to have? If not, change the test. Hone in on the areas of primary value or concern with test questions that address those directly.

PRO TIP

Creating your own test can be time-consuming. There are many testing sites and premade tests in the market. Take the time to do some research and use someone else's test to start. Be sure your recruits do not know which test you will use to avoid cheating. After you have some experience with what you like and what you would change, you can build your own.

Offer Effectiveness

We are clear with candidates up front, before they formally apply for our entry position of Bookkeeper, that our offer is the same to everyone who applies. We pay the same hourly rate regardless of a staff member's location, and we are careful to select highly skilled candidates so we do not adjust the rate based on experience or pedigree. If we aren't capturing the attention of qualified recruits, our offer may need to be adjusted.

PRO TIP

Different places have different opportunities and different costs of living. By offering a universal hourly rate and recruiting in areas where similar compensation opportunities do not exist, you can gain a competitive edge that only virtual companies enjoy. One of the great advantages of offering work from home is the reduction of rates based on the fact that the staff member doesn't have to spend money on fuel, meals, parking, or childcare, or miss work because of a sick child, car problems, or office-closing pandemics.

Staff Availability

Having qualified candidates who have accepted your offer waiting to contract with you is priceless. It can be tricky to hold them in a talent pool until a Bookkeeper position opens up because they most likely applied for other jobs at the same time they applied with you. If they have multiple offers and a chance to start making money now, they might get impatient and move on. It's a chance you take, but I think it is better to constantly recruit and lose a few good prospects than to need talent and have none at all. Hiring out of desperation is never a good strategy!

EXECUTIVE TEAM

KPIs are important at all levels of a company and the executive team is not exempt. Company-wide, I knew what KPIs I wanted access to because I was looking them up myself and, because of that, I wasn't getting them as frequently as I wanted. I addressed this by putting tools and tasks in place for the KPIs to be delivered to me. As you have seen, it is not always possible to have a tool deliver KPIs automatically, but wherever you can achieve that level of automation, you should. When stats need to be delivered as a task, they are delivered by the accountable person in charge of achieving the goals those KPIs are measuring. The great thing about the accountable person delivering KPIs to you is that the very act of gathering and monitoring that data for you heightens their awareness of that critical piece of the picture over which they are responsible.

Chief Financial Officer

Our CFO heads up Recruiting and Account Services. Her KPIs give us a broader view of the health of our business. I receive a weekly Account Services report from her compiling KPIs from her department and others. I suggest you choose a day and frequency for delivery of KPIs so you can begin to see trends from period to period. This will help you to better identify areas that need a deeper look. The Business Health KPIs that follow are making it to her via QuickBooks or Baton Pass, and they make it to me on that weekly report.

Business Health

KPI: Number of new customers. **Tool**: Account Services Weekly Report

KPI: Number of thirty-day notices. **Tool**: Account Services Weekly Report

KPI: Number of upgraded or downgraded customers. **Tool**: Account Services Weekly Report

KPI: Number of onboardings completed. **Tool**: Account Services Weekly Report

KPI: Number of customers by service level. **Tool**: Account Services Weekly Report

KPI: Number of customers on hold/suspended. **Tool**: Account Services Weekly Report

Gross Profit – KPI: Our gross profit as a percentage of gross revenue. **Tool**: QuickBooks

CPA Outreach – KPI: Number of outreaches and number of referrals from CPA/Experts in common

Business Health

The weekly report from Account Services is truly my business health check. It gives me enough of a snapshot that I can feel the pulse of my business and dive deep into areas that need attention. For example, if we see a slowdown in the number of customer onboardings being completed, then we know there's a problem with stagnation. The Accounting team might be completing a large cleanup/catch-up scope. Or the customer could be nonresponsive and we need to use some of our communication protocols to shake the tree. If several customer onboardings are stagnant with the same Accounting team, there may be a problem with overload.

The important thing is that we notice there *is* a problem. This might not seem important as you start a new business or department, but being aware of issues will become increasingly more valuable when your business or department grows to the point where you can no longer know everything that is happening every day. It will allow you to delegate with assurance, rather than wondering what's going on—and pinpoint areas that need your attention rather than micromanaging.

Gross Profit

When the Bookkeeper Report Cards are delivered to our CFO, she has what she needs to predict our monthly period performance. She compares billable revenue (portfolio value + alt. rev.) against all of the costs (hours recorded + tech and tools costs) to have a pretty good idea of what our gross profit will be for that period. Watching these stats, capping training hours, capturing every billable action, and nipping inefficiencies in the bud are critical parts of her job. Her bonus is directly related to our closing the period having achieved the goal of 50 percent or greater gross profit.

CPA Outreach

If Client Relations cold calls a CPA/Expert and they give us their first referral, that is a milestone we measure on that side of the house. Meanwhile, we also need to nurture our relationships with CPA/Experts with which we already have a customer in common. Our CFO is the perfect person to perform this outreach because it is the Account Services department that, upon completion of an onboarding, first introduced the CPA/Expert to their cloud desktop and showed them how to access their customers' books and records.

We are reaching out to them, "How's it going with such and such customer? Can I remind you that we can do that for all of your customers? Do you want us to come to you, bring lunch, and do a firm presentation? Do you have some customers that are particularly cantankerous that we can take on for you?"

That approach has won us some great customers and some grateful CPAs.

Director of Operations

The goal of Operations is to maintain quality standards of practice and watch for potential innovations. Our Director of Operations personally directs company operations, including onboarding, technical operations, quality control reviews, and programs and training. She knows that reliable and high-quality service by skilled staff retains customers and helps us grow through referrals. Her compensation is tied to the total customer portfolio value across the entire company, incentivizing company-wide customer retention and growth. Imagine that, compensating the role based on KPIs that are meaningful to the company. I'm learning!

Onboarding—KPI: Number of customers onboarding, number of days from launch. **Tool**: Onboarding Update

Onboarding Cost—KPI: Number of onboarding hours expended as a percentage of onboarding complete value. **Tools**: Timesheet | QuickBooks

Training and Continuing Education—KPI: Number of staff members in training, number of staff terminations per week. **Tool**: Account Services Weekly Report

Succession Track—KPI: Number of staff members in Executive Bookkeeper position, number on the Controller track. **Tool**: Account Services Weekly Report

Change Management—KPI: Progress toward total adoption goals for new process or tool. **Tool**: Account Services Weekly Report

---

Onboarding Progress

This KPI looks at the total number of customers on the onboarding platform, dates of signing, staff assignment, and status. The status will indicate any customers that are on hold or have a pending appointment for their financial review by Operations, as required prior to leaving the onboarding phase.

If this list becomes long and customers aren't moving off of it regardless of assignment to an Accounting team, we know to look at what might be impeding progress. If the list is short, that's usually great news, but it can also mean that our customer acquisition is low. This report, delivered to me every Monday by end of day, tells me a lot about the health of our company.

PRO TIP

Notice that I discuss onboarding both here and in the CFO section. I did that to show you that receiving different KPIs delivered from different roles and measuring different aspects of the same task or process can be helpful. I picked onboarding, because it is complex enough to be influenced by myriad factors. If you have a critical process like this in your business, ask for KPIs from several departments to make sure you are seeing the whole picture.

Onboarding Cost

Inefficient onboarding costs the company money and lowers customer confidence. Our rule of thumb is that the onboarding cost should be less than 25 percent of setup fee income. If it meets that KPI, everyone is happy, the Controller gets a bonus for the profit on their onboarding when it is completed, and the company meets its efficiency goal. If the KPI isn't met, we take a closer look and promptly take steps to get things back on track.

Training and Continuing Education

Operations is charged with managing programs and training, which deals with staff training and continuing education. A great way to lose a staff member is to fail to train them properly. They will leave in a heartbeat, because they will be frustrated, won't know what is expected of them, and won't be able to meet their performance goals.

Operations is responsible for knowing the number of hours that are required for a staff member to receive successful training in our protocol and techniques and for setting the not-to-exceed limit. The responsibility does not stop there. The department must also provide training activities and materials for our monthly continuing education, and they need to monitor that each staff member is participating fully. Failure by staff to complete continuing education requirements is grounds for termination.

Executive Bookkeeper Track

Our Director of Operations is responsible for working with the CFO to determine whether or not someone who has expressed a desire to become an Executive Bookkeeper has met the requirements. If so, it's ultimately her decision to promote that person, and it becomes her job to monitor their progress through the track. As Executive Bookkeepers are introduced to onboarding new customers, they will be working with Operations directly for the first time. If they later choose the Controller track, the Director of Operations' involvement will increase as they will be on the path to work directly under her management.

At any given time, she needs to know how many Executive Bookkeepers we have and how many are on the Controller track. Her ability to manage customer load balancing depends on this knowledge, because the more Controllers we have, the more room there is for expansion. She has to manage keeping new Bookkeeper portfolios growing, while giving Executive Bookkeepers on the Controller track a chance at onboarding new customers and additions to their Accounting team.

Change Management

One of the most difficult things to do within any organization is introduce change. For a company that is constantly innovating, change management is critical.

There is a joke in the accounting world that perfectly illustrates our resistance, "How many Bookkeepers does it take to change a lightbulb?........ @#*&$ CHANGE!!??

Over the past three years, we have introduced at least two new tools, internal and external, per year. In 2017 we introduced our password vault and checklist database. In 2018 came our new vendor bill management and payment system and the mobile app, and 2019 brought the inception of our new reporting dashboard and a move toward higher QBO utilization. For 2020 we rolled out the reporting dashboard to customers and made the virtual filing cabinet available via the phone app.

These aren't minor process tweaks; they are total rearrangements of the way we perform certain tasks and require entire staff and customer adoption for success. New members are easy because they never knew the old way. It's our existing members that can be grumpy and resistant. To overcome this, we lay out a process for change management that we believe will ensure adoption by a certain date. It addresses the value proposition, staff training and certifications, process for new members, perks for early adopters, customer training and benefit education, penalties for late adopters, and a lot of babysitting and coaching in between.

 PRO TIP

The key to introducing a new tool is making sure the staff adopts it. You have to create the path, define how it's best used, make it easy to pick up, show how it enhances or enriches their life or the service they're providing, and ask for feedback on function. If the staff knows and understands it, then the customer will adopt it because the staff will champion for it. If you fail to teach and win over the staff, you will fail to change.

With any new product adoption, we break the process out into phases and our Director of Operations reports back on the progress of each phase. For example, we recently adopted an advanced reporting tool, MoreReporting, and the entire team had to be trained and certified in this new product.

We also had to create a path for new hires to get that same training and decide what level of reporting each service plan was going to carry. Next, we had to integrate customer QuickBooks files with the new app and train the staff on what reports to run for the initial customer presentation of the new tool. We broke these adoption tasks into bite-sized pieces and set goal dates for completion. Our Director of Operations reports weekly on progress toward those goals.

Always innovate, but watch carefully as you do. Be sure your changes are being adopted and your vision is shared with the team so they can carry the torch.

Director of Client Relations

Our Director of Client Relations heads up the sales and marketing teams. While he manages all of the Client Relations KPIs discussed previously, he also oversees our marketing budget, and his job is to understand the amount of capital we have in the coffers for customer acquisition. Customer acquisition costs include all of the marketing and sales efforts to generate leads, advance those leads, and get that customer in the door. Specifically, he wants to see that the initial setup fees we charge the customer, minus the cost of onboarding, leave enough capital in the coffers to cover the costs of acquiring that customer. This is one very important KPI.

Customer Acquisition Cost KPI: Setup fees received net of onboarding costs for the period. **Tool:** QuickBooks

Customer Acquisition Cost

For budgeting purposes, we break our initial setup fee into three components. The first is generally allocated for technology, including system work, licenses, and the Help Desk. The second is allocated to cover the costs of the onboarding work to be done by Operations Tech, Operations, and the Accounting team. The third portion is for customer acquisition, including the compensation to the Client Relations representative who signed the customer.

This is not an exact science, but it gives us a framework from which to make other critical calculations, including determining if onboarding was efficient.

PRO TIP

When deciding what to charge your customers to initiate your service relationship, I encourage you to play around with your numbers until you feel certain you have landed on an amount that is 1) fair and equitable for its stated purpose, and 2) covers your costs to acquire that new customer plus any costs to onboard them. That way your ongoing subscription or fees can be applied to the services you perform going forward. This makes it much easier to determine your profit per customer without having to factor in a loss to acquire them.

Since our calculation is not hard and fast, we don't care if we spend all or none of our initial setup fee. We aren't trying to make a profit on initiating the relationship. At the same time, we want to be sure we aren't spending more than we planned.

We learned this by trial and error. We've tried a number of tactics to increase customer acquisition, including billboards, radio and television advertising campaigns, Yelp listing boosters, even Google ads. At one point, we brought in a marketer and implemented a Google ad campaign where we created landing pages, did the campaign work, used various keywords, and watched the statistics closely.

After experimenting for a few weeks, the marketer came back to us with something very helpful. He said, "Listen, customer acquisition is going to be higher than the value of the customer in that first year. Is that acceptable to you? Because for some companies, it is."

For a company that just got $10 million in seed capital, it might make sense. Their primary concern is to prove the model with really strong customer acquisition numbers. They don't care how much they have to pay for those customers, because they're trying to build top-line revenue and get another round of funding.

We're a different story. We're an established company that doesn't want to give away any equity and is not willing to take on any debt to acquire customers. So, our model must be different. We don't want it to cost us a year's worth of work to acquire a customer. That doesn't make sense for us. Our goal is steady growth and long-term survivability. What is your customer acquisition strategy?

 Killer KPIs Spotlight: Acquiring Customers

Many firms have the same challenge of wondering how much they should pay to acquire customers. In the beginning, we had strong customer acquisition, doubling our customer base year over year. You might do the same. It's possible when you are small. But once you become larger, those numbers aren't going to make sense anymore. Instead, you will want to set goals for acquisition that are based on an increase to monthly or quarterly income or number of customers net of attrition.

If you are a business owner, you will have to decide if you are going to take on debt or give away equity to have the capital to acquire customers more rapidly. Or will you find a model that helps your business become self-sustaining?

Your approach to customer acquisition may depend on your exit strategy. If you're positioning for acquisition, you might want to go out and get some growth funding, so you can get yourself lined up for a higher valuation. In this instance, you'll want to increase that growth trajectory so you can get higher multipliers.

But if you're just looking to create a machine that is profitable period over period, producing a steady annuity, then you don't necessarily need debt or equity capital. What you need is a tried-and-true way to bring in those customers at a cost that is manageable using your customers' initial investment in the relationship. This formula also ensures true scalability in economic downturns.

Keep in mind, when the economy suffers a recession or depression, you might not feel it immediately, but within a year, you will. Customer attrition will increase and acquisition will slow. At a time like that, you don't want to be overpaying for customer acquisition. If you plan well now, you can weather any storm.

I realize that I have shared a lot of information with you in this chapter. As you can see, it requires many KPIs to monitor progress toward the goals for each role, and when analyzed across multiple departments, we can see how departmental interdependence plays an important role in the overall health of the business. If one department is performing poorly, it may affect another. The sooner we know this, the sooner we can take action.

The fundamental way to use KPIs for monitoring the pulse of your cloud-based business is to watch long enough to know what you are expecting to see. Then investigate anything that deviates from that expectation. It is in the deviations that you will find happy discoveries of how something unexpected has affected your business in a positive way, and root out problems before they become insurmountable.

Pen to Paper

You have taken all of the necessary steps to develop a cloud-based business model replete with processes, interdependent roles, scopes of work, and tools to support them. You have a vision and understand how the business makes meaning to everyone it touches. Now, how do you keep your finger on the pulse of this beautiful thing you have created? How do you know when it's sick and needs your help? How do you discover hidden gems that turn into new opportunities? KPIs, of course.

In this chapter, I shared our KPIs by role. I like to break it down this way because by task is too detailed for me and by company is too general. You may decide to use a different method for breaking down your KPIs in a way that makes sense to you.

In this activity, start working on your own KPIs:

- ☑ List your roles. List the goals you want to set for each role.

- ☑ Determine how to best measure performance toward that goal. You can have several KPIs that measure a goal from different angles. This is not the time to hold back. You can refine later. For now, just write them down.

- ☑ Once you have your desired KPIs on paper, determine what tools you will need to access the data you want to measure. Even if you do not yet have that tool, put it down. Now you know you need it.

Some data can be delivered to you automatically and some will have to be gathered manually. As you mature in your KPI development, find the tools that provide the automation you will come to love, so you can stop gathering data and get busy analyzing it.

PART SEVEN

MAKE IT PERSONAL

*"At the end of the day, it's not
what you say or what you do, but how you make
people feel that matters the most."*

—TONY HSIEH

18

FINDING PROSPECTS

Build Your Street Cred

IN YEAR FOUR OF Complete Controller, I participated in a mentoring program through the National Association of Women Business Owners, and my mentor, an executive at Coca-Cola, really set the stage for me.

She said, "Do you know what is most important to Coca-Cola? Every time someone opens that can or bottle, what they find inside is exactly what they expect. Consumers come back to purchase their products time and time again because of standardization."

She was telling me this because I needed to provide that same experience for my customers, staff, and CPA/Expert users if I hoped to make Complete Controller a national brand. In this part of the book, I am going to take you through the customer experience. I'll start with how we position ourselves to find prospects. Next, I'll share how we convert them into customers. Then you will get an inside look at the customer journey. And I'll wrap up by showing you how we nurture and build the customer relationship every step of the way.

POSITION YOURSELF AS AN EXPERT

*The customer journey
begins long before they sign up
for your services.*

Before a customer signs, we have to create an environment that makes them comfortable with handing over their financial management. We have to establish the brand and messaging, gather trust elements, and position ourselves as experts in the market.

As a business professional, your job is to make your service accessible to your customers and show them how you can meet their specific needs. You do this by approaching your customer relationships from a position of being the expert. After all, you have provided (or will provide) these services to so many people and companies that you know (or soon will know) your own best practices. When it comes to process and technique, your expansive experience, coupled with an intimate knowledge of your customer and their needs, uniquely positions you to bring the value they expect, but on your terms. As an expert, you're not just doing whatever the customer wants you to do, when they want you to do it. Those days are over.

Once you have a business model and all of your processes are standardized, you will need two other foundational elements to differentiate yourself—strong branding and trust.

DEVELOP A STRONG BRAND

Be consistent with your branding. People have been telling business owners this for years. Everything must reflect your brand colors. That's a no brainer. But tone and voice are important too. Are you sassy, witty, and approachable? Do you put on an elitist air and make your brand a cut above? Maybe you think it's best to be professional and factual. Whatever branding image you choose, be consistent throughout your website, marketing pieces, social media, and events.

What if you are launching a virtual department within a larger firm? While you do not need to make the department a separate legal entity, I suggest you create a brand that separates your department and stands out from the parent firm. This branding creates separation in the customer's perception, relieving the customer association with the parent firm and allowing your department to stand out and be creative without compromising the firm's brand. It can also provide a layer of protection for the firm relationship if the separate department you are creating fails to meet the customers' needs.

Anybody can Google "branding" and get a whole host of strategies and tactics. Some will work for your industry and some won't. Here are some of my tried-and-true tips around creating strong branding.

Be intentional. Choose a strong and memorable logo. We chose our logo—an orange checkmark on a green graphic that looks like old-school ledger paper—because it's a play on what accountants know and love. No matter how virtual our business might be, that image still resonates emotionally within our industry. It's a powerful image. Complete Controller is a strong name, and it gets people thinking about what that might be. And that's all we need to do—say our name, have them see the logo, then watch for the light to go on when they figure out what it means.

Be visible. We have an active website. We're out there at trade shows. We go to CPA firms to bring lunch and talk about our offerings. We attend events hosted by our partners. We always say we're a great add-on or talking point for our partners at any presentation they give to generate customer acquisition. So, get out there as much as possible and let others see what you have to offer them.

Be social. Get on social media. Just do it. For our customers who are small business owners, this is the way we connect with them regularly. We give them encouragement, guidance, and tips on how to run their business more effectively and profitably. Social media is free, and it's a great way to continuously get in front of your customers with content they may find valuable. Know your target audience and create content that will be valuable to them. And post often so you stay top of mind.

Be well positioned. In our line of work, we can cover a lot of customer needs. To position yourself well, be clear on what you do and then price accordingly. For example, do you offer interior design or decorating services? What kinds of customers do you want to work with? Do you only want to work with customers with a million dollars of gross revenue or higher? Do you want your customers to have a certain number of properties? Think about how you are positioning yourself. That is going to save you some big headaches. It will help you figure out who you are marketing and talking to as it relates to your unique messaging.

BUILD TRUST WITH FUTURE CUSTOMERS

All of these branding pieces funnel into the next foundational element—trust. This is the glue that holds everything together. Once you have strong branding and know how you are positioning yourself in the market, you can figure out how to establish trust with your potential customer.

Trust is the magic wand that opens doors, which is why you need to create trust factors that you can point to during the prospect nurturing process: expert content, referral partners, and testimonials. Once you have established these trust factors, someone looking into your company can pull your website up and think, "These guys look like they really know their stuff."

CREATE VALUABLE TOOLS

Social media, website content, and blogging help to build your credibility. But nothing says "expert" like a tool or method. You really have to know your stuff to create such a thing. For us, it used to be a calculator or QuickBooks lesson, now it's our MyBookkeeper phone app, a full financial toolkit. Create something new, different, and unique. And remember, if you have it, then you must be big enough, smart enough, and trustworthy enough to have it. That's the impression you are trying to make. What could it be for you?

ESTABLISH REFERRAL PARTNERSHIPS

*Referrals are great, but they won't happen
unless the person making the referral trusts
and believes in you and your company.*

That's because making a referral is basically putting their brand next to yours. They are vouching for you. Our easiest sales to close are those that come in from a referral. Some referrals come naturally because someone in a trust position likes what you do and wants their friends or customers to use your service. But sometimes you have to help it along.

It's smart to establish a referral partnership program that offers compensation to referring partners and asks them to put you on their website. They may have a section for helpful resources, or they may decide that your offering is so compelling that it should be part of their menu "powered by you." Now you have something to point to that shows prospects how much other people trust your brand—enough to make you a part of their network and use you to fill a need for all of their customers. That's a big deal.

ASK FOR TESTIMONIALS AND REVIEWS

The best way to build trust is to leverage the experience of past and current customers and colleagues. How many times have you bought something or decided on a service because of stellar online reviews? The key to gathering these trust factors is to always be listening for kudos, because when you hear something you like, you want to make sure it is captured. Do not discriminate—it doesn't matter who they are praising in the company. Praise can come from anyone at any time, from a brief interaction with the client services team at a trade show to a customer who is terminating services because they are shuttering their business. We are always listening and ready to capture those kudos by asking for them. Here's an example of what we might say when we hear someone say something great about us:

> "Wow. Thank you for saying those things! That just means the world to us. Would you be so kind, if I were to send you an email, to click on the link and put that in an actual review for us? I mean, you know how hard it is to be a small business. Everything helps!"

Another great source of testimonials is all of the people who work with you. Chances are, you don't only work with customers. You work with vendors, colleagues, staff, and referral partners. Anyone who interacts with your business does so for a reason. If you are bold, you will ask them, "Why do you work with us?" and when they answer, you can capture the kudos by asking them for a review.

Take it from me: Vendors would love to give you a review. They see it as an opportunity to build rapport with you. All you have to do is ask. And be reciprocal, if their service or product is awesome too, give them some kudos! Here's what one of our vendors had to say about us:

"What a great company, and their employees are such a joy to work with. They all showed up for our training today and interacted well. We just love working with them."

Yet another group to hit up? Spouses of staff members. They are willing because they want their significant other to get the praise of collecting another positive review. But what would they say? Here is a five-star review we got from the spouse of one of our team members:

> "My wife works for this company and she has never been so happy. She loves working from home. We love having free time. We've saved three hours out of the day that she would normally be on the road commuting."

Regardless of the source, testimonials and reviews are impactful trust factors. When people hear and read good things about you, it lets them know that you are trustworthy. It shows them that you know your stuff and treat people well. Trust is paramount to winning business and building your customer base. It matters.

GET THE WORD OUT

Obviously, customers and potential referral partners will not come to you if they do not know that you exist. Yes, we have a sales team that makes cold calls for outreach. But we also have a steady stream of incoming leads from Google, our relationships, and other exposure. Here are some of the ways we generate those leads:

- ☑ **Blog, Chat, Email.** Our blog posts generate a lot of traffic on our website. There is always a call-to-action in our posts reminding readers that if they need help with bookkeeping, they should check us out. There is also a chat function on the site and a pop-up form where they can quickly subscribe to our relationship touch email drip campaign.

- ☑ **Valuable Giveaway.** In our blog posts and on our main website you will find calls-to-action to download our MyBookkeeper phone app. Our phone app financial toolkit is a super fun thing that we give away for free. We work with a vendor that builds cell phone apps especially for CPA firms. If you are thinking about an app, I recommend you build one that comes with push messaging so you can reach your audience with info about your services or latest promotions.

- ☑ **Sponsorships.** While everyone loves free exposure, when you sponsor an event, podcast, or content, you have more control. You can usually have a guest spot or give an educational talk. You can also cosponsor a booth or event with a partner to share the financial burden. Or add content to an event that a partner is already organizing. This can get you in front of an audience that otherwise would never cross your path.

- ☑ **Trade Shows.** This one is as old as dirt! Try it. Even if you cannot afford a booth. Network. Get seen. Sometimes there are activities you can do for free. Make friends and ask your new friends where else they are networking. Go where they go as their guest and be sure to return the favor.

PRO TIP

I recommend not joining the networking meetings you attend. I realize this sounds horrible but the reality is, once you've gone, you've gone. They know who you are. All you needed was that branding touch. Some groups only refer people if they are members, but I am going to call that out. Because look, once those members know you were there and that you have this really cool offering and you can do something that other group members can't do, they aren't going to be loyal to the group. You have differentiated yourself. They think you are cool and because of that, they are going to call you.

Test this out yourself! Go to a networking group and don't join. Go as many times as they will let you without joining. Branding 101 says you just want them to see you, hear of you, and see you again. All it takes is three touchpoints. So when they think of what you do, they will think of you.

Also, you will have all of their cards and build relationships with the members that might become lifetime referral partners. You don't know unless you try.

If you are part of an established firm launching your own department, the sentiment is similar. First of all, every single person in the firm needs to know how cool this new development is, what services you will be offering, and how you are marketing them. The new department should be able to send out separate emails and information to the firm's staff and customers for marketing purposes. Make yourself known.

Pen to Paper

This section is all about positioning your company to develop fulfilling relationships. You want to earn trust and offer your prospects and customers an experience that is personal. To accomplish this, start thinking about the following:

- ✅ What will your branding look like?

- ✅ How is your partner referral program structured?

- ✅ What trust factors will you create and collect to show that your brand is trustworthy?

- ✅ How will you gather testimonials?

- ✅ How does your website convey your value?

- ✅ Are there capture points where visitors can get in touch with you or sign-up to receive your marketing materials?

CHAPTER
19

THE PROSPECT'S JOURNEY

THE GROUNDWORK HAS BEEN laid for prospects to find your business and decide that it is trustworthy. Now the sales process must reinforce their findings. The way you treat a potential customer early on sets the tone for the whole relationship. Understand that for a prospect, the choice to work with any professional service provider requires trust and confidence in that provider's ability to meet their needs.

> *That is all the sales process is: an opportunity to show them that we understand them and can meet their needs. To do that, you have to make it personal.*

We allow people to sign up for our services right from our website. This is a convenience we provide for those who do not trust interaction with a salesperson and prefer to make uninfluenced decisions. We respect that choice and give them a path. A large percentage of prospects, however, will want to speak with someone before signing up, and we need to make those interactions evoke a very important action: signing on the dotted line.

The Personal Touch

Every incoming call to our Client Relations department is treated using the same loose agenda:

- ☑ Find out why they are calling to talk about bookkeeping today.

- ☑ Show them how we can make meaning.

- ☑ Let them select a service plan that meets their needs and budget.

But the first thing we do is ask for the caller's full name, email address, and phone number, in case we get disconnected. At least that's the explanation we give. Asking for this information up front culls out the salespeople and the people who aren't willing to engage in an exchange, which means they are not ready to buy. They are just fishing.

We provide a wealth of information on our website for anyone who wants to learn more about our service, and we don't mind talking with someone who is lukewarm. All the same, we don't need our sales team wrapped up in calls with people who aren't even ready to tell us who they are.

If the caller is willing to share that information, we pop it into our CRM and start asking them why they are calling. To break the ice, sometimes we will use a little humor, "So, tell me what's going on in your life that we're here on this phone call talking about bookkeeping today, what some might say is the most boring subject on the face of the earth?"

Really, it's about getting the prospect to feel comfortable spilling the beans about their pain points. As you listen to a prospect's pain points, participate in active listening by staying engaged and asking follow-up questions to dive deeper to see how we can best help them. Remember to ask about the hamburger.

People don't always come to us with everything in good order. Imagine that! Sometimes there is some shame around the topic of their books being a mess, someone embezzling from them, or not being able to afford their in-house staff—any number of pain points. They need professional help, and that is why we are here.

PRO TIP

As your business grows, create a separation between the person who is handling the inbound calls and the person who will be doing the work. I realize that separation between the sales process and the work process is a luxury of larger businesses, but I encourage you to do it as soon as practical to avoid giving in to pushy prospects or giving uninformed free advice.

 Make It Personal Spotlight: Lesson Learned

We do the bookkeeping for a customer who owns carwashes, and he was launching a new venture in mobile home parks. The plan was to take over distressed parks and figure out how to standardize the management process. He wanted to build a well-oiled machine. So, he called me to talk about his new venture and bounce ideas around, one of which was how to manage expenses and time. Founder to founder, we were swapping ideas and talking shop.

Well, he wound up signing up the mobile home parks with Complete Controller for bookkeeping services. And he developed a process for tracking and reimbursing expenses that he implemented based on our conversation.

Soon after, the bookkeeping team was conducting the process streamlining that we do for all of our customers, and they decided it would be best to unravel what he had set up and start fresh with a different solution. They knew of a method or software that would make it more efficient and easier to manage.

What did he say?

"Well, Jennifer said the other way would work great! Can't you work around it?"

I was in trouble. My staff had been cut off at the knees.

Not only that, he was frustrated. He had already implemented the process and spent all this time learning it and making it happen. All because I didn't keep the sales process separate from the business of giving bookkeeping advice.

I ate some crow and at first he was a little put out, but my team was able to get things back on track. Ever since, I've learned that bookkeeping advice, methodology, process streamlining, and tech stack recommendations belong in the onboarding part of the relationship, not in sales.

OFFER SOLUTIONS

When Client Relations is on that initial call with the prospect, they are learning about the prospect's pain points. This is an information-gathering process. We don't make recommendations. Instead, we share our value propositions— usually during a screen share meeting so they can see the user demo. We *ask* the prospect if they think we have a solution that could meet their needs. Then we take them to the service plans, go over the various features, and *ask* them where they see themselves within that spectrum.

We're going to let them make the decision. The formula is simple—seek out their problems, let them know our solutions, ask if they think we can add value, and if so, where. Part of the magic in working with prospects is the ol' card trick. We create the illusion that they are making decisions while guiding the entire conversation. In performing a card trick, you give a person two options, tell them what their other options are, and then, while appearing to rely on their decisions, guide them to where you wanted them to go to begin with. Why? Because anyone who has been doing this for a while knows what level of service will meet a prospect's needs. But in the act of letting them choose, we create a collaborative decision-making environment that builds trust. It's easier for someone to invest in something that they decided they wanted as opposed to something someone told them would work for them.

BRING IN ANOTHER PERSON

Sometimes our prospects ask questions that require a deeper level of expertise or industry experience than our salesperson can offer. If there is a whole list of such items, the salesperson will schedule another call and bring in an accounting professional to field those questions. If it's only a question or two that is stumping them, rather than losing momentum, they will try to get a team member on the call who can lend support right away. We have designated team members who are always willing to answer a quick question, if they are available.

Every once in a while, that person ends up being me. But I learned my lesson about being the CEO on the call, so I become my helpful alias, Rebecca Stone, a.k.a. the resident accountant at the call center. If Rebecca happens to be walking by during such an opportunity, she will hear, "Oh, I have an accountant right here, let me just ask if we do that." I know Rebecca sounds like a character in a book, but she's knowledgeable, friendly, and humbly does not carry the same risk as a conversation with the company CEO.

As my helpful counterpart, I have to discipline myself to answer the question and then set the conversation to move back to the rep, being careful not to try to close the deal. After all, the person who has been building trust by active listening and sharing information is the best one to finish the job.

SIGN THE SERVICE AGREEMENT

Once a customer has selected a service plan, we move them right to the sign-up process. The goal is to make it easy and strike while the iron is hot. If they dig their heels in at this point, we know they aren't ready, and we find out what they need to be ready. Usually it is more time, more money, or approval from a counterpart. That's fair, and we give them the space they need accompanied by follow-up on their terms.

If they are ready, we walk them through the steps to download our MyBookkeeper phone app. The app provides them with the tools they will need to be successful during our relationship. It also gives us another branding touchpoint. And, if they don't want to download it, we know they do not intend to become a customer.

Once the app is installed, it's time to prepare the service agreement. If they are already on a screen share meeting, we keep them there so they can view the process and we can reiterate the features as we enter their selections. If they were not on a screen share meeting, we ask them to join one. We want them to be a part of this important process. Keeping our prospect on the web meeting while we prepare the service agreement does several things:

1. It lets them be a part of the process.

2. It makes room for them to ask more questions.

3. It provides an opportunity to reiterate the features of their selections.

4. It allows us to talk about some of the agreement terms, such as our methods for managing billing and hourly customer requests.

5. It keeps the customer engaged.

You know what life is like as a small business owner. The minute that prospect hangs up that phone they have to return the three calls that were missed while you were talking. They also have somebody who's been knocking on their door, waiting for them to get off the phone. And guess what happens? The prospect gets distracted and forgets to sign that document they committed to while on the phone. They know this too, which is why the ones that have truly made their decision will typically stay on with you through the end, if you let them.

PRO TIP

Use electronic signing software if possible. Most will let you upload the static parts of your agreement and create templates with form-fill areas that provide for customization. Electronic signing reduces friction when the prospect receives the agreement. It removes the need for them to 1) be savvy and have their own method to sign the agreement electronically, and 2) print the document, sign it, scan it, and send it back—a time-consuming process that will likely be pushed off until "later." Electronic signing helps you to keep your momentum with the sale and will show your prospect that you are tech smart, which will increase trust.

As soon as the agreement is filled out, we use our electronic signing software to send it to the prospect. We stay on the phone while we wait for the customer to tell us they have received the email. We tell them to go ahead and open it and go through it while we are on the line so they can ask any questions as they arise. We give them space to review the terms and ask more questions. Occasionally they need to go and want to review the agreement later. If that's the case, let them go with a plea to be detailed and thorough when completing the new client briefing section at the end so we can match them to the Accounting team that has the experience to match their needs.

Once the prospect reviews the agreement, completes all of their fields, and submits it to us, we confirm that it is received, celebrate this momentous event, and tell them about next steps. Be sure your salespeople understand what the customer experience looks like after signing so they can provide accurate information about what to expect. The best way to establish trust is to tell someone something that another person tells them, and then to have that thing happen just the way it was told.

Pen to Paper

The first contact most people will have with your business is with your sales department. Sales is your lifeblood, so it is important to consider who is going to do what and how it will be done. Here are some questions to ask yourself:

- ☑ Will you be handling sales or will you have other people learn that role?

- ☑ What tools will you use to support the process?

- ☑ Can customers sign up without assistance?

- ☑ What agenda will you use for calls?

- ☑ How will you track follow-up efforts?

20

THE CUSTOMER JOURNEY

When a Prospect Becomes a Customer

IN THIS CHAPTER, WE are going to dive into how we personalize the experience for each customer. In earlier chapters, we covered all of the aspects of building a standardized model that can be operated by anyone with the user manual. I like to think of it as the well-oiled machine in a high-performance vehicle. The machine is reliable, performs as expected, and has mechanisms for monitoring its own health. The vehicle becomes personalized when the customer gets to pick the color, tint, seats, and custom packages.

In the last chapter, the prospect signed up for the service plan they thought would best meet their needs and budget. Now, we want to continue to create a boutique, customized, and individual experience on the front end for them as a customer, while the efficient machine operates behind the scenes.

BE WELCOMING

Once the agreement is signed, a new customer's first contact from us is a call from Account Services to review the service plan they selected and make sure they know what to expect, reinforcing what the salesperson said and building that trust. Account Services also tells the customer exactly how much their first payment will be and outlines the billing cycle.

That conversation is followed up by a nice welcome email from Operations welcoming the customer and laying out the next steps they have to take to be ready for their launch meeting. This is their "what to expect" in writing. This email is written as a series of steps, each having instructions of its own. An accounting onboarding is complicated, and it is important for us to simplify it for the customer while still getting through all of the hoops.

Think about your own onboarding process. You may have to gather information or documents from your customers before you can create their plan. Whether it's a food plan, a workout plan, or a legal strategy, what information do you need to have at that first consultation to bring value?

We try to make the process simple and use tools to ease the way when possible. Here's what we cover in our welcome email:

- ☑ **Access to their QuickBooks file.** We prompt the customer to tell us what type of files they have, if any, and request access to them. We provide a ShareFile ✖ link to convey their existing QuickBooks file, Excel spreadsheets, or whatever they have to us.

- ☑ **The MyBookkeeper App.** We include the phone app to make sure they have it downloaded so we can message them critical information.

- ☑ **Access to their desktop.** This is where all the magic happens. They get their username and instructions to call our Help Desk to set up cloud desktop access on as many computers as they like.

- ☑ **Talk2cc customer-specific email address.** This is the email address they use to stay in touch with their Accounting team, including sending over receipts from the phone app, bills to pay, and any special requests.

- ☑ **Explaining who does what.** This just offers clarity about who's who on the team.

☑ **Setting up a launch meeting.** Now they are ready to launch! A calendar link gives them access to set an appointment.

It has taken us years to refine this process. We used to send multiple emails, one after another, each discussing a separate to-do item. Then we realized that it would be helpful to have all of this information in one email, in case the customer needed to reference it later.

When creating your own welcome email, think about how best to guide your onboarding process. Does it begin with a phone call? Forms to complete? Establishing access to your cloud? How can you design it to be simple and intuitive? Your customer will appreciate this. Especially if it's complicated!

TELL THEM WHAT TO EXPECT

When customers arrive at their launch meeting, we want them to be ready and we want to be ready. They are meeting their Accounting team for the first time, and we want that to be a good experience. Because the technology stuff, like establishing access to their desktop and their QuickBooks file, has already been handled, we can use the launch meeting to do a fun desktop orientation. Plus, we should already have their accounting file, so we can provide feedback about the current state of their accounting and talk about any needed cleanup/catch-up scope, which lets us get off the phone and immediately jump into valuable work product.

For the desktop orientation, the first thing we point to is the onboarding checklist, which includes the following items:

PRO TIP

Using a checklist helps the customer visualize the onboarding phase so they aren't wondering in the back of their mind, "What's next?"

- ☑ Tech Stuff—QuickBooks Users, MyBookkeeper App, Talk2cc Email
- ☑ Launch Meeting
- ☑ Make Connections
- ☑ Who Does What When
- ☑ Processes, Tech Stack, Integrated Apps, Tools
- ☑ Critical Documents and Dates
- ☑ Cleanup and Catch-up
- ☑ Financial Review
- ☑ Custom Needs, Special Reporting, Cost Savings

This checklist serves as a guide for the customer, letting them know they are not done with onboarding until everything is checked off. And it's a bit satisfying that during the launch meeting, they can already check off the first two items.

SHOW ALL THE BELLS AND WHISTLES

During the orientation, we get to show off all of the helpful tools and resources we provide to the customer on their cloud desktop. For some, it will be a repeat of the features that Client Relations shared during the user demo, but seeing those tools come to life on their own desktop reinforces that what they were sold is actually unfolding as part of their experience with our company. We're building that trust bond.

LISTEN AND LEARN

Next, it's time to learn about the customer's business processes so we can best support them. We need to know where we fit in and set the expectation about what will be done and when. At the end of every service agreement is an integrated new client briefing. Remember, Client Relations prompts the prospect to fill it out as thoroughly as possible so we can match them with an Accounting team that knows their industry and can meet their needs.

We use that briefing to guide the conversation about the business we are onboarding. We learn the industry, legal formation, how the accounting has been done until now, what services the customer currently uses, and what the process is for generating revenue, collecting that revenue, and paying expenses and staff.

Having learned about the customer's company history, goals, hopes, and fears, we are now better suited to recommend products and services that will meet their needs. This is when customers learn more about our desire to integrate all of their tools. Our rule of thumb is, "Keep doing what you are doing until we change it." That helps us prevent having a customer treat a discussed item as an implemented one and let their current process fall through the cracks.

Think about what information you want to discuss with your customers before starting services. Do you need to learn more about them? If so, how will you guide this conversation?

MAKE THEM FEEL SECURE

Because we offer bookkeeping services, some of the first integrations we require are those to all of the customer's financial institutions and business services. This is a vulnerable step for most people and it is up to us make them feel safe and secure. Best practice dictates that we have our own login, rather than using the customer's, so we can maintain a clean authority audit trail. We take great care to store our credentials for customer access securely in our password vault, protected from unauthorized use.

Once added, the passwords become encrypted and can't be viewed by our bookkeeping staff with access to change a password limited to only top-level team members. Think about your own customer security. Are you PCI (payment card industry) compliant? Is your staff trained in HIPAA (Health Insurance Portability and Accountability Act) compliance procedures? What about standards of practice for your profession? On the cloud, your security is your customers' security. Be sure security protocols and governance are built into your internal processes and use of tools.

To serve our customers, we need to gain access to the following:

- ☑ Online bank account
- ☑ Business credit cards
- ☑ Merchant account for payment processing
- ☑ Other e-payment accounts used for business (like PayPal and Venmo)
- ☑ Point of sale or practice management system, if appropriate
- ☑ Invoicing system
- ☑ Inventory management system
- ☑ E-commerce site
- ☑ Time tracking system
- ☑ Payroll processing login

Now you can see why establishing trust with the customer is so important to the ongoing relationship. We insist on having direct access to all of the information that is going to be flowing into accounting, because we want to provide an efficient, standardized service. Access equals efficiency, as it helps us to avoid delays chasing documents or reports. Our pricing is based on having access. If we don't have it, until we do, we charge the customer manual hourly rates to perform work. Manual entry and waiting for information doesn't play well with our business model. We want to discourage that behavior by hitting their pocketbook. And if direct access is not provided by the time the customer is ready to exit the onboarding phase, we will terminate the relationship, because we're built on a subscription-based model that was developed on efficient practices. This goes back to not compromising the business model just to make one person happy.

Deep Dive

Prior to the launch meeting, our initial review, or health check, of the customer's books helped us to determine if any scopes of work were necessary to bring the accounting current and complete. During the launch meeting, we discuss our findings with the customer and afterward, we get written approval for any cleanup/catch-up scope that is needed. This health check is important because, although we ask on the new client briefing if there will be a cleanup/catch-up scope, occasionally there is a discrepancy between those responses and what we find to be true in the books. Imagine that!

If cleanup/catch-up work is needed, we ask the customer how they would like us to handle it. If the customer wants to handle it internally, we set a date from which all prior transactions will be the customer's responsibility and future transactions will be Complete Controller's responsibility. We set a deadline explaining that we cannot move forward with our work until theirs is caught up and reconciled. We need to know at what point we will have control over the books.

If the customer wants us to do the cleanup/catch-up work, we are happy to do so. In fact, it's a specialty of ours. Depending on the nature of the scope, we will get it done as a fixed-fee project or hourly custom request. All of these options are discussed with the customer and laid out clearly in a CYA email with a request for written approval before we proceed.

Keep Them Informed

Any time we do hourly work that is more than just a one-off task, we provide daily updates to the customer on our progress and number of hours spent to avoid blindsiding them with a big bill at the end of the month. Cleanup/catch-up work falls into this category, as it can be vast and unpredictable. Yes, the work needs to get done, but no one likes surprises.

This open communication empowers the customer with information and the ability to say stop, if the scope is exceeding their anticipated budget.

At that point, they can choose to complete the scope themselves or suspend our work until they feel it is prudent to continue.

When the cleanup/catch-up scope is finished, we review the books again to make sure the numbers are matching source documents and their financial reports are showing the true performance of the business. Now we are ready to show them our work and get their feedback.

Do any scopes of work need to be completed before core services can be provided in your business? Do your customers need to do some homework to prepare? Are you willing to help complete the work? How will you manage the process and billing?

Get Feedback

Once we have had a chance to review the books and records together internally and decide that everything is in good shape, we schedule a financial review with the customer. Just like the agreement signing and launch appointment, the financial review is a web meeting. This way, the Controller and Bookkeeper can share their screen with the customer and go through the bookkeeping together regardless of where any of them are in the world. We start by taking a peek into their virtual filing cabinet to see where we store those documents they sent over and where we will store their financial report packages, vendor bills, and receipts.

Then we say, "Let's go through these reports together, and tell me if you think this reflects your business operations. Where did we screw up? Where did we make the wrong assumption? What do we need to fix?"

This is always a great opportunity for learning. The reality is the customer could not possibly have told the Accounting team everything they needed to know on that first launch meeting call. Even in subsequent calls and emails as they were completing the cleanup/catch-up scope or getting the general ledger in order, there's always a chance that something wasn't discussed.

This is how we cultivate a collaborative relationship with the customer. They go through their reports and start picking things apart. Maybe they find this thing or that. And that's good—because that means we're getting close to perfect. We're getting to the point where they have enough information to be picky about the details.

Finally, we confirm their report distribution list. These are the people who will receive copies of their periodic financial reports. This usually includes the customer themselves and sometimes a partner or manager. Occasionally, a customer will want their bank included, which can be especially helpful if they have an active line of credit or other business loan that requires regular reporting. In fact, we have several bankers who refer to us repeatedly, because they need reliable and accurate reporting or work-in-process calculations and their customers aren't getting it done. Sometimes customers want to include their CPA and have them keep an eagle eye on our work. CPAs will generally charge a management fee for this service.

Cherry on Top

Once the customer is satisfied that the books accurately represent their business and they understand what's going on, the Controller will open that onboarding checklist on the desktop and check off those final items. A discussion then takes place around the last item on the list: custom needs. This is where we make sure the customer knows that we are available to help them with any needs they may have, including custom reporting, budgets, and cost savings.

We show them reports that are generated by our custom reporting dashboard for cool analytics functions like cash flow projections, industry benchmark comparisons, or debt readiness. This begins another conversation about advisory level services that can lead to recommending solutions from our partner network. We let them know that they can have direct access to their reporting dashboard and it can be upgraded if they would like more sophisticated reporting at their fingertips. This is also a chance to talk about what KPIs they would like to see for their business and discover if they have any custom reports they would like prepared periodically. More and more

CPA/Experts are using the tools on our cloud platform to provide advisory services and they may be the ones to encourage the customer to upgrade.

Once that conversation takes place and the final box is checked on the onboarding phase checklist, we congratulate the customer. Their onboarding is complete! We ask them how they think we did and let them know we are ready to reach out to their CPA/Expert and give them access to the books and records via a desktop of their own.

When you present your initial plan, strategy, or deliverable to your customers, ask yourself: Are there tools or services that can stem from that core product? And can you add value by offering these, even at additional cost?

BE TRANSPARENT

When onboarding is complete, we remove the customer-facing onboarding checklist from the desktop and replace it with the status report. If there are any discrepancies, anomalies, or unfinished business in the customer's file, we record it there. The customer, as well as their CPA, has access to the report. This allows us to be transparent with the concerned parties and eliminate head-scratching, wondering why the books aren't up to date or the trial balance is incorrect, because the status report lets them know that the customer hired us just last week.

If you plan to collaborate with resource partners or other experts on your customer's behalf, be sure you have a way to let them know the status of your work. These valuable contacts can either be your best advocate or your worst critic. Do not miss an opportunity to be transparent and CYA.

BE COLLABORATIVE

Speaking of the CPA/Expert, when we complete an onboarding, if we have not already established open communication, we do it now. Account Services makes a courtesy call to let them know that we have finished onboarding their customer. If they referred us, we tell them their customer is all set and offer to make an appointment to go over the books. We also recommend that they look at the books on their own and tell us if there is anything more we can be doing.

This part is so important. We've talked about how CPAs are gold around here. Connecting with that CPA is key. Sometimes a customer comes in from Google, a trade show, or refer a friend. In that case, we now have an opportunity to develop a brand-new CPA relationship. CPAs are our best referral partners because they get it, and because they can produce multiple customer relationships.

 ## Make It Personal Spotlight: A Model for Success

When possible, lean on an expert who is already part of the customer's team for input. Before you can home in on the proper technique for solving a need, you have to know the possible solutions. If a customer has complex needs, loop in their tax accountant, attorney, marketing guru, wealth manager, spouse, or other trusted advisor to help. This will breed a team spirit between you and that other professional and increase the chances that you will have a complementary, rather than adversarial, relationship.

It shows the customer that they should allow their advisors to be collaborative and allows you to mitigate the risk by sharing the solution with another advisor. And it can eliminate a potential critic as you are aligning with rather than challenging them.

The best partnerships are with colleagues who understand the value of a team and encourage collaboration. The best referral recipients are the ones who understand the value of relationship loyalty. Every time we get a question about an area of expertise that is handled by a customer's CPA or other expert, we see it as an opportunity to push the customer back toward that relationship.

For example, Mary starts asking us about an audit. We email her CPA and include Mary, and let them know she was asking about an audit and that we wanted to pass that along. This is a much more powerful action than simply telling Mary, "We don't do audits. You'll have to call your CPA."

Every time you can bring value back to a referral partner or even pull in an expert on the customer's team who did not refer you, trust is built. They begin to see you as an ally, and it is likely they will want to get to know you better and send more business your way.

FULL CIRCLE

At the end of a customer's onboarding, the Client Relations specialist who signed them reaches out to make a congratulatory call. Why does Client Relations care that their customer has completed onboarding? They have already been paid for the sale, so they're onto other things, right? Not at all. The relationship that person has with our customer has value. This is someone who established a trust bond with the customer and can get straight answers to important questions.

The call might go like, "Hey, John Smith! I just heard that you completed onboarding. How did it go? Do you love your Controller? Do you love your Bookkeeper? You can tell me all your secrets! What's going on?"

Again, this is strategic. This is another person who is completely separate from the Accounting team that can learn early on if the customer has any doubts or unmet expectations, or if they are thrilled. Client Relations lets the customer know this is an opportunity for them to be honest and give us the scoop. This is when the customer chimes in and says, "I really like my Controller. She's a rock star. She's so cool. She did this for me and she did that for me, and I feel like we're on track."

Then guess what happens? Client Relations recognizes the kudos and says, "If I were to send you an email with a link, would you be so kind as to leave us a review?" Sound familiar?

*It's important that you gather trust factors
at every opportunity of the customer journey.*

When the customer wants to refer a friend, they will inevitably remember that their Client Relations specialist cared enough to check in, and that is good business for everyone!

Pen to Paper

Customers are precious assets to your business. They have decided to trust you to meet their needs. Once they have been acquired, it is up to you to maintain and strengthen that trust. The early phase of the relationship is the most important. You do that by keeping them informed, honoring promises, performing on time, openly communicating, and providing multiple avenues for feedback. Along the way, watch for kudos and leverage those trust factors to earn more trust in the market and so forth.

As you lay out your onboarding process, consider these points:

- ☑ What is your process for onboarding customers?

- ☑ How will you keep communication active?

- ☑ At what point do you produce a deliverable and what is it?

- ☑ In what ways do you elicit feedback

STRENGTHENING CUSTOMER RELATIONSHIPS

Find a Rhythm

ONCE A CUSTOMER FINISHES onboarding, the cadence of their service plan begins. The Bookkeeper manages the entire cycle, sometimes working alongside the customer's staff to complete all necessary tasks. Depending on the customer's subscription level, they update the books with any nightly, weekly, monthly, or quarterly activities coming in from the bank, the point of sale system, credit cards, payment processing system, e-commerce site, or any other integrated programs. When downloads don't correlate directly with statements, the Bookkeeper performs a soft reconciliation by going through and making sure everything is posted. They also maintain the customer's virtual filing cabinet and make document requests as needed to fill gaps.

I've mentioned the electronic filing cabinet a few times before but haven't really talked about what a cool feature it is for customers at all service levels. We store all of a customer's financial documents in it, just like you would in a filing cabinet at your office. It's safer than Dropbox-like solutions for storing sensitive documents like payroll and human resources records, tax records from past years, asset documents, and any other important business-related information. Plus, it's accessible via the cloud desktop and our mobile app.

We encourage customers to send us their business-related documents throughout the year and we gather them as well, because by the end of the year we want the virtual filing cabinet to be filled with all of the source documents needed for audit or tax preparation. Audit readiness is a big deal for many of our customers, such as nonprofits and mortgage companies. In fact, we consider it our job to keep our customers audit-ready and to get them in the habit of submitting their documentation in real time.

The MyBookkeeper phone app supports this. Using this tool, customers simply pick up their phone, snap a photo of their receipt, label it, and send it to us. They can set the default send email address to their talk2cc customer email. Then they never have to think about it again. And if they don't want to take a photo of the receipt with their phone, for whatever reason, they can stick it in an envelope and send it to us. We want them to send us everything they would normally keep in a shoebox or crumpled up and on the dash of their truck. We have a scanning department and will do it for them.

This is especially helpful for the Bookkeepers when doing the soft reconciliations, because they can grab those receipts the customer has sent in, match them to transactions, making sure they are posted and labeled properly, and file them away. The more the customer can do this in real time, the more efficient the Bookkeeper can be.

At this phase of the relationship, internal processes are supporting the customer experience and tools are augmenting that support. What tools or resources can you put in place to support your customers? How will those facilitate the processes you have designed?

Set Communication Expectations

Communication is greater at the beginning of the relationship as discoveries are being made, but then we fall into a nice pattern of activity. Hopefully, both the customer and the Bookkeeper are responsive, and they find a symbiotic way to work together based on their preferred mode of communication.

Our customers need us to be proactive. We have to follow up with them. We warn them about our level of communication right from the start. We tell them, from sales all the way through the entire relationship, "Listen, we are going to bug you. We are going to bug you because we know you are busy. So, we are just staying on your radar. Please don't get offended. Even if it's the fifth time we've asked you for last year's tax return, we're actually not going to stop asking until you send it to us, because we want to make sure we get it right for you." We bug them because we care about them and their business.

It is important to set expectations for and facilitate communication. I have colleagues who like to use Slack channels for customer communication. We prefer email, but sometimes we have a customer who responds better to text. For us, the method isn't a sticking point. We use what works, and when it comes to documenting approvals and directives, we use a CYA email to establish a communication trail.

Make Their Life Easier

Our goal is to provide services to the customer for years to come. During the launch meeting, the team discussed current processes and areas for improvement, telling the customer not to change anything they are doing yet. Now it's time to return to that conversation. This is when we begin to make recommendations, and because of our resource partner relationships, those recommendations can create alternative revenue for our company. If the customer isn't ready to look at streamlining yet, they will be by the time the Controller's first quarterly call comes around.

In discussing areas for change, we recommend ways to improve and simplify processes for the customer, which means integrated solutions. This could entail a fully integrated timekeeping and payroll solution, an on-the-go invoicing solution, a more robust inventory solution, or a less expensive payment processing solution. We get feedback from the customer about what they would like to change and what they don't want to touch.

The fewer actual hands that touch the data, the better—we want technology touching technology, with the human component providing oversight of the data through reconciliation. This improves efficiency and enhances accuracy.

If we are working with a restaurant owner, we might say, "Hey, that's a great point of sale system, but it doesn't integrate directly with your payroll. This one over here charges a subscription instead of thousands of dollars up front, and it integrates directly with your payroll company. When your current system pops up for renewal, let's take a look at your options."

This type of conversation gives them something to consider, something to look forward to, and gives us a reason to come back and let them know we are thinking of them. Since we work closely with small businesses in myriad industries, we get to see what solutions work best for our customers and which ones are failures. We hope our customers will not rely on the vendor to tell them what works, and instead ask us.

Sometimes we get a customer who is very tech-savvy and they come to us fully optimized. A couple of chiropractors came to us through their CPA once, and I was blown away by their billing and customer intake process. It was all set up and everything talked to each other. We were able to gather information very quickly. It was perfect.

But that is not typical. There are usually some things that need to be addressed. So, at the very least we recommend that if they do make a change, to please talk to us first so they can understand how that change will affect accounting. What we want to avoid is a customer making a big broad stroke change and then coming back to tell us they did it. We will grin and bear it if they do, but behind the scenes, we will be wondering why they squandered such a great opportunity to have us help them develop a fully integrated tech stack.

In your industry, what tools or other services augment the core service you are providing to your customers? How would you approach your customers to share that expertise?

Double Check for Perfection

We have talked about how our internal peer review process ensures standardization and quality. Since we dive deep into the books anyway, we decided to turn this process into a value-added feature for our daily service plan customers. We prepare insights into areas that we are reviewing and set it up like a report card from school, using the following grading scale:

Excellent—No Action Items
Good—One Action Item
Somewhat—Two Action Items
Poor—Three or more Action Items

Then, in the customer's key areas, we look at the following:

- ☑ Transparency
- ☑ Confirmation of balance sheet accounts
- ☑ Accounting controls and fraud prevention
- ☑ Industry standard general ledger or chart of accounts maintained

We provide a summary of performance/findings, as well as action items, or suggestions for improvement, for each area. It is our hope that the customer will find this information valuable, and it can strike a conversation about their business that may lead to add-on services, changes to the tech stack, or process streamlining. All of these benefit our customer and us.

What is your quality control process? Can you leverage that work to bring greater value to your customers in the form of a deliverable? Do you pay for other nonrevenue-generating work that you can use to generate revenue by changing the way it is delivered?

Leveraging Actionable Intelligence

There is nothing more empowering than having your customer pay you to have access to the information you need to determine what other goods and services they want. You discovered this advantage when you created your cluster diagram back in Part One.

When you work hard to create and maintain a trust bond with your customers, your recommendations matter. In our case, they have shared their hopes, fears, and goals for the future and given us access to their financial data. By carefully introducing conversations of value, we are able to recommend auxiliary goods and services in response to their needs and data.

What if you set KPIs for your customers and used those indicators to tell you when to introduce a tool, resource, or service from your cluster? By setting triggers, you can maximize your alternative revenue potential. Suppose we notice that one of our customers has client invoices that are very past due. Their customers are not paying on time, and in fact they aren't paying beyond ninety days. If your cluster contains a collections app, as ours does, this would be an ideal time to mention it to the customer. We are working on a solution for accounting firms that will allow them to gather that actionable intelligence from their customer data and use triggers to make those recommendations automatically. Your industry may already have such a tool. If not, make one. It might turn out to be a bigger success than your professional service business!

> ## The trust bond is built by small acts that affirm our value and transparency.

Ask for prior approval, overcommunicate, collaborate openly with other team members, stay transparent, produce reliable work, recognize when tools will help the process, and make recommendations for improvement. This might be easier to do in good times than bad. Let's take a look at how we address trust when that situation is not ideal.

Handling an Unhappy Customer

Another way we strengthen the trust bond is how we handle times when the customer is unhappy. It is inevitable in a service business customer relationship. Customers express their frustration in different ways. Some send an email, some request a meeting, and some call you on the phone and just rip you a new one for twenty minutes straight.

When a customer is unhappy, the best thing you can do is remain calm and respond to their concerns in a timely manner. Prompt communication is a matter of respect.

They need to know that you want to resolve the issue at hand. Sometimes it's a matter of the customer just needing to unload and then they are over it. You just have to hold the space for them.

Acknowledging that you know they are unhappy can go a long way. You would be surprised at how much that does for someone. Anyone who has taken de-escalation training knows this is very important. For example, when they are complaining to you, you calmly say, "Wow, I can tell that this is really frustrating. Let me see if I can help you. Let's dig right in."

Whether you get an email, text, voicemail, or letter, call them. Do this so they can hear your voice and recognize you are human. Once the customer tells you their problems, they are now your problems. It's important not to shy away from that conversation. It's not, "Oh my God, somebody is upset. Let me gather all the information I can possibly gather and then write an email."

Instead, face it directly. Don't gloss over or make light of the issue. It's not a he said/she said, gather-the-facts situation. People remember with emotion, so it can sometimes be tricky to get to the crux of the problem. And no matter what, don't lose your temper! Even if you have to wind up getting "disconnected" by ending the call or take a breather by muting the phone call.

If you can't make the call promptly, find someone who can. This method of forwarding complaints and concerns to another team member is possible at any level. It can help to quicken the response time, allowing the customer to feel heard without having to immediately find a solution because the person who can solve the problem is unavailable.

Make sure that you explain the situation to the person you're forwarding the complaint to. Don't just abandon the customer to have to retell the story, because every time they tell the story, they are reliving it. Literally. Their brain chemistry does not know that the frustrating thing is not happening again and having to repeat themselves not only reinforces the bad feelings, it also frustrates them further because their time is being wasted.

By addressing the issue promptly and calmly, you will cultivate trust. If you don't call them and instead try to handle it via email or shove it off onto someone else without a show of acknowledgment, you will lose trust. Don't let fear get the better of you. Fear is a thousand feet tall and a thousand feet wide, but when you walk right up to it, it's often paper-thin.

PRO TIP

Once you've resolved an issue, let a settled matter stay settled. We have noticed that bringing it back up in a later conversation can reopen the wound, as can repeating the behavior or issue that set them off in the first place. Also, if customer service waits too long after resolution to check in and see how things are going, that can sometimes stir up a settled problem. Make sure the follow-up call is prompt and timely, just like your resolution call, to show respect and concern for your customer while maintaining their trust.

Adjusting to the Seasons

I believe it's important to treat people the best you can, both coming and going. The business journey is anything but linear, and we want to support our customers in this. Sometimes there's a season when they need to pull back on our services. Maybe they decide a weekly plan isn't necessary anymore, so they downgrade to monthly. In our business model, customers can always scale up or down to meet their needs and budget and use add-ons to fill the gaps.

Our "Service Plan Menu" provides the backbone service plans, while add-ons offer customization. Truth be told, we'd rather the customer stay with quarterly service on a minimal plan than leave our service entirely. We've had customers think they were going out of business, pull back to quarterly and go into a holding pattern. And then having experienced a revival, they bump right back up to a higher level of service. Other customers are seasonal—agriculture, for instance. If you gather and sell truffles during a certain period of the year and the rest of the year there are no truffles, it doesn't make sense to keep your accounting service chugging away at the same cost. So they do what is sensible for them—they scale back, reduce the cost, hunker down, and wait for the busy season. And they know we will be ready when they are.

Scaling back is different than suspension. Suspensions are allowed for a customer that is having trouble with payment and unsure of their future. Maybe the business is in negotiations to be sold. Or perhaps the business owner is sick and has placed their business on the back burner. We had a customer who was diagnosed with a brain tumor, and he closed the door on his business temporarily, not knowing if it would turn out to be permanent. I'm happy to report that his case is a success story because he got the treatment he needed, came back, and reopened his business.

Suspensions can also be for people who haven't paid. These are involuntary and the suspension status is set the moment their payment doesn't clear the bank. They won't receive any service at all during the period that is unpaid, and they lose access to their cloud desktop. When they get right with us and the suspension is lifted, they have to pay for the period of suspension to get the bookkeeping caught up.

The longest a nonpaying customer can be on suspension is ninety days, at which time they are automatically terminated. By then they have received weekly touchpoints, emails, and calls from us to try to get things rectified. Termination means that the customer has to pay a new setup fee to be reactivated. We archive the customer's records and are happy to deliver them to the customer as soon as the make good on their unpaid bill.

Service Terminations

If a customer decides to scale, suspend, or terminate their service, they need to speak with Account Services. We don't allow them to make plan-level changes or terminate via email. They must speak to someone. We require the person who signed the agreement to be the person on the phone during the termination debriefing appointment. This call is a final opportunity to get feedback from them. We make it a safe place for them to tell us what their experience was with their team and the cloud platform, while asking what we could be doing better. We ask, "If you had a single sentence to say about how Complete Controller impacted your life or business, what would it be?" Again, we're trying to gather that testimonial. It's our final opportunity to get them to share the love or, yes, the dirt.

So, even as they are walking out the door, we are rolling out that red carpet. We never want to burn bridges. Yes, we have some customers that we never want to hear from again, but we've also had customers that left and then returned, only to say, "I have no idea why I did that. I'm back." Or maybe a customer terminated service because they sold the business and the new buyer loved how clean the numbers were, so now they've hired us. By the way, that's a smart move, because we know how the business is run and keeping us around retains valuable knowledge.

We have had many occasions where a customer terminates service for one entity and six months later signs up two more. Entrepreneurs rarely stop at one, and we are a ready resource that won't break the budget. And since they already know and like us, sometimes they even request the same Bookkeeper, which is so validating.

Foster Feedback

Feedback is so important. Sometimes a customer calls, and they are frustrated with this or that thing, and they say, "Why don't you just do it this way? It would have been so much easier!" And you get to thinking and realize, "Why aren't we doing it that way?"

It's a critical reminder that as you build your model, you don't know what it's going to look like as it's interacting with real, live people. You have to be nimble. You have to be willing to evolve. And the way you do that is by listening to your staff and customers.

Feedback is about creating a safe space. We take every opportunity to have these conversations with our customers. We are grateful they are communicating, whether it's good news or bad. Customers are like teenagers—as long as they are talking your ear off, you can keep a finger on the pulse of their world. It's when they stop talking that you have true cause for concern.

The quarterly Controller outreach is a great way to create space for feedback. This call is to check in, and we don't require customers to call us back. But we let them know if they'd like to, we'd love to hear how things are going with their business, household, or whatever else is new. It shows concern. It shows empathy. And it builds trust.

You'll be amazed at what you can learn about your customer's hopes, fears, and plans for the future during these calls. These are all things you want to know. But it's likely they are not going to bring them up in their day-to-day communications with you. By taking the time to check in with your customers and invite them to share how things are going, you can make recommendations that make their experience with your company more personal. And that's what it's all about.

Pen to Paper

Now that your customer's onboarding is complete, the ongoing relationship ensues. It's important to maintain trust during this process by having a plan for addressing the difficult situations that are certain to arise, providing tools to smooth the day-to-day processes, and reinforce open communication by intentionally placing touchpoints in the relationship timeline.

As you develop your customer journey, ask yourself the following:

- ☑ What is your ongoing customer relationship process?

- ☑ What tools do you use to support its success?

- ☑ In what way does your customer participate in the process?

- ☑ What do you do if they get off track?

- ☑ What special customer needs do you accommodate and how?

- ☑ Who receives complaints and how are they resolved?

PART EIGHT

GIVE IT AWAY TO KEEP IT

"Before you are a leader,
success is all about growing yourself.
When you become a leader,
success is all about growing others."

—JACK WELCH

GIVE IT AWAY TO KEEP IT

Gratitude is everything.

I FEEL BLESSED TO have been selected to steward Complete Controller out into the world. At the risk of sounding completely woo-woo, I feel the universe meant for this company to come to fruition as it did, as evidenced by the multitude of events that positioned me for success, followed by many serendipitous occurrences that sealed the deal. By now, you know my story, some of my juiciest secrets and slip-ups, and the cast of characters who have helped along the way and shaped this company with me.

Before I explain what *give it away to keep it* means to me and Complete Controller, I want to share a personal story that changed my mindset about blessings and became the guiding force of how I walk through this world.

I was nineteen when my first child, Sarah, was born. Thirteen hours after her birth, she had a seizure and spent fourteen days in intensive care. They released her, still undiagnosed, and for the first four months of her life, she struggled. She had seizures for what appeared to be no reason, an intolerance to formula, digestive problems, persistent jaundice, and eventually congestion and a cough that wouldn't pass.

One day I was talking with a wise woman who owned and ran the daycare that Sarah attended when I first went back to work. I was bemoaning my misfortune saying that I see drug addicts and irresponsible moms having babies that are just fine and wondering why I, who tried to do everything right, was given a baby who was sick.

She quickly righted me by saying, "Shame on you. God didn't give you Sarah by chance. She was given to you because you are the best mom to care for her."

That moment changed my perception of the blessings in my life that sometimes looked like burdens. This lesson has helped me to keep a positive attitude through financial challenges, technology crashes, staff resignations, and all of the little frustrations that come with running a business. Sure, right when it happens, I may need to vent, but pretty quickly I'm able to remember that everything I thought was a burden has turned out to be a blessing in the end. Even though I couldn't see it until it was behind me. This knowledge has kept me strong and purposeful when it would have been easier to give up or go along.

When Sarah was four months old, I grew tired of emergency rooms and pediatricians telling me that they could find nothing wrong and to just wait for her to grow out of it, while my child was suffering. I pulled out the health insurance booklet and looked up the closest gastroenterologist because it appeared to me that digestion was at the core of her symptoms. I took her to that doctor and she was the last patient of the day. In fact, his front desk staff had already left.

I remember walking into the exam room with her and seeing his kind, open face, what appeared to me to be full of wisdom. I was overwhelmed with the past four months of struggles and blurted out that I needed him to please help my baby, that I knew something was very wrong but no one would listen. Then, I unburdened all of her history on him.

He looked me dead in the eyes and told me to bring her to Children's Hospital of Orange County (CHOC) and intake would be waiting for her. He promised not to let Sarah leave that hospital without a diagnosis. Initial tests came back indicating a possibility of cystic fibrosis, a terrible disease that basically ensures the patient will die at a young age. But her dad was unconvinced and insisted they keep looking.

Every discipline tested her—neurology, pulmonology, endocrinology—CHOC was a teaching hospital and they had all gathered with the results of their testing in a section of the cafeteria to brainstorm the Sarah Brazer case.

A visiting endocrinologist from Children's Hospital of Los Angeles (CHOLA) happened to be there following his colleagues' rounds, and when he heard all of the symptoms and test results, he piped up. He said he had seen one eerily similar case at CHOLA during his tenure and he might have an idea of what we were dealing with, but it was very rare and the test to diagnose it could cause the baby to go into a seizure or coma, or die.

We gave them the go-ahead, and they performed a test that monitored her adrenal function when her blood sugar got to a critically low level. Most people's bodies would release adrenaline at that point to keep them alive, but hers did not. Eventually, they were able to confirm the diagnosis of de Morsier's syndrome, a very rare genetic condition.

Because of the nature of her condition, when she contracted the usual childhood illnesses, unlike other kids, she needed hospitalization. Years later during one of these stays at CHOC, we had medical students drop by her room to ogle her and when I asked why, I was told that the Sarah Brazer case is one they teach all new pediatric doctors at the hospital. The teaching had rendered an important lesson: When a child is under your care, it may be the one opportunity you have to diagnose and treat them. If the parent says to dig deeper, you dig deeper. In that moment, I began to see the blessing my daughter had given not just to me, but also to the staff at the hospital.

The moral of my journey was to keep seeking answers until I found them, even if I had to go outside of the normal path to get what I needed. I don't think that we should do things just because it's always been done that way; if we know something is wrong, we should dig in and find the answers or fix it. If we can't do so using the path that has always been used, it is time to leave that path.

I took this message with me as I built Complete Controller. And with it, I have an immense amount of gratitude, resilience, and faith in my beliefs. There is nothing more powerful than being in alignment with your beliefs, especially when they feel bigger than you.

Autonomy Achieved

Remember in Part One where I talked about wanting to build a business that could run without me?

My success came when I realized Complete Controller could run on its own—completely—without me.

I realized I could actually take a vacation and be completely cut off from the company.

Well, almost.

In September 2015, I went on a cruise. If you've ever been on a cruise, you know that the internet package is super expensive. I'm not a cheapskate, but I am a bootstrapper who doesn't believe in buying stuff I don't need. So, I let everyone know I was going and that they were not going to be able to get in touch with me unless I was at a port. It was my method to test the idea of being unreachable for several days at a time. Before this trip, travel had always been different—working a couple of hours every night checking in, guiding the Complete Controller ship, touching base, and getting my fingers in all the pies. This was going to be my first total disconnect. My staff was completely supportive and told me not to worry, that they had everything managed. And they did.

However, one customer called me directly, on fire, because he couldn't get access to technology he needed. I took the call and was able to transfer it to a staff member who handled the issue without me. As many of you may know, that's hard to do—to just let go. Because you want to jump in and just fix it. Instead, I disconnected and went back to my vacation.

That experience made me realize that we had built something that was bigger than me. It was bigger than the original staff who had created it and I no longer knew the name of each person working for me. I didn't know many of my customers.

But my staff did. And they take very good care of them. That's when it dawned on me. This thing is not just mine anymore. That helped me step back and realize all of the blessings and serendipity that had crossed my path, helping to launch this company into the world. I had reached my goal.

I had to ask myself, "Wow. This is great. But is this really it?"

I built a business with a recurring revenue model and it does very well. It would be easy to just let it do its thing and not think twice. But I know better. Another thing I learned from a mentor:

A business that isn't growing is dying.

I always talk about wanting to work with vendors that are nimble and innovative, but I'm telling myself this, too. If getting your business to its success goal, in my case, autonomy, is your end-all, then sit back and enjoy, but put people in place who can continue the innovation so it will not become obsolete. To let a technology-based business become complacent and stagnant is to sign its death warrant. For there will always be hungry entrepreneurs with the passion in their belly to do it better than you.

The Power of Mentorship

Now that you have learned how to build a successful virtual business, I want to talk about the importance of mentorship and the impact it has had on me and my career. I learned so much by seeing other successful women pioneering their own paths. I generally found that they were willing to give their time and knowledge to me so that I, too, could be successful. As I mentioned in Chapter 18, one of the places where I found great mentoring was through the National Association of Women Business Owners (NAWBO). I was a member of the Orange County chapter for several years, including serving as treasurer on the board of directors.

The Orange County chapter's mentorship program was headed up by Dee Elliott, an incredible woman who created a business that develops and supports corporate mentorship programs ✖. The program she developed for NAWBO connected less-experienced business owners with those who were more seasoned, and through those relationships, so many questions were answered for these new entrepreneurs, such as:

- ☑ How do I hire somebody?

- ☑ Where do I market my business?

- ☑ What don't I know that I should?

- ☑ What if I make a misstep?

- ☑ What if I get sued?

You know, all of the questions that burn in your brain that you are afraid to ask. I went through the mentorship program to see if there was anything I could learn and was paired up with the executive from Coca-Cola, who was exactly what I needed and who taught me all about standardization. Afterward, I gave back by participating as a mentor.

One of my best examples of mentorship occurred when I first started Complete Controller. I barely knew what I was doing. I was working on the company website and putting all the marketing materials together, and trying to figure out how to make meaning. Then at an event one evening, I met a woman through a mutual friend. She had made her career in the telecom industry and was very intelligent and ferociously passionate about empowering women. We just clicked. Despite her mama bear passion, her greatest contribution to me wasn't warmth and comfort. It was that she told the truth as she saw it. Without hesitation, she would tell me what she thought of my plans and designs, straight up. I loved this because at that point I was a sponge, soaking up the feedback and strategies. I wanted to do the best I could.

One day, we took a long walk, and I was telling her about all of these marketing materials I was making, including a flyer for my new pricing structure.

She asked me what I had worked on the day before, and I said, "Well, I have this flyer . . ." She stopped me right in my tracks.

"It doesn't matter," she said. "It doesn't matter how glossy your flyer is. It doesn't matter how flashy your website is or whether you say the right thing on the piece of paper. What matters is that you get out there and tell people you are here. Because no one knows you exist. Nobody knows you are doing this. Don't be afraid to tell people—pick up the phone, go door to door, and do whatever you have to do to get the word out." She continued, "Everyone's list contains A, B, and C priorities. And you're doing a whole lot of C priorities. What you need to be doing is A priorities. You need to be out there landing customers."

That's when I realized landing customers wasn't my forte. But that helped me get into more networking and led to my decision to hire a cold caller and eventually the man who was to become my Director of Client Relations. I am grateful for that mentorship. And for that conversation. I needed to hear the truth. I needed to know where my gaps were and fill them, not just keep moving forward like everything was under control. Because let me be real—it doesn't matter if you make the best flyer. If you don't have someone who can go talk to people about the flyer and land the sale, it's meaningless.

My main tips around mentorship are simple:

- ☑ **Find someone who has already hit the success bar.** And here's the double kicker: They don't necessarily have to be in your industry and they don't ask you to pay them.

- ☑ **Listen to them.** If what they are saying resonates with you, that's a strong sign that the person is a good match.

- ☑ **Give back.** Maybe you need a mentor for your own business or practice, but chances are you can already be a mentor to someone else. Think about the young people in your community. Do you belong to a church, an organization, or another group? Do you see someone trying to launch a business? Have you noticed a person who constantly brings up an idea, looking to get feedback? Maybe there's a young person who needs some education around their finances. Why not ask that person to share more about their dreams or answer some of their questions over coffee? You will make someone's day.

Some of the greatest business training from gurus of success like Dale Carnegie will teach you the same: The best way to learn is to get a mentor, and the best way to give back is to be a mentor. As you engage in this cycle of giving and receiving, you will build a network around you of people who know your core talents, projects, hopes, and dreams. And that network is where you will go for advice, talent, funding, connections, and more.

Giving Back in Business

I have found that in life, as well as in business, the best way to establish strong relationships, learn new things, and be accomplished is to share your success and empower others. I had plenty of people along my path who empowered me, and now it is my turn to give back.

When you reach a point where you've reached your business goals, your bank account is big enough, you are living where you want to live, your family is stable, you've done some cool things, and you are satisfied, you'll likely view yourself as successful. Success is defined by what you think. It's a mindset.

For successful people, continuing to do the things that got them there can start to become boring and stale. If you are not trying to get more recognition, more money or more power, what do you do? What I do, and what I encourage everyone within my company to do, is empower others. You keep being successful by helping others to be successful in their own right. You give it away to keep it.

BUILT-IN GIVING

As you develop your company to make meaning in the lives of others, it is my hope that you will find ways to give back both inside and outside of the business. Here are a few ways we have built the giving spirit into our business model.

Sharing Information

Collaboration and sharing knowledge are ways to give back. When we decide on the best way to do something, write it down, make it a process, put it on a checklist, and then share the updated information throughout the company, we empower all of our staff. Some staff members came from cutthroat corporate environments where sharing knowledge and mentoring were limited by the kind of ambition that pitted colleagues against each other. Others came from situations of total autonomy so they were only as good as what they learned on their own. When we teach our staff to share their knowledge and give them a method to do so, they learn how to give back.

Mentorship

Mentoring is built into our organizational structure and role succession. Rather than having an authoritative hierarchy, we flip the pyramid and make it the manager's job to support and guide their team members. Managers who create other great managers are rewarded for their dedication to the success of others. The Controller, for example, serves as the mentor to a new Controller, giving advice, sharing experience, and giving of their own portfolio to provide that new Controller with the core they need to build a thriving team of their own. In return, they have a path to earn the title of Executive Controller, which comes with opportunities for increased compensation.

 PRO TIP

When creating your business staffing model or making improvements to your existing model, look at how you can build mentorship right into your supervisory positions.

Buy 1 Give 1

We also participate in the Buy 1 Give 1 (B1G1) global community. This organization provides the framework for us to embed giving into our business transactions and create a giving habit. B1G1 ⚒ is a worldwide effort that supports the seventeen sustainable development goals created by world leaders in 2015. You can find the link to access the entire list in our Community section in the Appendix. Through B1G1, a small business can set a promise for giving that is calculated based on an accomplishment of the business. So, every time you conduct business, you enrich not only yourself but the world around you. Our giving promise is that, whenever we onboard a new customer, we provide meals for the hungry in New York City. Large companies give back in big ways, and some companies wait to see if they need the write-off to give. We want giving to be a habit that is enmeshed in our business process so it doesn't feel optional.

COMPLETE CONTROLLER COMMUNITY PARTNERS

Recently, a nonprofit organization was established that provides scholarships for businesses that are in need of our services. We know the small business community needs support and we know that small business supports the economy of this great country. With that knowledge brings the responsibility to make sure the services we offer, which provide financial empowerment and literacy, are available to small businesses that otherwise cannot afford them out of pocket. We work hand in hand with community institutions to bring this dream to life.

GETTING RID OF THE BOOGEYMAN

A wise woman once told me, "To receive, you have to give and to give you have to receive, and there can't be a place where you block it. Because when you block the giving outflow, you also block the receiving inflow on the other side."

It's a cycle. As you learned in the last section, it's all about giving it away and then seeing it come back. But it may come back in an entirely different form, and it may not look the way you originally thought it would. This concept is explained in another book I recommend, *The Go-Giver* by Bob Burg and John David Mann. Everyone has heard of the law of attraction—we know it works. *The Go-Giver* teaches you other laws of the universe that are just as powerful (it's a really fun book—I read it on an airplane). This book challenges you to look for opportunities that would benefit other people and how you can take this mindset into everything you do. When you think about how an act or an opportunity will enrich other people, you can't lose.

That's why I decided to write the book you are reading. In the past, the thought of helping my competitors succeed or telling them about my weaknesses would make me fearful. But now I realize that my mission is to help everyone succeed and that includes my competitors, whom I choose to call colleagues instead. I believe in being a go-giver, and we are at a point in our company's life cycle where I want to give away some of the good (and ugly) stuff we've learned. Rest assured, we weren't always like that. When you're in the startup phase, of course it's natural to keep your cards close to the chest. You don't want anyone to steal any of your proprietary information and blow you out of the water.

Once you're a mature company, everything changes. You can be more open. You can even write a book! You can take your experience, wisdom, bumps, and bruises and share them openly because it's not going to hurt. In addition, the idea of your competitors knowing how you stubbed your toe and how you fixed it is not that intimidating anymore. Being afraid to share those things was like fearing the boogeyman in the dark. Now, I'm just doing it, because I don't care if they know my weaknesses and frankly, I don't think they care either. Maybe I'm just not that important!

Pen to Paper

By now you have built, or are on the way to building, a beautiful model for virtualizing your professional services and delivering them on the cloud. If you have taken all of the steps outlined in this book, your business may be self-supporting, or it may not need your constant attention for much longer.

However, that does not mean you can stop working to make improvements or completely step back from your work. Instead, I encourage you to contemplate the following as your business continues to grow:

- ☑ How will you continue to innovate within the business and your industry?

- ☑ How will you give back to the profession, your staff, your colleagues, and your community?

- ☑ In what ways can you make giving back a part of your business fabric so that it becomes a culture, rather than an afterthought?

A WORD TO MY PROFESSION

A FRIEND ONCE SAID to me, "Don't you think it's odd that people will go to dinner with someone, date them for a minute, take them home, become intimate with them, and know every inch of their lover's physical body, before they know their credit score or how many dollar bills they have in their bank account?"

Think about that. We are protective of anyone knowing our financial health or lack thereof, and who is that helping? When we hide our financial strategies and challenges, we rob our children of the opportunity to become financially literate, to understand what it means to save for a long-term goal, and what it takes to run a household and family. We're also blocking ourselves off from the ability to monitor and help our elders and allow them to have independence with their finances rather than just taking them over at the first sign of a problem. They don't need us to necessarily take over; they just need us to keep an eye out so they can maintain their autonomy.

Transparency is huge. Block chain is here, and it is pushing all of us to be more transparent. I hope as you develop your company or department, you innovate with that in mind. Get ahead of it. Champion for it. So when people start demanding transparency as the status quo, you will already tout that value and leverage the cloud to provide it.

Intelligence is the future of business. Artificial Intelligence (AI) already handles many mundane tasks like importing and identifying transactions or reviewing contracts and constructing financial transactions that represent the terms. What are we to do with the free time we have by not spending it on mundane tasks that can be handled by AI? Some say advisory services.

I say take action on intelligence. We can be more effective to our customers if we are able to set KPIs based on their unique needs, goals, and fears. If set properly, those KPIs should turn on that light bulb prompting a conversation when there is a need. Whether it's about tax planning, labor management, technology, an upcoming audit, or the way your customer is processing payments, these conversations help you become an integral, valuable advisor to your customer based entirely on information gathered through CAS. Now you can recognize if a customer is ready for new services such as payroll processing, benefits management, tax planning, business valuation, and more. If your referral network has been properly set up to provide alternative revenue, the action need only be that referral. Simply feed other specialties both inside and outside of the firm to grow the top line.

And you won't pay a dime to get in front of these potential customers, because they are already paying you for the day-to-day accounting management (bookkeeping, record keeping, and financial reporting) that you provide. Your customer is paying to give you an inside look at how they manage their business on a day-to-day basis. You know their most intimate pain points, needs, hopes, dreams, changes, risks, and plans for the future. Since you know them so well, aren't you the best candidate to bring solutions?

At Complete Controller, we have begun to expand our Client Accounting Services Intelligence (CAS-i) platform to monitor KPIs and automatically feed customers and CPA/Experts a call to action when actionable intelligence has indicated a need. By automating the monitoring and notification, we strive to never miss an opportunity to present the perfect product or service at just the right time. All of this using the very data our customers are paying us to gather and manage for them.

So, rather than CAS being something that you stuff in the corner or do because you feel obligated, what if we change our minds? What if we put it right in the center of our practice and let it feed all of the other service areas?

Placing CAS at the heart of your firm can lead to great (not to mention, profitable) things.

APPENDIX

THE TOOLBOX

RECOMMENDED READING

Built to Sell by John Warrillow

Now, Discover Your Strengths by Donald Clifton and Marcus Buckingham

The Art of the Start by Guy Kawasaki

The Perfect Close by James Muir

The Go-Giver by Bob Burg and John David Mann

TOOLS OF THE TRADE

Calendar/Email: Microsoft 365, www.microsoft.com

CRM System: HubSpot, www.hubspot.com

Mobile App: My Firm's App, www.myfirmsapp.com

Work Tracker: WorkTime, www.worktime.com

Virtual Offices: Regus, www.regus.com

Digital Contract Management: HelloSign, www.hellosign.com

Video Host: Vimeo, www.vimeo.com

Digital Publishing: FlowPaper Zine, www.flowpaper.com

Password Vault: LastPass, www.lastpass.com

Virtual Filing Cabinet: Box, www.box.com

Web Meeting: Join.me, www.join.me

Website Monitoring Tool: FullStory, www.fullstory.com

File Transfer: ShareFile, www.sharefile.com

✖ COMMUNITY

Buy 1 Give 1: www.CompleteController.com/b1g1

National Association of Women Business Owners: www.nawbo.org

Corporate Mentorship Programs: DEC Strategic Mentoring, www.deeelliottconsulting.com

⚒ **MY CLUSTER**

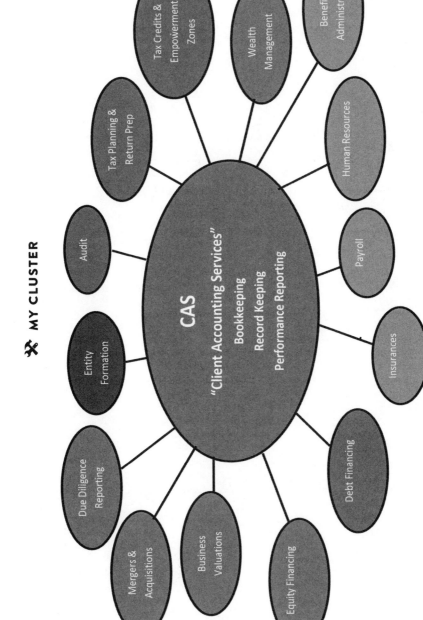

CAS
"Client Accounting Services"
Bookkeeping
Record Keeping
Performance Reporting

Tax Credits & Empowerment Zones

Wealth Management

Benefits Administration

Tax Planning & Return Prep

Human Resources

Audit

Payroll

Entity Formation

Insurances

Due Diligence Reporting

Debt Financing

Mergers & Acquisitions

Business Valuations

Equity Financing

⚒ THE SERVICE PLAN MENU

AFFORDABLE SOLUTIONS TO MEET YOUR BOOKKEEPING NEEDS

Love Us or Leave Us with 30-day Notice - No Long Term Contracts

Plan Features	MINIMAL	BASIC	COMPLETE	PREMIER	DELUXE
	$122 Per Month / Billed Quarterly	**$365** Per Month	**$885** Per Month	**$1635** Per Month	**$2740** Per Month
	Quarterly Bookkeeping Full Report Package	Monthly Bookkeeping Full Report Package	Weekly Bookkeeping Custom Report Package	Daily Bookkeeping Custom Report Package	Daily Bookkeeping Custom Report Package
Expert Bookkeeping Team	X	X	X	X	X
Accounting Basis	Cash	Cash	Accrual	Accrual	Accrual
Account Reconciliation Frequency	Quarterly Reconciliations	Monthly Reconciliations	Weekly Reconciliations	Daily Reconciliations	Daily Reconciliations
Number of Monthly Transactions	90 or Fewer	Over 90 Transactions	Over 90 Transactions	Over 90 Transactions	Over 90 Transactions
Accounts / Class Divisions Incl.	Up to 3	Up to 3	Up to 3	Up to 3	Up to 5
Tax Preparer Access	X	X	X	X	X
AP Management			X	X	X
Number of Vendor Bills Incl.			Up to 40	Up to 80	Up to 200

Payroll Mgmt - Twice Monthly	X	X			
Number of Employees	Up to 30 Employees	Up to 10 Employees			
Daily Sales Receipt Entry			X	X	
Document Renaming Service	Up to 5 Hours		X	X	
Period Close-Out & Review	X	X	X	X	X
Access to Forms & Templates	X	X	X	X	X
Process Review & Streamlining	X	X	X	X	
Custom Reporting	X	X	X		
Weekly Collaborative Mtgs.	X				
Financial Document Storage	X	X	X	X	X
CRM, POS, Inventory Mgmt Hosting — Web-based apps only	X	X	X	X	X
Triple Gateway Access	X	X	X	X	X
VPN SSL Security	X	X	X	X	X
QuickBooks Premier Desktop — $50/month Hosted License	X	X	X	X	X
QuickBooks Online — $40/month for 3 users — $125/month for 5 users — Training Included	X	X	X	X	

To see more, visit https://www.completecontroller.com/pricing-sign-up/.

Client Journey

| Client Relations | Acquired from CPA / Partner Referral or Search |
| Account Services | Acquired from Existing Clients or Client Recommendations |

Dir. Operations
Controller / Exec BK — Launch Mtg - Biz Model - CUCU Needs - Discuss Tech Stack - **Desktop Tour**

Op Tech
Controller / Exec BK — Intro to OP Tech - Facilitates File Transfer - Connect to Internal Tools

Bookkeeper — Meet the Team - Logins - BK Tasks
  - More Reporting
  - SmartAP
  - PDF Compressor
  - Est. preferred communication mode because we know you are busy - expect persistency

  - BK Preps Task Briefing

Gather Critical Info / Docs
Bring Chart of Accounts in line
Integrate Applications
Clean-up / Catch-up Scope - method / communication - Launch to Completion
Internal Financial Review

Controller / Exec BK
Bookkeeper — Client Financial Review - Onboarding Checklist Finalization

  - Status Report
  - Custom Reports - Budget Prep
  - Process Streamlining Recommendations - Partner Solutions

Onboarding Complete

Client Relations — Share the Love...or the dirt
Bookkeeper — Daily - Weekly - Monthly - Quarterly - Annual Tasks
  - Updates to BK Task Briefing
  - eFiling Cabinet Maint - Doc Requests

Client Support + Communication - Ask My Client - Period Close - Reporting
Report Package QC Reviews

Op Tech
Dir. Operations — Quarterly + Year End QC Reviews
Controller / Exec BK — Create the Space - calls monthly / quarterly
Feedback Tickle Email + Quarterly Call
  - Share the Love...or the dirt

Account Services — Upgrades - Downgrades - Suspensions - Terminations
Account Services — Complaints - quick to respond - bring in AS for resolution support
Termination Briefing - Share the Love...or the dirt

| Additional Support Roles - | System Admin / Web Admin | Recruiting / Human Reso | Programs + Training | Marketing |

QuickBooks File(s)	One for each entity
Contact Card	Easily find your team's email + phone
Onboarding Checklist / Status Report	Steps to take + the noteworthy conditions
Action Items	Your CC Team's inbox - work in process
eFiling Cabinet(s)	Secure document storage - soon to be accessible on phone APP!
SmartAP	Review and approve vendor bills - accrual basis clients only
Payroll Portal	Shortcut to your payroll service (or options if you don't have one)
Collect Payments	Shortcut to your payment processing (or options if you don't have one)
Integrated Svc/Program	Connection to ecommerce site / practice mgmt / POS / ERP
My Bookkeeper APP	Phone APP download instructions for all users (or if you switch phones)

⚒ CLIENT JOURNEY FLOWCHART

INDEX

ABOUT THE AUTHOR

FOUNDER AND CEO OF Complete Controller, a leading national business services firm, Jennifer Brazer believes that all business operators should have access to excellent financial data to fuel their critical decisions. She has developed efficient bookkeeping and records storage methods and a delivery system that allows businesses to stay securely connected to their financial data without being tethered to an office. Her solution promotes financial transparency and accountability, providing a critical foundation for success.

Jennifer's company, founded in 2007, has become the turnkey Client Accounting Services (CAS) department for CPA firms across the country allowing them to tap into her platform for single sign-on access to all of their clients' books and records, standardized practices, and unlimited bookkeeping talent. Offering both white-label and partnered solutions, the company becomes a strategic addition to any firm looking to add CAS to their service menu. Her #QueenofCAS hashtag references her journey, methods, and business model philosophies that have allowed CAS to move from a loss leader to an essential part of a firm, pumping revenue to myriad arteries.

Attributing her success to the support of willing advisors and mentors, Jennifer is always looking for ways to give back, empowering the small business community through financial literacy. An avid supporter of entrepreneurs, Jennifer has built an 82,000-plus social media following for Complete Controller, and she is a guest speaker to incubators, students, and associations. Her passion for women in business has fueled her membership in the National Association of Women Business Owners for which she served two terms on the Orange County chapter executive board as treasurer and a small business mentor. She is one of twelve elite members serving on the ADP accountant national advisory board and is well respected in the CPA community.

To learn more about the tools used in this book or to get started with building your own cloud-based business model, visit JenniferBrazer.com/workshops.